The Washington Post

DINING GUIDE

BY PHYLLIS C. RICHMAN

The Best-Seller by Washington's
Top Restaurant Critic

Published by
The Washington Post
1150 15th Street, N.W.
Washington, D.C. 20071

Second Edition

The text of this book is composed in Times New Roman, with
the display in Gill Sans.

Manufactured by Chroma Graphics, Largo, Md.,
in association with Alan Abrams

ISBN: [0-9625971-8-X]

EDITOR AND PUBLISHER: Noel Epstein
GRAPHIC DESIGNER: Robert Barkin
ILLUSTRATOR: Susan Davis
RESEARCHER: Susan Breitkopf
DISTRIBUTION DIRECTOR: André Denault

This book can be accessed online at
www.washingtonpost.com,
though it may be in somewhat different form there.

CONTENTS

INTRODUCTION

Restaurants, like wines, ought to be assigned vintages. Then we could begin to understand each other when we talk about our favorites.

"Remember Le Pavillon?" one might ask.

"Which Pavillon? The '90?"

"No, the '85."

"Ah, yes, that was a magnificent year."

Restaurants change. Their chefs move around, and even if they stay in one place, they mature or become tired, feel inspired or grow bored. Some chefs are better in particular seasons, some shine at lunch more than dinner, and every restaurant has its peak years and its valleys.

Thus guidebooks, too, must change. A mere two years after its first edition, this book has needed major reworking. Almost every one of its 225 reviews was altered in some way; nearly two thirds have been totally rewritten or are brand new entries. Restaurants open, restaurants close. Several prominent chefs who left the city have returned—note DC Coast and Sushi-Ko in particular—and the chefs of Washington also have been playing musical chairs to an unprecedentedly lively beat.

The fluid nature of restaurants should be kept in mind as you use this book, too. Menus nowadays are seasonal, so don't expect spring's morels nor summer's soft-shell crabs if you're choosing your menu in winter. Nor can you hope the tomato-mozzarella salad of January will measure up against the one you tasted last July.

The most I, as a critic, can hope to do is predict what a restaurant might be like at some unknown future date, and what it might offer for an unknown group of diners. Take it not as a promise but as a suggestion.

Much of your dining satisfaction is in your own hands. If you pick an uncrowded time, reserve ahead, specify your preferences, arrive on time and order according to the season and the chef's capabilities, you enhance your chances of dining well. And when you find a restaurant you like, reward it with your loyalty. You're likely to be treated all the better as a familiar face, and you'll help assure the continuity of the city's treasures.

This guide, then, is a place to start. It's an outline for you to color in with your experiences.

A word of explanation about the symbols accompanying the book's reviews (in addition to the ♿ indicating wheelchair access):

• PICKS: These restaurants are especially recommended as being the tops among their type, from the best of the pizza parlors or cafeterias to the standouts among the grand kitchens.

• BEAUTIES: These restaurants have beautiful or dramatic dining rooms or a delightful view.

• VALUE: Whether these restaurants are expensive or cheap, they offer particularly good value for the money.

Why no scores or 1-to-5-star rating system? I don't think you can compare an Asian noodle parlor to a full-dress, classic French restaurant. And if a French cafe serves stunning souffles but nothing else of note, should it get a higher or lower score than the full-dress restaurant that makes almost everything superbly save its dreadful souffles? What about restaurants that are better for lunch than dinner? Or serve terrific appetizers but dreary entrees? Or fall flat on Tuesdays when it's the regular chef's night off? Washington restaurants serve more than 50 different cuisines, as do those in most American cities. The variety, complexity and inconsistency of restaurants in this country makes rating systems irrelevant. That's why I limited my symbols to the above three.

I visited all the restaurants in this book without advance warning, and anonymously where possible. Even though I pay for my meals in cash or by credit card with a pseudonym and make reservations under another name, I am frequently recognized in restaurants nowadays. That's inevitable after 22 years of reviewing restaurants for *The Washington Post*, so I work at noting what is going on throughout the restaurant and ordering a wide variety of dishes, some of which must be prepared ahead. I also get plenty of feedback from other diners, so I can often compare others' experiences with my own. What changes most when I am recognized as a critic is not the quality of the food, but the service and sometimes the portion size.

Over these 22 years I have had to put up with some unspeakably bad meals. But I've also had countless exciting meals—prepared by talented chefs and served by thoughtful and intelligent staffs. I owe them gratitude not only for delicious afternoons and evenings, but also for what their craft has taught me. I thank them.

I also owe two decades' worth of gratitude to *The Washington Post*— not just for bankrolling this expensive education but also for providing me with a platform and absolute freedom for my opinionated prose. The *Post's* publisher, Donald Graham, has been endlessly supportive and even, on occasion, an uncomplaining lunch companion. The legendary Ben Bradlee, Shelby Coffey and the late Howard Simons and Marion Clark hired me, and I've remained enormously grateful to them. The *Post's* current executive and managing editors, Len Downie and Steve Coll——who's also been my editor at the Sunday Magazine—have continued to challenge and reinforce me.

Just as restaurants are group efforts, so are books. My thanks go to *Washington Post Books* publisher Noel Epstein. Bob Barkin and Susan Davis designed and illustrated my first *Post* writings, and now, two decades later and to my great satisfaction, designed and illustrated successive editions of this book. Susan Breitkopf gracefully accomplished the herculean job of gathering all the header material, organizing the lists, proofreading and coordinating other aspects of this book.

There are so many others to thank as well: my constantly interesting and entertaining colleagues at the *Post*, the friends and family who have gone anywhere to eat anything in order to help me do my job, my three children—Joe, Matt and Libby—who are now able to make jokes about growing up with a refrigerator filled with nothing but little white carryout boxes and aluminum foil swans. And most of all, Bob Burton, who always remains ready at home with a tomato-onion-anchovy sandwich or a properly baked potato when I need an antidote to restaurant food. Nor can I forget the readers who call, write and send me e-mail messages to tell me about new restaurants they've found, to chime in with their agreement or to accuse me of having the tastebuds of a doorknob. I learn from them all.

In recent decades, American cooking has come into its own, no longer in the shadow of the French. Thus, instead of *bon appetit*:

Good appetite.
Phyllis C. Richman

ADDIS ABABA
2106 18th St. NW, Washington, DC
(202) 232-6092

ETHIOPIAN

Open: Daily 11 am-1 am **Entrees:** $7-$10
Credit Cards: All major, DIS, DC, CB
Reservations: Recommended **Dress:** Casual
Parking: Street **Entertainment:** Ethiopian music F-Sat 10-3

I t's known as the Ethiopians' Ethiopian restaurant, and the crowd shows it. ADDIS ABABA is a plain, bare dining room with just a few home-country scenes on the walls and slightly frayed plastic placemats, but the tables are often full.

Service is critical if you're unfamiliar with this eating style—no utensils. The plates are just big, floppy pancakes topped with thick stews, and more of those same spongy pancakes are provided for you tear in pieces and use to scoop up your dinner. The server will show you how, and steer you towards the peppery or mild dishes, as your prefer.

Except for tomato *fitfit*—which is a kind of raw-tomato salad with green chilies and pieces of the pancakes to soak up the juices—even the spicy dishes are fairly mild. Try that refreshing tomato dish as an appetizer or an entree; it's the best of the menu. Lamb fitfit, too, is all the more flavorful for having the bread soak up the peppered sauce. The meats

". . . an entertaining and inevitably filling meal at the price of a mere snack."

themselves, even the chicken, are chewy. And the mild dishes, called *wats*, tend to be a little sweet. If you like more fire, you can add a bit of the thick red *berbere* paste to your dishes.

Details blur and flaws are forgotten in sight of the array of vegetables, stewed and mashed, that accompany those meats. The process of tearing up the seductively sour, slightly fermented pancakes and scooping up a little of this and that make for an entertaining and inevitably filling.

AL TIRAMISU
2014 P St. NW, Washington, DC
(202) 467-4466

ITALIAN

Lunch: M-F noon-2:30 **Entrees:** $11-$14
Dinner: Daily 5-11 **Entrees:** $14-$20
Credit Cards: All major, DC **Dress:** Nice casual
Reservations: Required **Parking:** Valet (fee) weekends
Metro: Dupont Circle

The name is perfect: Tiramisu has become more of an icon than a dessert. It's ubiquitous, as are mid-range Italian restaurants such as this, serving the inevitable modern Italian menu of carpaccio, grilled portobello mushroom, arugula salad, spinach agnolotti and veal scaloppine. It's got some built-in assets, namely the company of a lot of good restaurants on the block, a friendly looking bar at the entrance of the long, narrow white stucco dining room, and a glass-fronted fireplace in the back. It also has tables so close you have to squeeze between them and a low ceiling that makes the rear of the room seem airless.

The centerpiece of this dining room is chef Luigi Diotaiuti himself, wearing a red bandanna and a chef's jacket with pasta-bowtie buttons and cuffs printed with a food theme. Wandering the dining room in search of a birthday to celebrate, Diotaiuti seems determined to make AL TIRAMISU feel like a party.

The staff is genial, and so is the menu. Among the pastas, there are: house-made gnocchi in a mild yellow-pepper coulis, fragile pillows of spinach-ricotta agnolotti in mascarpone cream, handsome two-toned ravioli with an asparagus and ricotta filling. By the time the entrees arrive, plain and simple grilled fish looks particularly attractive. Nothing here beats it, though the osso buco comes close. Desserts are a list of crowd-pleasers, mostly chocolate, drizzled, striped, latticed and painted with sauces in contrasting colors. They fit the devil-may-care mood of this restaurant.

A & J RESTAURANT
1319-C Rockville Pike, Rockville, MD
(301) 251-7878

CHINESE   🚻

Open: Sun-Th 11:30 am-9 pm, F-Sat 11:30 am-9:30 pm
Entrees: $1.25-$4.85   **Credit Cards:** None; cash, local checks only
Dress: Casual   **Reservations:** No   **Parking:** Free lot
Metro: Twinbrook   **Dim Sum:** All day

L et everyone else complain about the homogenization of our food. I take heart from restaurants such as A & J. It looks like no more than a Formica-tabled shopping-strip storefront, yet it serves the kind of exotic dishes that once would have required a trip to San Francisco's Chinatown.

It's a plain, rock-bottom-priced, cash-or-check-only cafe that makes its own noodles for soups and fashions doughs into Northern-style Chinese dim sum by hand, then serves them all day long. The menu is a three-page list of big soups and small dishes, the Chinese version of tapas or *mezze*. You might find elsewhere a more flavorful broth, a less compact steamed bun filling or plumper smoked chicken, but the variety here—more than two dozen soups alone—is dizzy-

". . . the kind of exotic dishes that once would have required a trip to San Francisco's Chinatown."

ing. Among the dozen stuffed doughs are flaky turnip pastries, crisp and chewy pan-fried pork dumplings, sesame-topped buns sandwiched with pork or beef and picturesque breads such as thousand-layer pancake. For adventurous appetites, there are meaty steamed pork hocks or beef ten-dons with garlic sauce; accessible to every taste are light salads of bean curd skin with mustard greens and beans or dry bean curd with Chinese parsley and peanuts.

It's nibbling food: cold and hot dishes, robust and delicate, meaty and vegetarian, mild and spicy. And it's priced so that it would be a challenge to spend as much as $10 a person.

A.V. RISTORANTE ITALIANO
607 New York Ave. NW, Washington, DC
(202) 737-0550

ITALIANO   ITALIAN   ♿

Open: M-Th 11:30 am-11 pm, F 11:30 am-11:30 pm,
Sat 5 pm-midnight **Entrees:** $8.50-$14 **Closed:** Sun
Credit Cards: All major, DIS, CB, DC
Reservations: Recommended for 10 or more **Dress:** Casual
Parking: Free lot **Metro:** Gallery Place-Chinatown

This big, bare, unlovely set of dining rooms is the great-grandfather of our real Italian red-sauce restaurants. It's loved and hated, famous and notorious. Its menu is immense, but many of the dishes are never (and maybe never have been) available. The regulars know to order from the long list of daily specials scrawled on a board in the entrance hall.

The pizza is "thin-crusted and savory enough to make diners from New York stop complaining for a while."

A.V. can be cheap or not, and if you don't ask prices ahead of time, you might find some surprises at the end. Another trick the regulars know: These are huge portions, so order accordingly. Mixed meat platters, mixed seafood platters, sautéed vegetables all tend to be plain and good. The pizza is for purists, not adventurers, and it's thin-crusted and savory enough to make diners from New York stop complaining for a while. Pastas are straightforward and hearty, none better than Spaghetti Caruso, heavy with whole chicken livers, peppers, onions and mushrooms in a full-flavored tomato sauce.

The dining room is as dark as a cave (even at lunch), the service is offhand, the mood is hectic. Don't look for refinements in the decor or the food. But look for aromas and bold flavors to remember.

AFGHAN
2700 Jefferson Davis Highway, Alexandria, VA
(703) 548-0022

AFGHAN   ♿

Open: Daily 11 am-11 pm **Entrees:** $6.50-$9
Lunch Buffet: M-F 11-3, $5.95
Credit Cards: All major, DIS, DC **Dress:** Casual
Reservations: Recommended **Parking:** Free lot

It seems extravagant to eat at home when AFGHAN is nearby. A large platter of kebabs with bread or rice will leave two diners change from a $20 bill, even with tax and tip. And the bread is a sight to behold, a flat golden oval, well over a foot long, baked to order in a clay oven. AFGHAN'S menu is small, mostly meat or vegetable kebabs plus a few rice pilafs and dumplings as entrees. The kebabs, particularly the chicken, tend to be dry; lamb ribs are your best bet among the meats. But the highlights here are the appetizers. *Aushak*—so good you should consider ordering it as an entree—is scallion-filled dumplings that have a peppery bite under their yogurt-tomato-mint topping. *Bulanee* is a giant turnover filled with mashed potato and onion, oozing and fragrant. AFGHAN also does savory things with spinach and eggplant, which are side dishes or entres.

Though the dining room of this warehouse-district restaurant has all the finesse of a high school gym decorated for a prom, the long tables attract Afghan families for dinner and office groups for the $5.95 buffet lunch. You might find better kebabs elsewhere, but the bread here is as good as Afghan bread gets.

There is another Afghan location at 6271 Old Dominion Drive, Mclean, VA, (703) 734-0909.

AMAZONIA GRILL
4615 Wisconsin Ave. NW, Washington, DC
(202) 537-0421

BRAZILIAN

Lunch: Tu-Sun 11:30-4 **Entrees:** $6-$16 **Buffet:** F 11:30-4, $7.95
Dinner: Sun-Th 5:30-10:30, F-Sat 5:30-11:30 **Entrees:** $12-$20
Credit Cards: All major, DIS, DC **Reservations:** Recommended
Dress: Casual **Parking:** Street **Metro:** Tenleytown-AU
Entertainment: Brazilian music Sat 11:30-3 am

In good weather, the hub of this restaurant is the covered porch. The dining room inside is more dressed up, with stuccoed walls and large paintings of Brazilian life, forest-green tablecloths and vases of various red flowers. But the porch seems more innately tropical.

A large icy *caipirinha* also sets the scene. This is a jolting limeade made with clear Brazilian liquor, lots of lime wedges and a little sugar. It calls for immediate food to cushion the blow, particularly since this is one of the many restaurants where appetizers are the stars. *Carne seca* is chunks of cured dried meat cooked to crispness yet nearly falling apart. Mussels come drenched in garlic and dill and flamed with cognac—just right for dunking bread. Other seafood appetizers are flavored with coconut milk and palm oil, a theme that carries through the entrees. A nutritionist probably would recoil in horror, and many people find the strong palm oil an acquired taste. But if you've loved food in the tropics and haven't found any here that matches your memories, palm oil may be the missing link.

The star of a Brazilian restaurant is *feijoada*, a large pot of black beans crammed with ham, sausage and other varieties of pork. It's accompanied by a platter of toasted manioc meal, reminiscent of bread crumbs, with shredded collard greens and slices of orange. These unlikely components make a great amalgam. The less daring can have grilled steak or fried chicken, though with a Brazilian touch. More elaborate meat entrees run to chicken with pineapple; fried bananas and collard greens; duck with yucca leaves, cognac, olive oil and garlic; or *churrascada,* a mixed grill for two. Seafood dishes are variations on the palm oil theme. The colors are vivid, the aromas intense, the textures viscous and rich.

This is Brazilian food made for Brazilians, not tamed for North American tastes. For some that's a drawback. For most it's an advantage.

ANATOLIA

633 Pennsylvania Ave. SE, Washington, DC
(202) 544-4753

TURKISH   ♿

Lunch: M-F 11:30-3 **Entrees:** $7-$10
Dinner: M-F 5-10, Sat 5:30-10 **Entrees:** $10-$16 **Closed:** Sun
Credit Cards: All major **Reservations:** Recommended
Dress: Casual **Parking:** Street **Metro:** Eastern Market

This is an intimate restaurant run by a husband-and-wife team, Tildikim and Dilek Mit. He's in the kitchen and she's in the dining room, charmingly greeting and serving. Neighbors drop by, children are fussed over. ANATOLIA is a hometown kind of place with a lacy tearoom look, its tables covered with pink and pastel green cloths (unfortunately protected with clingy plastic). On the walls are Turkish rugs and over the tables are hanging lamps, cleverly fashioned from upended copper kettles.

You can sample most appetizers in one fell swoop with a *mezze* platter, with its tangy hummus, refreshing *baba ghanouj* and dill-perfumed stuffed grape leaves. My favorite part of the mezze platter is roasted eggplant, thick slices so soft they nearly collapse under a blanket of yogurt sauce that has garlic, dill and mint competing at top pitch. That yogurt sauce—thick and rich, sometimes with shredded cucumber and mint as well as garlic and dill—is a recurring theme. Most important, it's the binding element in a wonderful appetizer of shredded, sautéed carrots. The yogurt sauce weaves its way among the entrees, too. It moistens the bed of cubed pita bread for *yogurtlu* kebab (beef or lamb, sliced and grilled) or the spiciest and best of the meat dishes, Adana kebab, long sausages of ground lamb, teasing the tongue with cumin and garlic. Plain grilled kebabs are better elsewhere.

> **"The greatest appeal of Anatolia is among the appetizers."**

In sum, the greatest appeal at ANATOLIA is among the appetizers: anything with eggplant, anything sauced with yogurt, certainly those stuffed grape leaves and that brilliant carrot *mezze*. At the other end of the menu, ANATOLIA'S baklava is sensational. Follow it with Turkey's most famous contribution to cuisine: coffee, boiled in a tiny pot to a foamy few tablespoons' worth, thick, dark and nearly syrup. It offers a sweet, quiet ending to a gently pleasant meal.

8

AQUARELLE
Watergate Hotel
2650 Virginia Ave. NW, Washington, DC
(202) 298-4455

AMERICAN   ♿

Breakfast: Daily 7-10:30 **Entrees:** $14
Lunch: Daily 11:30-2:30 **Entrees:** $17-$26
Dinner: Daily 5-10:30 **Entrees:** $18.50-$32
Brunch: Sun 11:30-2:30, $38 **Pre-Theater Menu:** Daily 5-7, $38
Credit Cards: All major, DIS **Reservations:** Required
Dress: Jacket at dinner **Parking:** Free valet **Metro:** Foggy Bottom

The visual drama of this dining room takes place not in the room itself but outside: Long stretches of glass bring the Potomac River and the other Watergate buildings into the picture, framed by window boxes of geraniums.

Chef Robert Wiedmaier's presentations, too, are beautiful, with little skyscrapers of phyllo-wrapped mushroom rolls accompanying the quail, and sweetbreads formed into plump disks that look almost like crab cakes. His plates are complex: Meat and seafood entrees are dressed with vegetable purees; carved vegetables form spokes; sometimes a soft bed of cooked greens provides color contrast. Depending on the season, there might be an eggplant puree with the seared salmon appetizer, celery root puree with the squab, white bean puree beside the rack of lamb. One night, best of all, a pear-turnip puree had been matched with the duck. Thus, nearly every plate has some memorable component, and when all the parts work in unison his food is worthy of drum rolls and salutes.

Start with a gateau of crab or a small copper pot of fresh morels swimming in butter sauce with a hint of truffle oil—what could be more seductive? And squab cooked rare, on a celery root puree with a small mound of sautéed mushrooms—just fine. Continue with a salmon fillet coated with coriander and fennel seeds, cooked at a heat high enough to form a crust while leaving the inside nearly melting, or perhaps a quail, puffed with a lovely spongy and faintly meaty mousse, or skate when it is available. And definitely save room for dessert, whether the butter-rich three-chocolate terrine, the thin, crisp round of hot plum tart with cinnamon ice cream, or the most subtly impressive, a little dish of *crème brûlée*, as soft and silky, understatedly rich and perfect as eggs, sugar, cream and vanilla could hope to be.

ARDEO
3311 Connecticut Ave. NW, Washington, DC
(202) 244-6750

AMERICAN

Dinner: M-Th 5:30-10:30, F-Sat 5:30-11:30 **Entrees:** $11-$18
Brunch: Sun 11-3 **Entrees:** $7.25-$15.25
Credit Cards: All major, DC **Reservations:** Recommended
Dress: Casual **Parking:** Valet (fee) after 6 pm
Metro: Cleveland Park

Once you get past the cool, suave look of ARDEO, you realize it has an even greater distinction: It is packed with waiters. Even more astonishing, they know what they are doing.

The food is trendy New American. The meal begins with a basket of good bread and a white bean dip. Then you can go in many directions. You could have just a burger, accompanied by excellent fries. Or you could eat lightly with an entree salad of smoked salmon, smoked trout and scallop *seviche*.

The emphasis is on creativity, and the appetizers reflect that: Strawberries along with Stilton in the spinach salad and grill marks on the romaine. To balance disappointments such as scallops in a wan red-pepper coulis or too-vinegary portobellos, there's a smooth, spicy black bean soup.

With their long list of ingredients, the entrees are bound to offer something delightful—seasoned mashed potatoes, perfectly cooked asparagus—even if the whole dish doesn't succeed. Limp linguine can be ignored as you savor its marvelous shrimp and julienned vegetables. A huge soft-shell crab is fried so lightly that its mushy texture is hardly noticeable. Roast chicken is usually a good test of a restaurant. Here it's crisp-skinned and bursting with flavor. Why, then, is the rack of lamb flabby and bland? The double-thick pork chop chewy and steamed-tasting? Potato-crusted cod is just right, but its clam chowder sauce belongs on chicken a la king. A sure hand is evident in the desserts, though. One of the best is rhubarb soup with mango mousse, but the praline semifreddo is also good.

ARDEO is one of those restaurants that reverberate with promise. I'll look forward to its honing its dishes. But the crowds packing it, even on weekdays, aren't waiting for any such thing.

ASHBY INN
692 Federal St., Paris, VA
(540) 592-3900

AMERICAN

Dinner: W-Sat 6-9 **Entrees:** $17.50-$24.50
Brunch: Sun noon-2:30, $19 **Closed:** M-Tu
Credit Cards: MC, V **Reservations:** Recommended
Dress: Casual **Parking:** Free

This small inn has been the fulfillment of a typical Washington dream: Its proprietors, Roma and John Sherman, gave up jobs on Capitol Hill to run a country inn with a few rooms for overnight guests, yet close enough to Washington to draw those who merely want to dine. They change the menu daily, keeping it close to the season, and grow some of what they serve. John Sherman's passion for wine shows in the personalized and decently priced list.

You can dine on a terrace overlooking the garden, on an enclosed porch, or in rooms that look like colonial dining rooms or a tavern. The furnishings have a New England simplicity, turned romantic by hurricane lamps. The menu, too, shows restraint: not too many choices, nothing complicated. The vegetables shine on their own, in a roasted corn chowder or a buttery spinach accompaniment to a grill or a roast. A plain roast chicken is crackling and juicy, a memorable bird. And the region's local rockfish is served brown and crusty, silky inside.

This is not flashy cooking—it shows considerable reserve—and its plainness can highlight the flaws. But if you order whatever is most local, most seasonal and most simple, dinner is likely to be as satisfying as it is soothing.

ASIA NORA
2213 M St. NW, Washington, DC
(202) 797-4860

ASIAN

Dinner: M-Th 5:30-10, F-Sat 5:30-10:30 **Entrees:** $18-$25
Closed: Sun **Credit Cards:** MC, V, DIS
Reservations: Preferred **Dress:** Casual
Parking: Valet (fee) **Metro:** Foggy Bottom/Dupont Circle

The more I see of ASIA NORA, the more I miss the old City Cafe, whose M Street space was sacrificed for this pricey nouvelle Asian seafood restaurant. ASIA NORA is gorgeous, with deep green walls and brass-inlaid handmade tables, but increasingly its beauty is only wallpaper deep.

On one visit, the tuna tempura appetizer looked glorious but the fish inside was half cooked and half raw, all bland. Seafood dumplings displayed sauce artistry, but their filling was damp and bitter. Entrees were no better: A lusciously fresh fried sea bass was drowned in a mush of cooked vegetables and murky red sauce. Thai seafood curry had the opposite problem: The coconut-milk sauce was rich and satiny, but the seafood was scrawny, its textures unappetizing. I've found far better seafood curry at inexpensive Thai restaurants.

". . . increasingly its beauty is only wallpaper deep."

Even dessert, an array of sweets in a bento box, consisted of sweet spring rolls reeking of old oil, oddly flavored ice creams and a passable square of foamy coconut mousse cake. All this at some of the highest prices in town.

ASIAN FLAVOR
128 West Maple Ave., Vienna, VA
(703) 938-9800

THAI/JAPANESE

Lunch: Tu-Sat 11:30-2:30 **Entrees:** $5-$8
Dinner: Tu-Th 4:30-10, F-Sat 4:30-10:30, Sun 4-9:30
Entrees: $8-$17 **Closed:** M **Credit Cards:** All major, DIS
Reservations: Recommended **Dress:** Casual **Parking:** Free lot

I see ASIAN FLAVOR as a 1950s musical about a Japanese restaurant, with a set whose theme is green. Walls of green fabric, chairs of soft green vinyl, tables of green Formica. A gleaming sort of green—like lettuce, like pistachios, like lime juice, a green just short of the chartreuse satin warm-up jackets that shimmered through high school corridors in the '50s. Not acidic, though. The color is tamed by its surroundings of warm blond wood: sushi bar, window frames, hanging lanterns, slats dividing the dining areas. Sequined and quilted Thai hangings twinkle on the walls.

The blackboard tells us today there is *toro*, the prized fatty tuna. It shares the marquee with rainbow rolls, those rice logs striped with wrappers of tuna, flounder and avocado. That probably means the chef has made a run out to Dulles to pick up his shipment of the freshest sushi fish from New York. Even if the salmon-skin roll is sometimes too fishy or the eel isn't up to snuff, I'd detour to ASIAN FLAVOR just for the sushi. Its first attraction is its prices, many of them two-thirds to three-quarters the price I'd expect to pay elsewhere, and the daily specials are undoubtedly fresh.

The menu is both Thai and Japanese, and beyond sushi the best dishes are fried, particularly such appetizers as spring rolls or *tod mun*, the bouncy little Thai fried fish cakes, which may be the best dish in the house. These fish cakes are tender and airy rather than resilient, curry-spiced and juicy rather than processed-tasting, and lacy at the edges. They're worth a short detour from the sushi.

ATILLA'S
2705 Columbia Pike, Arlington, VA
(703) 920-8255

TURKISH   ♿

Lunch: M-Sat 11-2:30 **Entrees:** $5.25-$8
Dinner: Tu-Th 5-10, F-Sat 5-11, Sun 4-9 **Entrees:** $12-$15
Credit Cards: MC, V **Reservations:** Recommended
Dress: Casual **Parking:** Free lot
Entertainment: Middle Eastern music F-Sat 9-midnight

S ome people are satisfied to find one outstanding dish on a menu and just come back when they have a hankering for that favorite. Whether other dishes are good or bad doesn't concern these loyalists. ATILLA'S is the place for them.

It's hardly necessary to order appetizers, because the waiter automatically brings you the best of them when you are seated. A basket of house-made pita, deeply browned and heavily sprinkled with sesame seeds, arrives with a plate of hummus—tart and spicy hummus, smooth but not pasty, light despite a slick of oil on top. Nobody in the area makes better pita or hummus, and the first round is free.

You're not just stuck with hummus, though. The Albanian liver is a revelation, the tiny cubes coated with spices that make them sharp and tangy, sautéed until they are crusty and tender and accompanied, like almost everything else, by a pile of shaved red onion and parsley. Fried eggplant with garlic and tomato sauce tastes much like Italian *caponata* (even without the olives and capers), and it's good despite its oiliness.

The entree list looks long, but it's mostly variations of grilled lamb. Forget everything but the *doner* kebab. This mixture of thinly cut lamb, beef and veal is formed into a giant meatloaf and grilled on a vertical spit. You've probably seen something similar called a gyro in local carryouts, but that factory-made frozen version is as much like ATILLA'S as a hot dog is like homemade sausage. It's available as a platter, piled on pita or on damp, soft rice. So you don't really need to find out whether the rest of the entrees are juicy or dry, over-marinated or under-seasoned that day. The *doner* kebab is enough to bring honor to ATILLA'S.

AUSTIN GRILL
2404 Wisconsin Ave. NW, Washington, DC
(202) 337-8080

AMERICAN/SOUTHWESTERN

Open: M 11:30-10:30, Tu-Th 11:30-11, F 11:30 am-midnight,
Sat 11 am-midnight, Sun 11-10:30 **Entrees:** $6-$15
Brunch: Sat-Sun 11-3, $7-$8 (regular menu also available)
Credit Cards: All major, DIS, DC
Reservations: No **Dress:** Casual **Parking:** Street

One crunch of a chip and you know the food at an AUSTIN GRILL (and SOUTH AUSTIN GRILL) is far above ordinary gummy Tex-Mex cooking. These chips taste of corn, they're light, and they're fried in fresh oil. The two salsas on the table are not just hot, but flavorful.

But while all the cute stencils on the walls, the down-home decor and can't-keep-still music might lead you to expect that these are nothing more than taco palaces, the menu will convince you that an AUSTIN GRILL is more serious than that. Along with the inevitable fajitas, burritos and enchiladas, the AUSTIN GRILLS serve awfully good grilled fish (though I'd skip the little dish of sweet orange tequila butter), as well as shrimp and scallops. There are chili-and-garlic-marinated pork chops *adobado* and a rib-eye version of *carne asada*. And some days you might find *posole* among the specials.

For me, though, the stars of the menu are the crabmeat quesadilla, which is delicate and subtle, and the green chili, a wonderful, slow-burning stew with roasted *poblanos* and cilantro fighting for prominence and plenty of diced chicken and potatoes to keep them in line.

If you go for the quesadilla, a side order of guacamole certainly will be in order once you've scraped up the bit that decorates the plate. Then perhaps another order just to make sure it's as good as you thought it was. Surely you won't have room for an Ibarra chocolate brownie.

Also in DC: Austin Grill at The Lansburgh, 750 E St. NW, (202) 393-3776. For suburban branches: South Austin Grill, 801 King St., Alexandria, VA, (703) 684-8969; Austin Grill Springfield, 8430 Old Keene Mill Rd., Springfield, VA, (703) 644-3111; and Austin Grill Bethesda, 7278 Woodmont Ave., Bethesda, MD, (301) 656-1366. All Austin Grills, except the Wisconsin location, are wheelchair accessible.

B. SMITH'S

Union Station, 50 Massachusetts Ave. NE
Washington, DC
(202) 289-6188

AMERICAN

Lunch: M-F 11:30-4 **Entrees:** $9-$22
Dinner: Sun 5-10, M-Th 5-11, F-Sat 5-midnight **Entrees:** $11-$24
Brunch: Sat-Sun 11:30-3 **Entrees:** $9-$22
Dress: Casual **Credit Cards:** All major, DIS, DC, CB
Reservations: Recommended **Parking:** Validated, 2 hours
Metro: Union Station **Music:** Jazz Tu-W, F-S 8-10, Sat-Sun noon-4

When a restaurant is named after a New York model, the Oil of Olay girl, you expect skimpy salads and ascetic, dry-grilled fish. But that's not what you get at B. SMITH'S. The restaurant that has taken over the historic presidential waiting room at Union Station serves its bronzed salmon with butter-thickened bearnaise sauce and its salads with whole strips of bacon or plenty of Swiss cheese and Smithfield ham dressing. The menu is abundant with barbecued ribs and fried catfish, crisp onion rings and gravy-drenched mashed potatoes.

B. Smith's is a mood. The entrance has the feel of an art deco supper club, with a fan of burgundy fabric as backdrop to the maitre d's station and jazz wafting in from the lounge. The soaring, vaulted room, festooned with gilded and painted fancy work, is the match of many cathedrals. And along the side is an enclosed terrace with stone columns and wicker chairs, a hint of one of Paris' elegant squares.

The menu reads like a family album of Southern cooking, albeit with newfangled modifications. B. SMITH'S produces a full range of food, from simple to exotic, light to heavy, luscious to truly dreadful. I can't remember tasting better red beans and rice. They make me forgive the excess sugar in the corn bread that accompanies them and wish they were my full meal, not just an appetizer.

In a Southern restaurant it makes sense to save room for dessert. Both the Southern cheesecake—with cherries and nuts—and the pecan diamonds could hardly be richer, the diamonds' dough more like caramel than like cookie. And the coconut cake is about the sweetest dessert I have ever eaten—almost like fudge—but the coconut itself is fabulous, and I ate every bit to prove it. Washington might be a little embarrassed to have to import a Southern restaurant from New York. But I'll take my red beans and coconut cake wherever I can get them.

BACCHUS
1827 Jefferson Pl., NW, Washington, DC
(202) 785-0734

LEBANESE

Lunch: M-F noon-2:30 **Entrees:** $6.95-$10.50
Dinner: M-Th 6-10, F-Sat 6-10:30 **Entrees:** $12.50-$16.25
Closed: Sun **Credit Cards:** All major
Reservations: Recommended **Dress:** Casual
Parking: Complimentary valet at dinner **Metro:** Dupont Circle

Nobody's been serving *mezze* longer than BACCHUS, yet this restaurant is fresher than ever. The small downtown branch has been refurbished with crisply striped upholstery and fabrics draped from the ceiling to hint of a tent. The service, too, has new energy. And most of the food is as good as ever. The Bethesda location is newer and has always looked more luxurious.

While the entree list has stayed the same over the years—kebabs, rice casseroles and yogurt-drenched meat dishes—the list of mezze grows longer. Thus, more than ever, it pays to construct your dinner of a table of appetizers (at lunch, ordering an entree is required). The range of eggplant dishes alone is astonishing, and there are two kinds of tangy, spicy, house-made sausages. The phyllo pastries—stuffed with meat or cheese—are crisp and greaseless. And the chicken drumettes, charcoal-crisped and tart with lemon, are irresistible, particularly with the powerful garlic puree that comes alongside. I've been disappointed lately in the under-seasoned hummus, and the salads tend to be heavy on the vinegar. *Shwarma* is sometimes over-marinated, thus sour and mushy. Skipping over them would hardly be difficult, given the array of vegetable sautes and purees, the stuffed grape leaves and *kibbe*, the falafel and the fish buried in tomato and olives.

If you must, the lamb and chicken kebabs are probably as reliable as any, and they have the bonus of buttery noodle-studded rice pilaf. Rice topped with meat or chicken hasn't nearly the savor. To drink, there is always wine, or if that's not on your agenda, fresh lemonade.

Bacchus' Bethesda, MD, branch—at 7945 Norfolk Ave., (301) 657-1722—has an $8 fixed-price lunch, is open for dinner from 6 to 10 on Sunday and is wheelchair accessible.

BANANA CAFE
500 8th St. SE, Washington, DC
(202) 543-5906

CARRIBEAN/TEX-MEX   🚻

Lunch: M-Th 10:30-2:30, F 11:30-2:30   **Entrees:** $6.25-$9
Dinner: Sun-Th 5-10, F-Sat 5-11 **Entrees:** $7-$16
Brunch: Sun 11-3, $13 ($17 with mimosas)
Credit Cards: All major, DIS, DC, CB **Reservations:** For 6 or more
Dress: Casual **Parking:** Street **Metro:** Eastern Market
Happy Hour: M-F 5-7 at piano bar: $2 U.S. beers/rail drinks; free appetizers
Entertainment: Piano bar Tu-Th 5-11:30, F 5-12:30, Sat 7:30-12:30

The BANANA CAFE is a trip. It's a tropical dining room that pulsates with lime green, tangerine and pink walls hung with paintings by the owner and local artists, with the doorway outlined in tiny lights. It's decorated with plastic-and-wood bananas. The music sounds like old Havana nightclub hits. If for nothing else, it's become famous in the neighborhood for its margaritas.

Much of the menu is made up of Tex-Mex staples—enchiladas, tacos, tamales, burritos, quesadillas and fajitas. There's a fairly standard seafood section with indifferent paella, *zarzuela,* salmon and shrimp. But what sets this menu apart are dishes such as the Cuban *ropa vieja, carnitas* and *picadillo*, as well as a couple of Puerto Rican dishes made with sweet or green plantains. The codfish fritters could compete with any you'd find in the Caribbean. The other standout appetizer is seviche, an immense plateful of turbot chunks, marinated with a restrained mixture of lime, onion and chilies. The house specialty, though, is plantain soup, a strange but intriguing army-green beef stock spiked with cilantro and chilies, into which you squeeze lime to taste.

When it comes to the entrees, the earthier the better. The Cuban and Puerto Rican dishes outshine the soggy, bland enchiladas and tamales and the seafood. Far more satisfying are *carnitas*, crusty soft chunks of pork marinated with bitter orange juice and accompanied by raw onion and lime, or the sweet and savory ground-meat picadillo. The true highlights of dinner are the rice and the black beans.

For dessert, the kitchen makes cheesecakes and flans in flavors-of-the-day such as coconut, guava, passion fruit, banana and chocolate. Flan is flan, you say? Not here. It's a Puerto Rican-style flan, which means it's made with sweetened condensed milk and comes out dense, velvety and hinting of caramel through and through.

BAROLO
223 Pennsylvania Ave. SE, Washington, DC
(202) 547-5011

ITALIAN   ♿

Lunch: M-F 11:30-2:30 **Entrees:** $12.50-$15.50
Dinner: M-Th 5:30-10, F-Sat 5:30-10:30 **Entrees:** $13.50-$24
Credit Cards: All major, DC **Dress:** Nice casual
Reservations: Suggested **Parking:** Complimentary valet
Metro: Capital South

C hef Enzo Fargione has a taste for the baroque, and not only in his sometimes-zany dishes. The restaurant itself is decorated like a giant's hunting lodge, complete with a display of weaponry and chairs that are just short of thrones.

BAROLO'S menu changes daily, but you can always expect a profusion of flavors that stretch one's conception of Italian food. Sometimes the concoctions miss, but then there are delightful revelations: roasted lamb hearts with an inventive sauce; braised eggplant (beneath a peppery tuna) that goes beyond a mere vegetable. A "crayfish" appetizer turned out to be shrimp one day, but they were so flavorful that they made me want to stop right there and consider them dinner.

If only Fargione's achievements were predictable. How is one to know that the pheasant is going to be chewy and bland, while the squab will be just fine? Lamb loins are luscious, but their "light tomato broth" is overwhelming and tastes like a paste.

A recommendation: Unless you're a risk-taker, circumvent the more complicated entrees.

One certainty is that Fargione has no instinct for pasta, which often tastes vague and starchy. Risotto has the right texture, but it is correct without being delicious. A $20 bowl of rice ought to be glorious.

Whether the desserts are delicious or not, you'll be driven to order one by looks alone. They're like circus toys, and some are indeed luscious. The tiramisu is so good that it reminds me why tiramisu became popular in the first place. A mango mousse, though, slips into true rubberiness.

Finally, Fargione breaks the mold with the coffee service. Espresso isn't the highlight here, not when there is excellent coffee brewed in individual silver plunger pots. This is a restaurant that goes that extra step — even if it is sometimes a step too far.

BeDuCi
2100 P St. NW, Washington, DC
(202) 223-3824

MEDITERRANEAN   ♿

Lunch: M-F 11:30-2:30 **Entrees:** $9.50-$20
Lunch Special: M-F 11:30-2:30, $12.95
Dinner: M-Th 5:30-10, F-Sat 5:30-10:30, Sun 5-9 **Entrees:** $11.50-$20
Credit Cards: All major, DIS, DC **Reservations:** Recommended
Dress: Casual **Parking:** Complimentary valet at dinner
Metro: Dupont Circle

Owners Michele Miller and Jean-Claude Garrat show off the dining rooms like a couple who've just moved in to their first house. Here's the sun porch, with its slanted glass roof and walls, its brick floor, its sunny disposition even on gray days. Inside are three rooms and a bar, the main room furnished with sound-muffling carpet, dark wood chair rails accenting white walls, and an overlay of paintings, drawings and prints.

Their restaurant serves "Mediterranean style" cooking, which means you can choose from eight or more pastas, several couscous and paella variations, even entrees from Morocco, with fanciful names and flowery descriptions. The menu at BeDuCi—short for Below Dupont Circle—is one of those something-for-everyone conglomerations. With such a long and complicated list, it's hard to find just what the chef does best. Soups aren't in the running. Grilled portobello mushroom is more satisfying (how can a portobello mushroom be bad?), and an appetizer of carpaccio, gravlax and prosciutto is a heap of good things.

The handwritten list of specials is the page to scrutinize. One day the star of the meal was a bowl of steamed mussels and clams in an herbed lime broth, one of those dishes that tempts you to use up all the bread to sop up the sauce. When in doubt, order a pasta special such as sun-dried tomato linguine with fresh artichokes and olives or squid-ink noodles topped by a flavorful tomato sauce, with shellfish and artichoke slices. Among entrees, too, specials show the most care. Vegetarians can do well with "Heather's Roasted Vegetable Brique," a stew of mushrooms, red and yellow peppers, spinach, onions and carrots wrapped in a crepe-thin layer of phyllo.

Desserts are made by Michele Miller—the likes of homey brownies with nuts and birthday-cake-style fudge frosting; caramelized pineapple cobbler that's much like an upside-down cake; and dark, moist chocolate cake with raspberry jam between the layers.

BET ON JAZZ RESTAURANT
730 11th St. NW
(202) 393-0975

AMERICAN/CARIBBEAN   ♿

Lunch: M-F 11:30-2:30 **Entrees:** $8-$17
Dinner: M-Th 5-10, F-Sat 5:30-midnight **Entrees:** $16-$24
Brunch: Sun 11:30-3 ($26) **Credit cards:** All major, DIS, DC
Dress: Business attire **Reservations:** Recommended
Entertainment: Jazz F-Sat 9-midnight, Sun brunch
Parking: Valet (fee) **Metro:** Metro Center

BET ON JAZZ is a full-dress supper club, drawing an all-out decorative crowd. The dining room is outfitted in glove-leather banquettes and silky burnished wood paneling two stories high. A gigantic screen overhead shows jazz videos, while a bandstand awaits the live musicians who play on weekends.

The service needs a lot of work. One three-course lunch dragged out to nearly three hours. What's more, this is a restaurant where the hostess won't seat a party until it is complete (and turns away people in tank tops, T-shirts or sneakers).

If you ordered very carefully, you could skate right over the kitchen's deficiencies. A shrimp appetizer is two enormous and unusually juicy shrimp whose flavor is sealed in by filaments of fried pastry. Broiled mozzarella and portobello is homey. But otherwise, the ice is thin. Crab cakes are tired and dry. Barbecued ribs, served as an appetizer, are tender, with a pleasantly chewy-crisp surface, though too sweet and badly in need of a chili jolt.

Among entrees, any variation on jerk chicken is the best bet, because the spicing is seductive without quite searing your mouth. Strips of that spicy chicken also enliven penne with sun-dried tomatoes, shiitakes and basil. Fish is cooked nicely, left moist and tender, but suffers from its sauces. Such red meat dishes as pork chop and ostrich burger have been a challenge to a steak knife.

Except for the *crème brûlée*, the sweets are the highlight on this menu. Passion fruit tartlet is sensational, and a warm banana tart is a delicious variation on tarte Tatin. Chocolate terrine is irresistibly rich.

BET ON JAZZ is not satisfying as a restaurant, at least not yet. It works better as an event, a scene, an ode to great American music.

BIS
15 E St. NW, Washington, DC
(202) 661-2700

FRENCH ♿

Breakfast: Daily 7-10:30 **Entrees:** $6.75-$12
Lunch: Daily 11:30-2:30 **Entrees:** $8-$22
Dinner: Daily 5:30-10:30 **Entrees:** $17.50-$22
Credit Cards: All major, DIS, DC **Reservations:** Recommended
Dress: Nice casual **Parking:** Valet (fee) **Metro:** Union Station

A new restaurant on Capitol Hill is automatically big news. And when it's a spinoff from one of the city's top restaurants—Vidalia—and located in a chic new hotel—George—it's a major event. Thus BIS has been gathering Washington celebs since its opening day. Its owner-chef, Jeff Buben, has hardly had a chance to catch his breath, much less to put his new bistro in proper order.

It shows great promise. The dining room—with a balcony above the bar—is handsome in a dignified way, with acres of light wood, a glass-fronted kitchen to make a show of the cooking, and comfy banquettes with glove-leather seats. The spaciousness of the booths makes it impossible for the waiters to reach across to deliver plates to the far corners, but the comfort of a large table is worth a diner's assistance.

> **"It shows great promise."**

The wine list is a mesmerizing collection, just right for hearty bistro food and priced so low we might wish Buben to attack the federal budget in his spare time. And the menu reads deliciously: snails with artichokes, rabbit galette, Provencal vegetable tart, steak tartare, several traditional French soups or pate to start; entrees from the rotisserie or such classics as duck confit, veal stew, goujonettes of sole or mussels as entrees.

They don't yet taste as good as they sound, but BIS was still in its infancy when this book went to press. Buben's talent will surely bring it up to snuff eventually.

BISTRO FRANCAIS
3124 M St. NW, Washington, DC
(202) 338-3830

FRENCH   ♿

Lunch: M-F 11-6 **Entrees:** $8-$12
Dinner: Sun-Th 5-3 am, F-Sat 5-4 am **Entrees:** $13-$19
Brunch: Sat-Sun 11-4 ($14) **Credit Cards:** All major
Pre-Theater (early bird): Daily 12-4, $11.95 (lunch); daily 5-7
$17.95 (dinner) **Reservations:** Recommended **Dress:** Casual
Parking: Validation available at Georgetown Park Mall
Metro: Foggy Bottom

BISTRO FRANCAIS has always seemed to me like the little brother among French restaurants. It's small and noisy and not quite suave enough. The tables cling to each other under a canopy of hanging plants and amid a cacophony of leaded glass and mirrors. It doesn't have the smooth elegance of the big boys, but it's clearly part of the family. In fact, this is where local French chefs go to unwind after a night at their own stoves.

It looks unmistakably French, even Parisian. But its service is hesitant and hardly continental. What has kept it going strong for decades is the menu—long and interesting, catering to the onion-soup-and-minute-steak crowd along with the giblet-salad-and-marinated-tuna set. It's got all the traditional dishes: pâtés, melon with port, coq au vin, steak tartare and its signature rotisserie chicken with tarragon. And it has an extensive array of more inventive daily specials such as an appetizer of eggplant teamed with a zesty lamb sausage and pan-fried cakes of salmon mousse studded with scallops. If the cooking is not brilliant, it is certainly competent.

For such ambitious French cooking, BISTRO FRANCAIS is a bargain. Few restaurants in this price range serve such good bread and vary the vegetables with each entree. The real buys, though, are the fixed-price lunch and early-bird dinners, complete with a glass of wine, soup or a truly French salad, entree and a choice of desserts from a tray of French standards. Dover sole is priced here like fillet of flounder elsewhere. And BISTRO FRANCAIS has matured well. As the sun goes down, the mirrors sparkle and the wood paneling gleams, BISTRO FRANCAIS begins to look romantic, even quite grown up.

"This is where local French chefs go to unwind after a night at their own stoves."

BISTROT LEPIC
1736 Wisconsin Ave. NW, Washington, DC
(202) 333-0111

FRENCH

Lunch: Tu-Sun 11:30-2:30 **Entrees:** $10-$13
Dinner: Tu-Th 5-10, F-Sat 5-10:30, Sun 5-9:3 0 **Entrees:** $14-$18
Closed: M **Credit Cards:** All major, DIS
Reservations: Recommended **Dress:** Casual **Parking:** Street

S ome restaurants are loved for their food, others for their service, many for their style. BISTROT LEPIC is loved for, among other things, its size and shape. This small storefront has the proportions of a typical small-town bistro in France.

What's more, it has a disposition to match its sunny yellow dining room, a hostess whose enthusiasm is infectious and a reasonably priced menu that's inventive but anchored in French bistro tradition. No wonder it's often full for midweek lunch in Georgetown, where many restaurants are nearly empty at midday. BISTROT LEPIC feels good.

Its food is fine. Not wonderful, not memorable, but attractive and agreeable. And where else will you find a scrapple-like slice of boned and braised pigs' foot on the menu? Entrees also make much of bistro staples: kidneys with mustard, chicken *piperade*, beef with marrow and rabbit confit. Salmon is wrapped in a potato crust, its sauce sprinkled with caviar, and scallops are given an Asian touch of pickled ginger—

"Bistrot Lepic is a charmer, not a dazzler."

oddly sweet with their broccoli mousse. Liver is a favorite, though its capers, olives and sherry vinegar flavorings don't quite come together.

In all, BISTROT LEPIC is a charmer, not a dazzler. Unsurprisingly, it's considered by many Georgetowners to be their personal secret favorite.

BLUE PLATE
2002 P St. NW, Washington, DC
(202) 293-2248

AMERICAN

Dinner: Tu-Th 5-10, F 5-11, Sat 4-11, Sun 4-10 **Entrees:** $7.25-$19
Brunch: Sat-Sun 11-4 **Entrees:** $5-$13.75
Closed: M **Credit Cards:** MC, V **Dress:** Casual
Parking: Street **Metro:** Dupont Circle

BLUE PLATE, the Dupont Circle diner with handmade wooden booths and produce-crate labels on the walls, has begun to age nicely. From the start, it's employed a group of jeans-clad servers practiced in the attentive languor you'd expect to find in a diner along old Route 1, and it's refined its menu of lightened and updated down-home food.

On the other hand, the kitchen remains a small, low-key operation, which is a nice way of saying that it is easily overwhelmed and often slow. If you see a line to the door at BLUE PLATE, you might as well browse next door at Second Story Books for a while until the crowd thins, or come back another day.

Okay, so it's not your typical diner. It's a diner where everything is made in-house—the burger, the bun, even the ketchup. Blue Plate churns out ice creams and sorbets to suit the season, it pays attention to vegetarians as well as to meat eaters. No wonder it's a good bit more expensive than the classic diner.

The sandwich list is largely predictable—burger, club, meatloaf, grilled cheese (with vegetables). Main courses, the likes of peppercorn-marinated strip steak and grilled fresh fish, move up the scale to real restaurant prices and style. There are such homey classics as pot roast, pork steak and macaroni and cheese. The highlights of the entrees are often the accompaniments: chunky applesauce and sauerkraut, both made from scratch, real mashed potatoes with gravy that's not from a jar, green beans that are definitely fresh.

A diner with a wine list? BLUE PLATE has one. It's small but enticing, with prices in line with the diner mode. There are also interesting beers on tap, plus fresh lemonade, chocolate milk and egg creams. If that doesn't impress you, how about this: Did you ever expect to find a diner with great decaf?

BOMBAY BISTRO
3570 Chain Bridge Rd., Fairfax, VA
(703) 359-5810

INDIAN   ♿

Lunch: M-F 11:30-2:30, Sat-Sun noon-3 **Buffet:** M-F $6.95,
Sat-Sun $8.95 **Dinner:** Sun-Th 5-10, F-Sat 5-10:30 **Entrees:** $6-$12
Credit Cards: All major, DIS, DC
Reservations: Weekday lunch only **Dress:** Casual
Parking: Free lot **Metro:** Vienna

You can tell a lot about a restaurant by its fish. BOMBAY BISTRO'S whole Maryland rockfish is marinated in yogurt, ginger, garlic and other spices. The skin is scored, and the fish is cooked over charcoal so that it is very crisp outside and deliciously blackened in spots. It's a magnificent entree. At the homier end of the menu is a vegetarian peasant dish called *rava* onion masala, a huge wafer-thin pancake made of lentil and rice flour folded into a square with yellow potatoes and onions packed thickly inside. BOMBAY BISTRO serves all the curries, biryanis, tandoors and vegetarian dishes that form the common Indian repertoire. And at their best they have such refinement that they leave no doubt that India's is one of the world's great cuisines. On the other hand, BOMBAY BISTRO can miss, with overspiced tandoor shrimp, underseasoned curries and too-thick breads.

This is sophisticated cooking that attends to all the senses. If you've hit it right, your curry can be like a painting, with its own palette of seasonings, all carefully arranged and balanced. Lamb *rogan josh* has a sauce that is thick and velvety, intricately spiced but mild, its waves of fragrance gently lapping at your taste buds. Another lamb curry, *nilgiri khorma*, is quite different. Its sauce is a dark greenish brown, thick and grainy, more complex than hot, unfolding as you savor it. Vegetable dishes are more subtle, the spinach heightened with just a little sweetly fried onion and dotted with large, bland cubes of house-made cheese, the shredded eggplant a red-gold combination with bits of tomato and onion. And biryanis are distinctive. BOMBAY BISTRO is a warmhearted restaurant where the service is courtly, the cooking is aristocratic and the prices are proletarian.

Bombay Bistro's other location: 98 W. Montgomery Ave., Rockville, MD, (301) 762-8798.

BOMBAY CLUB
815 Connecticut Ave. NW, Washington, DC
(202) 659-3727

INDIN ♿

Lunch: M-F 11:30-2:30
Dinner: M-Th 6-10:30, F-Sat 6-11, Sun 5:30-9 **Entrees:** $7-$19
Brunch: Sun 11:30-2:30, buffet $18.50 **Pre-Theater:** Daily 6-7, $24.50
Credit Cards: All major, DC **Reservations:** Recommended
Dress: Nice casual **Parking:** Complimentary valet
Metro: Farragut West **Entertainment:** Pianist, dinner/Sun brunch

E xcept for the seafood, the BOMBAY CLUB'S menu is nearly identical to that of any other Indian restaurant. Whether they charge $5 or $50, Indian restaurants all serve *rogan josh* and *vindaloo*, tandoor chicken and *dal*. The strictly vegetarian ones, of course, skip the meats. The South Indian places serve rice-flour pancakes. And the upscale restaurants, like this one, add scallops, crab and lobster to their repertoires.

But while the choices sound the same, no other Indian restaurant, not even another pricey one, has quite the same spacious comfort, casual luxury, quiet elegance. The service here is as professional and suave as what we hope to find in the best French restaurants. And those ubiquitous Indian classics are at their most refined. The shrimp are said to be fresh—and they taste so juicy and sweet that I'm not inclined to doubt it. Vegetable curries taste clearly of their vegetables—neither overcooked nor from a can. Sauces are delicate as well as spicy, and never show a telltale rim of grease. Rice is fat and tender, each grain separate. Presentations are artistic. And most important, the spices are married thoughtfully rather than jumbled.

With all that, the standouts at the BOMBAY CLUB are still the dishes unique to the more lavish Indian menus: salmon marinated with yogurt and cooked in a tandoor, appetizers of piquant mussels and crab and scallops—though one Monday lunch, they tasted as if they'd had a rough weekend. Look for the right beverages here, too, whether an old fashioned Pimms cup or seasonal fresh juices.

And keep in mind that refinements don't always work. An appetizer of *sev puri*, a casual toss of fried thin noodles and potato with tamarind and mint chutney, is here tortured into cunning shapes and a sight to behold, but it's grown soggy while it's been dressed up. So order your usual tandoori chicken or lamb curry, consider a seafood luxury, and expect your dinner to remind you how well those British colonials lived.

BOMBAY CURRY COMPANY
3110 Mount Vernon Ave., Alexandria, VA
(703) 836-6363

INDIAN

Lunch: Daily 11:30-2:30 (Sun buffet $8) **Entrees:** $3.50-$7
Dinner: M-Th 5:30-10, F-Sat 5:30-11, Sun 5-9 **Entrees:** $7-$10
Credit Cards: MC, V, DIS, DC **Dress:** Casual
Reservations: Recommended **Parking:** Free lot

This small storefront Indian restaurant has responded to its popularity by brightening the dining room: Now it's a small storefront dressed for company. Still, it's far from fancy, with dark green vinyl tablecloths and modest decorations on the walls. More important, its prices are still pleasantly low and its service remains as friendly as ever — though at the height of a busy evening the small staff serves at a run.

On the surface, there's not much to distinguish the BOMBAY CURRY COMPANY from countless other little Indian restaurants. Its breads are pedestrian and its menu choices are standard. If you start with spiced tandoori chicken wings, though, you'll understand its attraction. They leave your eyes teary and your mouth tingling for more. The curries won't impress you with the quality of the meat, but with the complexity and skill of the spicing. Butter chicken is creamy and, at first taste, tomatoey and mild. Gradually your tongue distinguishes the ginger, then notes layers of other spices. They taste freshly ground and have more texture than dried powders. They build and develop and reveal themselves in waves of flavor.

Each curry is significantly different, and the hot ones are mightily hot. After a meal at BOMBAY CURRY COMPANY, you'll never again think of all curries as just one yellowish stew. The best time to study them is during the $8 Sunday buffet: half a dozen entrees, house-made bread, rice and salads, all for less than $8. What's more, that's when the chef takes the opportunity to make seasonal dishes and the foods that strike his fancy each week.

BREAD LINE
1751 Pennsylvania Ave. NW, Washington, DC
(202) 822-8900

AMERICAN/INTERNATIONAL   🚹

Breakfast: M-F 7-10:30 (leftovers till 11) **Entrees:** $1-$3.50
Lunch: M-F 11-3 (light fare till 5) **Entrees:** $3-$8
Closed: Sat-Sun **Credit Cards:** All major, DIS, debit cards
Reservations: No **Dress:** Casual **Parking:** Street
Metro: Farragut West, Farragut North

Many years ago, a beloved, now-gone relative told me, "I'm proud of what you do, even if all you write about is sandwiches." Sandwiches? What's wrong with sandwiches? I think there's nothing more worthy of attention than a great sandwich. No dish is more versatile, satisfying or routinely dishonored than the sandwich.

It's so easy to use floppy, tasteless bread, and who notices? Yet the BREAD LINE bakes its own, and there's no better bread in town. The fillings, too, are simply excellent, each in its own way. But owner Mark Furstenberg—who, I feel duty-bound to disclose, is a friend of mine—will say his place is not a sandwich shop. It makes stuffed doughs—*piadini*, knishes and empanadas, calzones and samosas as well as small pizzas, tartines and other topped breads. And they are wonderful.

The soups are as robust and elegant as any you'll find at restaurants with captains and sommeliers rather than self-service and carryout. The salads are hearty, creative and excruciatingly fresh. The breakfast pastries are "worth a trip," as the French put it. His cookies and desserts are homey and amusing. But what can I say? I

". . . there's no better bread in town," and the "fillings, too, are simply excellent."

can't resist the sandwiches. Not when the turkey is right out of the oven, aromatic and juicy; the Moroccan-spiced tuna has become a local legend; and the prosciutto for the sandwich with mascarpone, gorgonzola and fig jam comes from Parma. When I need a cheese steak, I wait for Wednesday; Tuesday is meat loaf day; and if I'm homesick for New Orleans I can find an honest *muffaletta* on Monday.

BRICKSKELLER
1523 22nd St. NW, Washington, DC
(202) 293-1885

AMERICAN   ♿

Open: M-Th 11:30 am-2 am, F till 3 am, Sat 6:30-3 am, Sun 6:30-2 am
Entrees: $5-$14 **Credit Cards:** All major, DIS, DC **Dress:** Casual
Reservations: Accepted for 6 or more **Metro:** Dupont Circle

Beer is big news these days. Some restaurants are brewing their own. Others are collecting impressive lists of microbrews. But still none can touch the BRICKSKELLER, which has almost a 40-year lead on these new beer purveyors. I don't know whether its claim to featuring the world's largest selection of beer is true, but its list of brews has climbed above 700, and the walls of this cellar are lined with their empties.

It looks like a fraternity hangout, but you don't have to be newly arrived at drinking age to enjoy the BRICKSKELLER. The service is friendly, and the food ranges from snacks (cheese board, pizza, tempura vegetable basket or spicy wings) to full meals (buffalo steak, rum and lime chicken, kalua pork or chicken flown in from Hawaii, or a shellfish assortment steamed in beer). There are even East European *pierogies*.

At the BRICKSKELLER, though, I turn conservative. Every time I order something adventurous, I wish I'd gotten a hamburger. The other foods are perfectly acceptable: The po' boy is stuffed with excellent fried oysters, even if the bread is flabby and the dressing is dull. The rainbow trout is fresh, and the pierogies are

> **"Its list of brews has climbed above 700."**

heart-warming. But I've learned the hard way: If anyone at the table has a burger, I'm going to want one. These burgers are terrific, whether the Brickburger with its bacon-salami-onion-cheese topping, the Down Home, combining ground beef with Italian sausage, or my favorite, the Ale Burger, seasoned with caraway and you-know-what. The fries, too, are dark and slightly sweet, clearly made from appropriately aged Idahos.

As for the beers, some people have a system. They might start with the A's, or make their way through one country or one brand. I just leaf through the book and zero in on a few new entries, then discuss the matter with my waiter. These waiters know their brews.

BURMA
740 6th St. NW, Washington, DC
(202) 638-1280

BURMESE

Lunch: M-F 11-3 **Dinner:** Sun-Sat 6-10
Entrees: $6-$8 **Credit Cards:** All major, DIS, DC
Reservations: Recommended **Dress:** Casual
Parking: Street **Metro:** Gallery Place-Chinatown

Chinatown has spread its wings to encompass Cantonese, Shanghai, Hunanese, Mongolian and Taiwanese cuisines. It has incorporated several Vietnamese restaurants. Yet the most exotic cooking in this enclave is at BURMA, a small upstairs restaurant that keeps adding unusual dishes to its long menu. The bare-bones dining room has just a bit of polish, and the service is reasonably communicative, if hesitant. Most disconcerting, though, the kitchen seems flummoxed by having to prepare for more than four people at a time.

If you plan your visit at least a day ahead, you can order a whole spiced duck. Otherwise, try the mango pork. It's lean chunks of braised meat permeated with red spice paste—a moderate hit of chili peppers included. Tamarind fish is also chili-heated, as well as tart, but fish is not BURMA'S strength, particularly on a Monday before the week's catch is in. The curries and kebabs aren't half as interesting as such less familiar dishes as sour mustard plant, the pickliest of pickles, sautéed with bits of pork. Often, though, the main dishes are hit-or-miss.

"The most exotic cooking [in Chinatown] is at Burma."

Among appetizers, fried vegetables feature eggplant in a light puffy batter, meltingly soft inside and irresistible, even though it's too greasy. It's the equal of gold fingers, a favorite that translates as fried squash, and both are served with a tart, salty, wonderful dipping sauce. BURMA serves half a dozen soups that are distillations of the restaurant's strong seasonings—chilies, lemon, tamarind, mustard plant. It has vegetarian entrees and intriguing noodle dishes. But its glory is salads, whether tofu, papaya, seafood, tea leaves, herbs, eggplant or ginger. The ones that sound the strangest taste the best. Consider the entrees an exploration and the appetizers and salads home base.

BUSARA
2340 Wisconsin Ave. NW, Washington, DC
(202) 337-2340

THAI

Lunch: M-F 11:30-3, Sat-Sun 11:30-4 **Entrees:** $6.25-$9
Dinner: Sun-Th 5-11, F-Sat 5-midnight **Entrees:** $10-$15.25
Credit Cards: All major, DIS, DC **Reservations:** Recommended
Dress: Nice casual **Parking:** Valet (fee) at dinner
Happy Hour: M-F 5-8, half-price tropical drinks

B USARA has a glossy modern set of rooms with sensational furniture—plastic-coated tables in crayon colors in the dining room and, in the bar, metal tables that reflect in psychedelic hues. On a winter day it could cheer you instantly. In fall or spring, the back garden can soothe you, with its tables set around a tiny pond lush with greenery.

The menu, too, is unusual, with some mild attempts at fusing Eastern and Western cuisines. Many entrees are served Western style, with vegetables and salad greens filling out the plate. Like all Thai restaurants, though, BUSARA serves a range of mild to incendiary dishes—designated by one, two or three chili peppers on the menu.

If I'm eating with a group and willing to risk a disappointment or two, I order some of the more original and multinational dishes. If it's just myself and a friend, we play it safe with traditional Thai cooking. The old standard *larb gai* is just right at BUSARA: The minced chicken has plenty of lime and hot peppers, with lettuce leaves to fold around it. If you like dough-wrapped appetizers, the list is satisfying, from Shrimp Bikini—wrapped in spring-roll skin—to spring rolls to crab and chicken wrapped in bean-curd sheets. Then there are salads, not small appetizers as in most Thai restaurants, but large platefuls, enough for a table to share or one diner to make into a meal.

The list of entrees is immense—if you want to make it easier to navigate, just concentrate on the curries. And for contrast, a noodle dish like *pad thai* is mild enough to tame the curries' heat. In short, BUSARA combines modern sophistication with tradition, comfort with festivity and neighborly warmth with professionalism.

For this restaurant's Tysons Corner branch, where parking is free and closing time is slightly earlier: Busara, 8142 Watson St., McLean, VA, (703) 356-2288.

C.F. FOLKS
1225 19th St. NW, Washington, DC
(202) 293-0162

AMERICAN/INTERNATIONAL

Lunch: M-F 11:45-2:45 **Entrees:** $4-$10
Closed: Sat-Sun **Credit Cards:** Cash, check only
Dress: Casual **Reservations:** No
Parking: Street **Metro:** Dupont Circle

It's been years since I've ordered from the menu at C.F. FOLKS. This tiny luncheonette—just a counter, a handful of tables inside and a few on the terrace—thrives because of its daily specials, listed on a blackboard.

The four or five entree options might include contemporary grilled chicken in yellow pepper sauce on pasta, or old-fashioned meatloaf with mushroom gravy and mashed potatoes. One day the theme is Cajun, another day Southwestern or seafood. There's always house-made soup—any French restaurant in town could profit from this recipe for saffron garlic soup, while the clam chowder tastes like New England's best, and typically there's a fresh-fruit cobbler or pie for dessert. It might be a soft-shell crab day or a day for pan-fried catfish with spicy tomato sauce on a bed of grits flavored with black beans. The macaroni with cheese, ham and asparagus is even better than childhood memories.

C.F. FOLKS serves the kind of food that usually comes with a waiter and a white tablecloth, but since the entree prices are under $10, regulars are glad to serve themselves and to carry their crab cakes or curry back to the office or to a park bench. How many lunch counters have a Paul Prudhomme cookbook behind the cash register and host informal debates about the city council in between ringing up orders?

CAFE ATLANTICO
405 8th St. NW, Washington, DC
(202) 393-0812

LATIN AMERICAN/CARIBBEAN   ♿

Lunch: M-Sat 11:30-2:30 **Entrees:** $8.50-$14
Dinner: Sun-Th 5:30-10, F-Sat 5:30-11 **Entrees:** $15.50-$20
Light Fare: M-Sat 2:30-5:30, $6-$9.50
Pre-Theater: Daily 5:30-7, $20 **Credit Cards:** All major, DC
Dress: Casual **Reservations:** Recommended
Parking: Valet (fee) at dinner **Metro:** Archives-Navy Memorial

If Jose Andres is cooking this exquisitely at age 29, what will he be doing by 35? No chef in America creates Nuevo Latino or New Caribbean food with a surer hand or a finer sensibility. And he keeps getting better.

CAFE ATLANTICO is a three-story festival of bright colors, with an open kitchen and artwork in sizzling hues. It's a vibrant place, with service so charming you might be tempted to book your table permanently.

Start with a tart jolt of lime in a *caipirinha* or a milder pisco sour decorated with chevrons of spice powder. Or go right to the wine list, which explores our Southern Hemisphere and comes up with liquid gold.

The appetizers are all so compelling, you might want to look into a tasting menu. The tuna seviche—served oh, so fashionably, in the bowls of spoons—is enriched with coconut milk and crunchy with corn nuts, yet its taste stays focused on the buttery raw fish itself. Soft-shell crabs swim in passion fruit, which heightens the sweetness of these sweet, crisp-edged little delicacies. Scallops are bedded on creamy white-and- black rice, concealing surprises of texture. Entrees team salmon with papaya and a crab-corn stew, or steak with malanga and tamarind. While I've been disappointed with the texture of the pheasant, its deconstructed mole sauce is intriguing, as is a tian layering avocado, the hauntingly delicious corn fungus called *huitlacoche*, and slices of lamb. But one dish continues to stand out: a tropical rendition of duck confit, its skin crackly with a crust of brown sugar and allspice, its richness balanced by tart passion fruit.

Nor does Andres neglect desserts. They're lush and whimsical remakes of chocolate bread pudding, hazelnut mousse and such. What this adds up to is a meal of such imagination and quality that it would cost 50 percent more anywhere else in town—if you could find it.

CAFE BERLIN
322 Massachusetts Ave. NE, Washington, DC
(202) 543-7656

GERMAN   ♿

Lunch: M-Sat 11:30-4 **Entrees:** $7-$17
Dinner: Sun-Th 4-10, F-Sat 4-11 **Entrees:** $12.50-$17
Credit Cards: All major, DC **Reservations:** Preferred
Dress: Casual **Parking:** Street **Metro:** Union Station

Washington has only a couple of German restaurants, but even if there were more, CAFE BERLIN'S sweet little dining room would stand out from the crowd. You'd hardly know you were in the shadow of the Capitol at this small town house restaurant. It has such a European lilt, from the flowered tablecloths with pink underneath to the soft accents of the staff. This is a hospitable restaurant with Old World charm. There is enough space between tables to suggest privacy and a peaceful air that encourages conversation.

"One might be inclined to start and end with dessert."

The most seductive food is on the pastry display, so one might be inclined to start and end with dessert, from black forest cake to strudel. In a more conventional vein, CAFE BERLIN offers wiener schnitzel, sauerbraten and paprika-tinged stews. There are wursts, of course. And spaetzle are handmade here. Even vegetables are dressed up with the likes of dill sauce.

Some dinner entrees cost three times as much as at lunch, but it's still moderately priced. And in the evening the dishes' taste is fresher and the choices are more extensive.

CAFE BETHESDA
5027 Wilson Lane, Bethesda, MD
(301) 657-3383

AMERICAN ♿

Lunch: M-F 11:30-2 **Entrees:** $7-$14
Dinner: Sun-Th 5:30-9, F-Sat 5:30-10 **Entrees:** $16-$25
Credit Cards: All major **Reservations:** Recommended
Dress: Nice casual **Parking:** Valet (fee) at dinner **Metro:** Bethesda

In its expansions and contractions, CAFE BETHESDA has sometimes lost its way. At its best, it serves light, fresh and sophisticated American food with French underpinnings, and even at its least, it is a simply pretty little restaurant.

The menu runs to classics such as chicken marsala, grilled fish, perhaps a veal dish, a seafood salad. Crab cakes are dressed up with magenta-marinated red cabbage and a scattering of finely diced tomatoes and peppers on a stark white lemon cream. And the creamy crab cakes themselves are unorthodox but delicious, particularly since they are

". . . as scrumptious as a Monet, no matter what's being served."

sharpened by the lemon, the cabbage and a few capers. The vegetables served with the entrees give me hope: wonderful, lumpy, red-skin mashed potatoes, perfectly cooked fine matchsticks of carrot, a few impeccable snow peas.

Still, the food wouldn't carry the day if CAFE BETHESDA'S service were less endearing. And on a sunny afternoon, surrounded by flower-laden window boxes and potted flowering trees under a flowered umbrella, a meal at CAFE BETHESDA is as scrumptious as a Monet, no matter what's being served.

CAFE DALAT
3143 Wilson Blvd., Arlington, VA
(703) 276-0935

VIETNAMESE   ♿

Open: Sun-Th 11-9:30, F-Sat 11-10:30 **Entrees:** $7-$10
Lunch Special: M-F 11-2:30, $4.25, $5 (buffet)
Credit Cards: MC, V **Reservations:** Recommended
Dress: Casual **Parking:** Free lot (after 6) **Metro:** Clarendon

All of the Vietnamese restaurants in Arlington's Little Saigon serve the standard dishes: *cha gio*, summer rolls, *pho*, grilled pork, lemon grass chicken and more. Thus, clearly the survivors are good enough to meet the competition. So how to choose? It depends on what you want to eat.

CAFE DALAT is one of the smaller restaurants, with a menu that is not as extensive as Queen Bee's down the street. Given the unadorned look of the place, you can guess that the prices are low. Most of the dishes are grilled, and that's what draws me back to CAFE DALAT: simple, lightly seasoned grilled meat or seafood.

The sweet-soy marinated pork is crunchy, chewy and flavorful. Even better is the skewered seafood. The menu doesn't quite explain the dish, but it's a kind of mixed-seafood mousse, formed into small balls and threaded on skewers with squares of onion and green pepper. Unlike most ground-seafood dishes, this one tastes fresh and clearly of shellfish. It's light and airy, faintly caramelized, and is meant to be wrapped with cilantro, shredded vegetables and white rice noodles in leaves of lettuce, then dipped in a golden fruity peanut sauce. A beer and a platter of Vietnamese skewered seafood, pork, beef or chicken—that's heavy competition for American fast food.

CAFE DELUXE
3228 Wisconsin Ave. NW, Washington, DC
(202) 686-2233

AMERICAN   🦽

Lunch: M-Sat 11:45-3 **Entrees:** $8-$13
Dinner: M-Th 3-10:30, F-Sat 3-11, Sun 3-10 **Entrees:** $8-$19
Brunch: Sun 11-3 **Entrees:** $6-$10 **Credit Cards:** All major
Reservations: No **Dress:** Casual **Parking:** Street
Happy Hour: $1 off drafts, 25 cents off rail drinks

CAFE DELUXE looks like a French brasserie. Even better, it looks like one that's been around a while. The tile floor, chunky glassware and thick white dinner plates delivered to your table without fanfare identify this as a casual, drop-in-for-a-snack kind of restaurant. When it's crowded it has a buzz, a burbling of conversation, but even at its noisiest you can converse without strain. Maybe that's why it seems so comfortingly broken-in.

Think of this as an American diner: Would you order sea bass with lemon pepper crust in a diner? Or grilled tuna burger with pickled ginger mayo? No, you'd probably go for the bacon cheeseburger. And you'd be guessing right.

I'd also suggest another item that's in diner mode: grilled meatloaf. And the sugar snap peas are a distinct improvement on anything green you are likely to find at a diner. The menu nods to vegetarians with a grilled vegetable antipasto, a vegetable pizza and fettuccine. There's an agreeable spinach and cheese dip with terrific, crackly, thin tortilla chips for people who want to hang out without being involved in a serious meal. While the soup might not be exciting, it is house-made and meal-sized. Desserts are rich and homey, such gooey sweets as chocolate-chip cookie pie or fruit cobbler.

A micro-brewed draft beer or thick white mug of perfectly decent American coffee, sipped slowly in a calm dark booth, or a martini and a burger at the bar—those alone are good reasons to visit CAFE DELUXE.

CAFE MILANO
3251 Prospect St. NW, Washington, DC
(202) 333-6183

ITALIAN   ♿

Lunch: M-Sat 11:30-4 **Entrees:** $8-$15
Dinner: M-Th 4-11, F-Sat 4-midnight, Sun noon-11 **Entrees:** $11-$28
Late Night: M-Th 11-1 am, F-Sat midnight-1 am **Entrees:** $7.50-$15.50
Dress: Casual **Credit Cards:** All major
Reservations: Recommended **Parking:** Validated at lunch

It's an Italian fashion show: designer neckties on the walls, terracotta tile floor and umbrella-shaded outdoor tables, comfortably and expensively stylish. The crowd, too, looks like the imaginings of a fashion designer, ever more European, more chic and more deafeningly sociable as the evening wears on.

The food is also haute couture. It's got very good ingredients and clean lines. This is a salad crowd, appreciative of bright, crisp simplicity, as in shaved fennel, bitingly fresh arugula,

"It's an Italian fashion show."

sharp and earthy Parmesan, lemon and olive oil. Carpaccios of meat or fish offer protein as refreshing as a salad. And pastas tend to be rich in vegetable flavors, the likes of wild mushrooms and spinach with chopped raw tomato on silky house-made pappardelle. I seek my pizzas elsewhere, and save CAFE MILANO for light dishes—perhaps a plate of prosciutto, with all the nuances of aged wine, or a *vitello tonnato* that's creamy and haunting even if the veal is sliced too thin to maintain its character.

When I've ventured into the entrees, they've surpassed my expectations. Chicken breast rolled with sage and prosciutto is plump and juicy on its bed of ratatouille, and a grill-striped paillard of veal, still on the bone, is a succulent background to oil-slicked spinach and olives, which bodes well for veal Milanese and the double-cut veal chop. But some of the entree prices are so steep that concentrating on salads and pastas makes several kinds of good sense.

CAFE OLÉ
4000 Wisconsin Ave., Washington, DC
(202) 244-1330

MEDITERRANEAN   🚻

Lunch: M-F 11-3 **Entrees:** $5-$7
Dinner: M-Th 3-10, F 3-12, Sat 11-midnight, Sun 11-11
Entrees: $5-$12.50 **Dress:** Casual **Reservations:** 8 or more only
Parking: Validated all day **Metro:** Tenleytown-AU
Entertainment: Guitar F-Sat 8-midnight (summer only)

CAFE OLÉ is not just at the other end of the price scale from Jacques Van Staden's usual haunts (he's worked at Lespinasse, Citronelle and Jean-Louis). It's also as casual as they are formal. There's not a necktie in the house, unless some diner has come right from work.

At first glance, CAFE OLÉ seems like another fast-food, snacks-and-wraps place. But something far more interesting is happening here. CAFE OLÉ is creating its own environment. The bar has that convivial feel of an authentic wine bar: People seem to be there for tasting and conversing rather than hard drinking.

The food also plays a significant part. Bright colors, hard edges, intrusive music and self-service aren't usually accompanied by such luscious little salads. The *soujouk* salad, crunchy and spicy, is like none I've tasted. Shankleesh is a dice of ripe tomatoes made wildly delicious with creamy sheep's cheese, red onions and a tingle of seasonings. These are small dishes, but they have such flavorful impact that they leave you satisfied well before you're stuffed.

Of the *mezze* I've tried from the long list, I like the cold ones best. The hummus has guts. The *panzanella* is that irresistible mix of good tomatoes with basil, garlic and cubes of toasted bread infused with olive oil. Toscana salata has bits of mortadella, artichoke and olives tossed with silky orzo in a lemon aioli. French, Italian, Greek—a little of everything is in this one little dish. Others are more North African, or French, or Israeli or even Spanish. These foods have big flavors, well suited to small portions and to slow nibbling. They far outshine the complicated and sometimes mushy sandwiches and wraps.

Desserts are showy sweets, rich and stolid. Giant brownies are achingly sweet and sometimes stale. This is a kitchen that accomplishes more with subtlety than with extravagance.

CALIFORNIA GRILL
1090 Vermont Ave. NW, Washington, DC
(202) 289-2098

AMERICAN   🚹

Breakfast: M-Sat 6-10:30 **Entrees:** $1.75-$3.25
Lunch: M-Sat 10:30-5 **Entrees** $3-$7
Closed: Sat-Sun **Credit Cards:** All major
Reservations: No **Dress:** Casual
Parking: Street **Metro:** McPherson Square

Only in America do French, Mexican and Southern California cooking add up to bargain-priced fast food. The CALIFORNIA GRILL is a self-service cafeteria and carryout where you get not just a sandwich but a meal—light or substantial, hot or cold—for well under $10.

The salads are the ubiquitous Caesar, but also a California Cobb made with chicken, avocado, eggs, two cheeses and bacon. The tostadas come with traditional fillings as well as mahi mahi. The sandwiches include BLT, egg salad, roast beef and turkey, but then there's a grilled tuna steak. And kebabs—the highlight of this menu—are well marinated, nicely charred on the grill yet moist, and they come with herbed roasted new potatoes that could make french fries seem boring. The chicken kebab, my favorite, can compete with any you'd find at triple the price.

"Only in America do French, Mexican and Southern California cooking add up to bargain-priced fast food."

This is a New Wave cafeteria, one with an emphasis on fresh vegetables and bright flavors. It's so trendy that it has an espresso bar. And the espresso bar is so trendy that it serves tapas. What will California think of next?

There is another DC location: 1720 M St. NW, (202) 463-4200.

CAPITOL CITY BREWING COMPANY
1100 New York Ave. NW, Washington, DC
(202) 628-2222

AMERICAN ♿

Open: Sun-Th 11 am-11 pm, F-Sat 11 am-midnight
Entrees: $8-$20 **Credit Cards:** All major, DIS, DC
Reservations: Accepted for 15 or more **Dress:** Casual
Parking: Street **Metro:** Metro Center

These immense, handsome brewpubs have been installed in some of the most magnificent historic buildings in the city. That's enough reason to have a look. They also feature delicious amber-tinged brews—you can get a sampler of four if you don't have an immediate preference. With them comes a basket of soft pretzels and horseradish-mustard dip. Who needs more?

Yet there's a long menu, too, that runs the gamut from light (salad with grilled chicken breast, grilled or poached fish) to heavy (a variety of sausages, ribs, pork chops). Surely the dishes were devised to sell beer, as some of the best are hot enough to send you gasping for a cold draft—the chili has a real kick, and even the wonderful corn crab chowder has a hit of pepper. Not all is spicy, though. Some dishes err on the bland side; vegetable-topped pasta with pesto, for example, can taste of little more than starch.

Habits die hard, and most people seem to stick to burgers at pubs, but then these thick, char-striped, cooked-as-ordered burgers (beef or turkey) can be worthy of the beer. They're served with thin fries, rather tasteless and chewy but so crunchy they seem as if they've been coated with flour. Po' boys are also popular, and the oysters have a pleasantly crackly cornmeal crust. Too bad they don't have a more authentic po' boy roll, though. Excellent fried catfish fares no better as a club sandwich on unfortunately soggy toast. The sleeper on this menu is the mushroom quesadilla, listed as an appetizer but certainly enough for lunch. It's rich and gooey with cheese and comes with a brightly flavorful tomato salsa. More than Cobb salad or grilled salmon, it's a dish that seems like beer food.

Other locations: Postal Square, 2 Massachusetts Ave. NW, Washington, DC, (202) 842-2337; 2700 S. Quincy St., Shirlington, VA, (703) 578-3888, and 7735 Old Georgetown Rd., Bethesda, MD, (301) 652-2282. There is live entertainment on Thursday nights at Shirlington.

CAPITAL GRILLE
601 Pennsylvania Ave. NW, Washington, DC
(202) 737-6200

AMERICAN/STEAKHOUSE   &

Lunch: M-F 11:30-3 **Entrees:** $9-$28
Dinner: Sun-Th 5-10, F-Sat 5-11 **Entrees:** $22-$23
Credit Cards: All major, DIS, DC **Reservations:** Recommended
Dress: Jacket & tie preferred **Metro:** Archives-Navy Memorial
Parking: Complimentary valet at dinner, validation at lunch

THE CAPITAL GRILLE, the third branch of a Providence, R.I.-based chain, shows its dry-aged steaks not only in the raw but in the throes of molding—part of the aging process. The aging room is in full view of the street. From a distance the rows of uncut porterhouses look richly abundant. But look too closely and you'll probably order fish. Inside, the dining room has clubby dark wood and money-green window shades, hunters' prize heads on the walls and big tables set with steak knives. This is a he-man environment.

If you can overcome your introduction at the aging room window, the overriding reason for dining at the CAPITAL GRILLE is the steaks—sirloin and porterhouse. Don't look for butter-tender steaks. These have some bite and a full meaty flavor. The portions are gigantic—baked potatoes a pound each, mashed potatoes family size, and cottage fries portioned for a tableful, then piled with french-fried onions.

Light eaters will zero in on the seafood: swordfish and salmon, grilled just past rare, or large grilled shrimp on linguine. Lobsters can be steamed or broiled and generally come in giant sizes. All the seafood looks impressive, whether inch-thick fish steaks (even two inches on occasion) or the monster-sized shrimp and lobsters. And they are cooked so gently that undercooking is a far greater likelihood than overcooking. But none of the seafood has much taste; it's just nice, bland stuff. And the pasta under the shrimp is limp and soggy. Lamb and veal chops are better entree alternatives, though not nearly the match of the steaks.

Wisdom might dictate that you start a meat-heavy meal with a salad, and there is a properly zesty Caesar. Even so, passion might direct you to the fine smoked salmon or greaseless pan-fried calamari with hot pickled peppers. Should you find room for dessert, you can top off your fatty escapade with a flourless chocolate cake that tastes like fudge with an extra dose of butter.

CAPITOL VIEW CLUB
Hyatt Regency Hotel
400 New Jersey Ave. NW, Washington, DC
(202) 783-2582

AMERICAN ♿

Dinner: Daily 5:30-10:30 **Entrees:** $19.50-$27
Credit Cards: All major, DC **Reservations:** Recommended
Dress: Jacket preferred **Entertainment:** Pianist Sun-Sat 7-11
Parking: Complimentary valet **Metro:** Union Station

Except for a picnic, you couldn't have both good food and a monumental view in this city—until the CAPITOL VIEW CLUB opened. Even from the farthest table of this rooftop restaurant, you can see the drama of the illuminated Capitol dome and the charm of the Library of Congress' aged copper roof—although admittedly you have to peer beyond a dreary boxy office building in the foreground. The dining room is unmistakably hotel style; there is little interior decoration to compete with the scene, except for etchings of the Capitol lining the entrance. Tables are spacious and well spaced; chairs and banquettes are comfortable. Table lamps shaded in black silk flicker with alcohol flames to intensify the romance of the evening. That romance is disrupted, though, by waiters who try hard but don't necessarily understand much English, and tables of loud conventioneers.

"Where else have you seen an elk chop?"

At lunch the CAPITOL VIEW CLUB is just that — a private club. Only at dinner is the restaurant public. The menu is American and modern, full of adventures. Where else have you seen an elk chop? CAPITOL VIEW CLUB goes to the trouble to get good breads and serve a fine selection of wines by the glass. It offers plenty of seafood and brags outrageously about its crab cakes, but it needs better smoked salmon and trout. And meats such as buffalo rib eye and rack of lamb are best left bare, since the sauces tend to be overreduced and sticky. In fact, vegetables are typically the highlights of the entrees.

THE CAPITOL VIEW CLUB, atop the Hyatt Regency Hotel, extracts a price to pay for this feasting with a view, as in most hotel restaurants. But even with its deficiencies, it succeeds beyond our usual options for rooftop dining.

CARAVAN GRILL
1825 18th St. NW, Washington, DC
(202) 518-0444

PERSIAN

Open: M-Th 11:30-10:30, F-Sat 11:30-midnight, Sun noon-10
Entrees: $7-$20 **Lunch Buffet:** Daily 12-4, M-F $7, Sat-Sun $8
Dinner Buffet: Sun-Th 4-10:30, $10; F-Sat 4-12, $11
Credit Cards: All major **Dress:** Casual **Reservations:** Recommended **Parking:** Street **Metro:** Dupont Circle

Given the CARAVAN GRILL'S hidden basement entrance, you'd almost expect an eatery that's small, dark and perhaps a bit grubby, the proverbial hole-in-the-wall. Instead, you're greeted by a quietly dignified host in a long white tunic and pants, or another wearing a colorful shirt and an exuberant smile.

One side of the restaurant is devoted to the buffet—quite a stretch of dishes for around $10. The host shows you the day's creations, which run to a dozen or more and include everything from three kinds of eggplant and stewed meats to chicken kebabs and light salads. You can even order single dishes off the buffet for a small price, or fill a container and carry it out, priced by the pound.

CARAVAN GRILL'S buffet is a playground of exotic aromas and mysterious combinations. Even though some of the dishes are soupy and soggy, others are unmistakably delicious, while still others grow on you after a bit.

Look for yogurt soup. All the soups are hearty and satisfying, but if you find a creamy green soup thick with four kinds of beans, lentils, rice and yogurt, you've hit the right day.

The fat little pieces of chicken on the buffet kebabs are juicy and tender, more flavorful than the a la carte chicken kebab. And the eggplant dishes are fine. Meats are better when ordered a la carte. In all, the vegetables survive the steam table best, and the salads are a refreshing contrast.

Beyond the buffet, which despite its flaws is an astonishing bargain, there are even greater deals on the a la carte menu—*kubideh* kebab and lamb kebab are the match of any in town at twice their price.

The desserts are bought from a Middle Eastern bakery, so they're no reflection on this kitchen. Besides, after you've had your fill from the buffet, dessert is not likely to loom as much of a temptation.

CARLYLE GRAND CAFE
4000 S. 28th St., Arlington, VA
(703) 931-0777

AMERICAN   ⓖ

Lunch: Daily 11:30-5   **Entrees:** $7-$13
Dinner: Sun-Tu 5-9, W 5-10, F-Sat 5-11   **Entrees:** $9-$20
Brunch: Sun 10:30-2, $7-$13   **Pre-Theater:** M-Th 5-6, $10
Credit Cards: All major   **Dress:** Casual-formal
Reservations: Recommended   **Parking:** Free lot
Happy Hour: M-F 4:30-6, complimentary chips & salsa

This large contemporary restaurant's ground floor, with its vast bar and sea of cafe tables, is only for those who can stand near the speakers at a rock concert without earplugs. I'd certainly head for the upstairs. There the place still has all the backdrop of a party — glowing wood with matte black accents, decorative glass, immense art nouveau posters and even piped music — but it also has the comfort of upholstered booths and modulated noise. The eclectic-American menus of the two floors are not identical, but close enough. And the prices are the same.

This kitchen does well by fish. The lightly smoked grilled salmon is said to be the most popular entree. No wonder. The smoking is delicate and the salmon is cooked carefully so that the surface is nicely browned while the interior is pale pink, tender and juicy. It's topped with diced raw tomato and onion vinaigrette, which nicely cuts the sweetness of the honey-mustard cream painted in zigzags across the fish. Chicken is often a tasteless thing these days. But the chicken paillard at the CARLYLE GRAND CAFE recalls why Americans once dreamed of a chicken in every pot. Not so with the shrimp. They are large and accurately grilled but totally tasteless. Crab cakes, too, are watery and bland. Grilled pork chops are likely to be dry, saved only by basil mashed potatoes and a tart, spicy apple chutney with appealingly firm fruit. There is plenty more to explore here, from sandwiches to steaks, and the salads look like clear winners.

When in doubt, stick with the familiar. The quesadilla weaves fragrant roasted peppers, spicy chorizo and mild cheese into a fine gooey filling for crisped tortillas, and the mound of lightly spiced onion rings served with a bottle of house-made mustardy steak sauce can deliciously serve as dinner.

CASHION'S EAT PLACE
1819 Columbia Rd. NW, Washington, DC
(202) 797-1819

AMERICAN

Dinner: Tu 5:30-10, W-Sat 5:30-11, Sun 5:30-10
Entrees: $14.50-$19 **Brunch:** Sun 11:30-2:30 **Entrees:** $7-$9
Closed: M **Credit Cards:** MC, V **Dress:** Casual
Reservations: Recommended **Parking:** Valet (fee) after 6:30

This Adams-Morgan restaurant is like a friend. Its space and menu are small, the mood is casual and the room is decorated with photos that look straight out of a family album. The menu, written in chef Ann Cashion's script, reads as if she just went to the market and decided on the spot what to serve her friends for dinner. Unfortunately, Cashion's is a moody friend, and sometimes short-tempered or inconsiderate. It's not the place to try on a crowded night.

Nothing is excessively elaborate. This is straightforward cooking with French underpinnings and an American sensibility. The favorite dishes stay on the menu, so you can expect to return to the lovely gold-and-green curried mussels with spinach, or the fragile and tangy leek and goat cheese tart, the credible gumbo or the painstakingly fresh fried shrimp and calamari with house-made tartar sauce.

There are always a couple of fish dishes with seasonal vegetables, lamb is often teamed with its natural allies—garlic and eggplant—and duck breast with a garnish of *foie gras* is likely to be dressed in something right from the orchard (which means sour cherries in summer). Most surprising are the appetizer pastas. Nearly anyplace else, whole wheat pappardelle would taste more like punishment than indulgence; here it is supple and flavorful, a delicious base for grated cheese and wild mushrooms.

Sometimes Cashion serves unfathomable disappointments—a chewy and unseasoned pork chop in recent memory. But who doesn't? And if you've been wise enough to order a side dish of crisp, buttery potatoes Anna, you'll never go hungry. Besides, the rustic, homey fruit desserts will make it up to you afterwards.

CESCO TRATTORIA
4871 Cordell Ave., Bethesda, MD
(301) 654-8333

ITALIAN

Lunch: M-F 11:30-2 **Entrees:** $10-$15
Dinner: M-Th 5:30-10, F-Sat 5:30-10:30, Sun 5-9 **Entrees:** $14-$22
Credit Cards: All major **Dress:** Casual **Reservations:** Suggested
Parking: Valet (fee) at dinner **Metro:** Bethesda

Bethesda has more than enough Italian restaurants, some might say. But it has pitifully few good ones, I'd respond. CESCO, with chef Francesco Ricchi in the kitchen, is the best of them I've found. After many years at his family restaurant in the hills above Florence, he moved to Washington to run I Ricchi downtown. Then, after some bouncing around, he took over this cozy whitewashed corner restaurant in Bethesda.

The place has its limitations: The dining room is forgettable, and the service can be harried. And, to be blunt, the cooking is not as sparkling as it was in the early days, and it's still prone to oversalting. More complaints? The bill adds up to quite a bit if you aren't careful.

The best of Bethesda's Italian restaurants.

Now that the carping is out of the way, here's what makes it worthwhile: Ricchi is inventive but never strays far from the classics. His wildly popular Parmigiano salad is wrapped in a crusty sleeve of baked cheese. His pastas skirt the obvious to include pappardelle with duck as well as various handmade stuffed noodles. His risotto shows the hand of an expert. Ricchi could teach American chefs how to roast—and spice—a baby chicken, and his fish dishes are straightforwardly excellent.

Few plates are decorative; mostly they rely on taste rather than design. CESCO serves the long-cooked dishes such as rabbit stew and osso buco that are eternal if not fashionable. And for dessert, though the creamy tiramisu, *zuccotto* and profiteroles (here called *bongo bongo*) are much in demand, they can't hold a candle to pretty, delicious strawberries sliced and arranged like a flower over a bed of pear puree.

48

CHADWICK'S

5247 Wisconsin Ave. NW, Washington, DC
(202) 362-8040

AMERICAN

Lunch: M-Sat 11:30-4 **Entrees:** $6-$10
Dinner: Sun-Th 4-midnight, F-Sat 4-1 am **Entrees:** $6-$17
Brunch: Sun 10-4, $7-$12 **Reservations:** Accepted
Credit Cards: All major, DIS, DC, CB **Dress:** Casual
Parking: Validated after 5 **Metro:** Friendship Heights
Happy Hour: M-F 4-7, various drink and food specials

Years ago, when I called the branch of CHADWICK'S in Friendship Heights to ask whether it offered a Saturday hamburger special, I was told, "We have hamburgers, and they are special." It's still true.

These burgers are thick and juicy, carefully handled and cooked as rare as requested, striped with grill marks and stacked on a very good golden, chewy, sesame-seed bun with lettuce, tomato, red onion and a dill pickle. In fact, they are one of the best burgers in town, regardless of price. The fries are limp and boring, but plentiful. And the rest of the pub fare tends to be well priced, decently cooked and served with breezy good cheer.

CHADWICK'S in Georgetown, with its dark old wood and homey service, is worth remembering when you've been walking on the canal or strolling at Washington Harbour and want a quiet retreat from the crowds —or don't want

"One of the best burgers in town, regardless of price."

to pay harborside prices. The other branches are appreciated by families, since children are treated like valued customers and their parents have learned to count on efficient service. The three Chadwick's are now independently owned, but they are all cozy pubs that have been brought up well and have so far aimed in the right direction.

THE CHEESECAKE FACTORY
5345 Wisconsin Ave. NW, Washington, DC
(202) 364-0500

AMERICAN	&#9855;

Open: M-Th 11:30 am-11:30, F-Sat 11:30-12:30 am, Sun 10 am-11 pm
Entrees: $6-$18 **Brunch:** Sun 10-2:30, $6-$9.50
Credit Cards: All major, DIS, DC, CB **Reservations:** No
Dress: Casual **Parking:** Garage, 2 hours free
Metro: Friendship Heights

This jam-packed, family-friendly eating place could have been called the Salad Factory, but would lines have formed and crowds have waited through half the lunch or dinner hour if lettuce accounted for its fame? While small mountains of greenery sit before most everyone at lunch and many at dinner, they're largely an excuse for indulging in cheesecake: Eat all your vegetables—*then* you can have dessert.

Frankly, I prefer the vegetables. The menu lists more than a dozen salads, and each combines so many ingredients that it's hard to imagine them all fitting in one bowl. The Santa Fe salad, for example, has diced marinated chicken with lettuce (nearly all the salads start with chicken and greens), tossed with black beans, corn, fontina cheese, olives, tomatoes and crisp tortilla strips with lime vinaigrette, cilantro pesto and spicy Asian peanut sauce. It's Santa Fe by way of Rome and Bangkok.

The concoction that most captures my fancy, though, is the Tuscan chicken salad—with the tomato-basil vinaigrette on the side. Like the other salads here, it looks like a medium-sized Alp in a bowl. The bottom layer is penne, buried under an avalanche of awfully good greens. Sweetly roasted chunks of eggplant, a few strips of roasted peppers and a lone Kalamata olive are threaded through the greens, grated cheese is sprinkled on top, and clinging to the side of the mound are three very thin and nicely charred slabs of boneless chicken breast. You've got to cut them up and distribute them throughout the greenery for best results, because on its own the chicken is dry and cindery. But when the chicken bits are mixed in, their charred flavor is an asset to the fluff of vegetables. Some salads may be short on substance and high on volume, but that must be so they can leave you feeling light, healthy—and ready for cheesecake.

There is also a local branch in White Flint Mall, 11301 Rockville Pike, N. Bethesda, MD, (301) 770-0999.

CHING CHING CHA
1063 Wisconsin Ave. NW, Washington, DC
(202) 333-8288

CHINESE

Open: 11:30-10 **Tea Meal:** $10; appetizers: $1.50-$4.50
Credit Cards: All major, DIS **Dress:** Casual
Reservations: Recommended **Parking:** Street

W inter or summer, there's always an excuse for making lunch time an escape. Ching Ching Cha is just that. It's a Chinese tearoom in Georgetown, on Wisconsin Avenue below M Street, a surprise of spaciousness, beautiful details and sunshine from a large skylight.

Tables and chairs are gleaming rosewood with mother-of-pearl inlays, and you can opt to sit at low tables with pillows instead of on chairs. Along with the teas—some rare and costing $12 to $20 a pot, others a more modest $4—you get a lesson in brewing and a charming array of utensils.

You can also lunch lightly, on just a dish of wonderful crunchy five-spice peanuts, a single, delicious, tea-and-spice boiled egg, perhaps a small pastry. There's a handsome "tea meal" for $10, of miso soup and a lacquered tray of three tangy dressed cold vegetables, rice, a tiny salad and morsels of either soy-ginger chicken, salmon with mustard-miso sauce or steamed teriyaki-sauced tofu. The difficulty is reentering the jarring outside world after such a serene interlude.

CIELITO LINDO

4305 Kenilworth Ave., Bladensburg, MD
(301) 699 5787

MEXICAN

Open: Sun-Th 11 am-9 pm, F-Sat 11 am-10 pm, Sun 11 am-9 pm
Entrees: $5.25-$10 **Closed:** M **Credit Cards:** All major, DIS
Dress: Casual **Reservations:** Recommended **Parking:** Free lot

CIELITO LINDO is a real Mexican restaurant, not Tex-Mex or chain-Mex. It's a family-run, mom-and-pop kind of place that's about as close as a restaurant can get to home cooking. It's also a kind of home away from home for Mexicans yearning for familiar tastes and smells.

CIELITO LINDO has the best qualities of a mythic Mexican hole-in-the-wall without the drawbacks. It's spacious rather than cramped, spotless rather than grubby. The place is decorated with garish gold- and silver-braided sombreros, but the walls and floor are a soothing pink and gray.

The menu is a long list of predictable Mexican standbys: burritos, quesadillas, enchiladas, plus a few deep-fried things such as chimichangas and flautitas. None can hold a candle to Mama's specials: Michoacan-style empanadas, big fat baked ovals of faintly sweet yeast bread stuffed with chicken and vegetables; house-made yeast rolls, perhaps stuffed with cheese; or mole, that startlingly black, grainy sauce that builds up a gradual heat in your mouth, weaving an elusive sweetness and satisfying bitterness in its wake. You can get mole with chicken, or it makes for great enchiladas. So does the tangy, modestly hot green chili sauce for the everyday enchiladas. And don't pass up the roast pork—*carnitas* Michoacan-style, cooked for 12 hours until the meat collapses into soft strings—or barbecued lamb.

> **"It's . . . a kind of home away from home for Mexicans yearning for familiar tastes."**

Alongside the platters come tortillas, warmly exuding the smell of cornmeal. Most of the meats are also available in soft tacos, quickly heated on the grill and a little greasy but less so than the deep-fried kind.

CITIES
2424 18th St. NW, Washington, DC
(202) 328-7194

AMERICAN/INTERNATIONAL   ♿

Dinner: M-Th 6-11, F-Sat 6-midnight, Sun 5-9 **Entrees:** $17- $28
Brunch: Sun 11:30-5, $25 **Reservations:** Recommended
Credit Cards: All major, DIS, DC **Dress:** Casual; no sneakers
Parking: Complimentary valet for dinner
Entertainment: European dancing Th 9:30-2 am, F-Sat 9:30-3 am

The shtick here, for many years, has been that the restaurant changed its decor and menu every few months to transform its theme to a new city. Nowadays, though, CITIES seems permanently settled in Paris, though the dining room looks French only by way of South Beach. The chairs are wicker or covered in white cotton shrouds, the lighting is dim, the music has an Adams Morgan beat and the front, in good weather, is open to the street.

Thus CITIES is an odd mix of French tradition and American informality. The menu runs to appetizers of duck confit (fine, on a crisp potato pancake) to foie gras (bitter and almost raw, with cherries and spinach). There are salads with truffle vinaigrette or *mosto* oil, extravagances of caviar or shellfish on ice, and an assortment of cheeses—priced daily. The entree list is shorter, honoring such traditions as bouillabaisse and mixed grill. Dover sole is pristine, boned at the table and accompanied by a puff pastry topped with spinach and oysters; halibut, deliciously teamed with leeks, is supposed to be garnished with sweetbreads, but sometimes the chef forgets.

That's the crux of the problem here. The elaborate and pricey menu is fulfilled by a slapdash staff. The kitchen is slow, the dining room has a laissez-faire attitude, and there's no telling which dishes are going to be given the attention that the prices would suggest. The clue to dining well here is probably not the $49 raw bar "Plateau Prestige for Two" at the top of the menu but the $4.95 "Pommes Frites w/Dijon Mustard" prominently featured in the center.

CITY LIGHTS OF CHINA
1731 Connecticut Ave. NW, Washington, DC
(202) 265-6688

CHINESE

Lunch: M-F 11:30-3 **Entrees:** $4.50-$13
Dinner: M-Th 3-10:30, F 3-11, Sat noon-11, Sun noon-10:30
Dinner Entrees: $7-$26 **Credit Cards:** All major, DIS, DC
Reservations: Recommended **Dress:** Casual
Parking: Validated after 5 pm **Metro:** Dupont Circle

A s Chinatown shrinks, CITY LIGHTS OF CHINA keeps growing. It's now tripled its original size, and it depends on little more than pale green walls and mirrors to set the mood. The entrance crowds up, the service bogs down, but the cooking seldom falters. It's bright, and it's crunchy where it should be and tender where it counts—and the flavors hit all the right buttons.

Over the years I've built a list of favorite dishes—eggplant with garlic, stir-fried spinach, crispy fried beef with its caramelized glaze and red-pepper heat, and garlic-spiked salt-baked shrimp. The star of the show, however, is the Peking duck, as much for the dining room's performance as the kitchen's. The skin is as glossy as lacquer and nearly devoid of fat. The meat is moist and not overdone, and it's always available freshly cooked, even at lunch. The carving is a dance of considerable grace.

CITY LIGHTS OF CHINA has a broad menu, yet the kitchen can handle the range with competence. Its sauces aren't greasy, its vegetables are rarely overcooked. On the down side, prices have edged up and service is more efficient than attentive. This is not a place that cossets its diners, and it might rush you if there are people waiting for your table. But if there are shortcomings in the service, there are none in the quality of ingredients. It's the food that counts here.

> **"The star of the show is the Peking duck, as much for the dining room's performance as the kitchen's."**

CLYDE'S OF CHEVY CHASE
70 Wisconsin Circle, Chevy Chase, MD
(301) 951-9600

AMERICAN

Lunch: M-Sat 11-4:30 **Entrees:** $6-$14
Dinner: Sun-M 4:30-11, Tu-Th 4:30-midnight, F-Sat 4:30-12:30 am
Entrees: $6.75-$19 **Brunch:** Sun 10-4 **Entrees:** $7-$14
Late Night: Sun-M 10-11 pm, Tu-Sat 10-midnight
Credit Cards: All major, DIS, DC **Reservations:** Recommended
Dress: Casual **Parking:** Validated for 2 ½ hours
Metro: Friendship Heights **Happy Hour:** M-F 4-7, drafts $2, $3
house wine and rail drinks; menu $2.50-$4.50
Entertainment: F (DJ), Sat (pop covers) 9:30-close

It's the Orient Express. It's the Indy 500. It's the Air and Space Museum. It's CLYDE'S OF CHEVY CHASE. One of the largest Washington restaurant investments since Red Sage, this CLYDE'S is an extravaganza complete with a model train circling overhead and a reproduction of an Orient Express parlor car as your booth. These aren't second-rate imitations but luxurious replicas, with glove-soft leathers and inlaid woods.

Downstairs the menu is more casual and pizzas are available, as is a bandstand for live music behind the gigantic bar. Upstairs isn't exactly formal, but the dining room is conversation-friendly—bustling but not noisy. The menu offers every indulgence. Vegetarians are wooed with curry, couscous and a melange of lentils, brown rice and pasta. Meat eaters will find rotisserie duck and chicken as well as steaks in three sizes, while seafood fanciers can have their rockfish wild, their mahi mahi with tropical fruits and their shellfish Thai-style. Most of the menu reads better than it tastes, and you'd be safest ordering one of CLYDE'S justly famous hamburgers. Another hint: The kitchen copes better with fish than with meat.

"It's the Orient Express. It's the Indy 500. It's the Air and Space Museum."

It's all probably a plan to leave room for dessert. You can leave happy if you finish your meal with the chocolate bread pudding, warm and sufficiently bittersweet, with ice cream and whipped cream melting over it. And the cappuccino custard mousse cake is adorable, constructed as a coffee cup with a cookie handle.

CLYDE'S OF GEORGETOWN
3236 M St. NW, Washington, DC
(202) 333-9180

AMERICAN   ♿

Lunch: M-F 11:30-4:30, Sat 10-4   **Entrees:** $6.50-$14
Dinner: M-Th 4:30-10:30, F-Sat 4:30-11 pm, Sun 4-10:30
Entrees: $6.50-$19   **Pre-Theater:** M-F 4:30-6:30, all entrees $11
Brunch: Sat 10-4, Sun 9-4, $4.25-$14
Late Night: Sun-Th 10:30-midnight, F-Sat 11-1 am
Credit Cards: All major, DIS, DC   **Dress:** Casual
Reservations: Recommended   **Parking:** 2 hours discounted during concierge hours at Georgetown Park
Happy Hour: M-F 4-7, half-price drafts, menu $2.50-$4

Who would have expected Georgetown's first big-time saloon would become known for its produce? CLYDE'S has been reinventing itself. The atrium now has a 16th-century stone chimney piece, and large vintage model planes hang from the glass ceiling. The Victorian omelette room has been converted to a cherry-paneled tavern with oil paintings of sporting life over the booths.

Burgers are still featured—beef or turkey. And CLYDE'S chili is, too—though that is also available in cans from your neighborhood fancy food shop. Yet the mainstays are not beef but those contemporary light protein hits, chicken and salmon, appearing as appetizers, salads, sandwiches and entrees with an abundance of local vegetables to accompany them.

The menu changes daily, giving the chef a chance to react to the market. But sometimes I wonder if the chef changes from minute to minute. Rarely have I found such wide swings in a restaurant's food. The service is at least as erratic. CLYDE'S still makes a fine burger, and it has mastered rotisserie chicken. If I had to bet blindly, though, I'd put my money on appetizers: Chicken tenderloin strips sautéed with aromatic vegetables. A succulent eggplant terrine. Or the hidden gem of the menu, rings of tender white squid served in a hot iron skillet. CLYDE'S has a nifty draft-beer list, as one would expect, and a wine list that's value-conscious. It even boasts of serving filtered water in its pitchers.

Suburban locations: Clyde's at Tysons Corner, 8332 Leesburg Pike, Vienna, VA, (703) 734-1901; Clyde's at Mark Center, 1700 North Beauregard St., Alexandria, VA, (703) 820-8300; Clyde's of Reston, 11905 Market St., Reston, VA, (703) 787-6601, and Clyde's of Columbia, 10221 Wincopin Circle, Columbia, MD, (410) 730-2829.

COPPI'S VIGORELLI
3421 Connecticut Ave. NW, Washington, DC
(202) 244-6437

ITALIAN   ♿

Dinner: Sun-Th 5-11, F-Sat 5-midnight **Entrees:** $9.25-$16
Credit Cards: All major, DIS, DC
Reservations: Recommended **Dress:** Casual
Parking: Street **Metro:** Cleveland Park

The great accomplishment of this Cleveland Park spinoff of a U Street cafe is that as soon as the opening-months' crowds died down it took on the mood and patina of a long-loved neighborhood restaurant. The dark wood booths are cozy, the walls of photos add character, and the servers are matter-of-factly pleasant.

Beyond its comforting environment, COPPI'S has one of the most unusual Italian menus in town. Pastas and pizzas—baked in a wood-burning oven—are commonplace, but who else serves Ligurian dishes? And which other restaurant cooks all of its entrees in a wood-burning oven? The menu is full of unexpected twists, such as dried smoked tuna with the gnocchi and preserved lemons in the rice. Flavors of the Middle East— *merguez* sausage, cumin—weave among the baked chops, roasted fish, ravioli and hearty soups. Clams are not just baked—they are drenched in herbs and garlic and clustered in a casserole of bread so their juices form a kind of redolent, savory bread pudding.

If only the dishes tasted as good as they sound, I'd be a regular. I'm delighted by the salads, unprecedented combinations of meats or fish with greens, as in favas and *sopressata* or smoked tuna with arugula and caper pesto. Pastas tend to be too understated (where was the rabbit in my raviolini?), and casseroles scream themselves hoarse with garlic, basil, oregano—too much of whatever sounds seductive about them.

So you need to order cautiously. And of course save room for dessert, most irresistibly the oozy, chocolatey warm Nutella calzone.

For the U Street branch, located near the U Street-Cardozo Metro station: Coppi's, 1414 U St. NW, (202) 319-7773.

COSTA VERDE
946 N. Jackson St., Arlington, VA
(703) 522-6976

PERUVIAN

Open: Daily 10-10:30 **Entrees:** $8-$16 **Buffet:** M-F 11-1:30, $7
Credit Cards: All major **Reservations:** Accepted for 5 or more
Dress: Casual **Parking:** Free lot **Metro:** Clarendon/Courthouse
Entertainment: Peruvian music F-Sat 7-10, Sun 2-6

C OSTA VERDE is a Peruvian festival nearly every night. Thursday is Chinese food, a popular specialty in Peru. Friday and Saturday nights there's piano music during dinner and a dance band later. And Sundays the specials include *pachamanca*—a huge platter of chunks of beef, chicken breast, hunks of pork, potatoes (sweet and white), corn on the cob and a large tamale, all drenched in pan juices and resting on a bed of banana leaves. Even on plain, ordinary Tuesdays and Wednesdays, COSTA VERDE offers a standing menu of a dozen fish and seafood entrees, plus meat dishes ranging from lamb stew to tripe.

The best way to join in is with a pisco sour. Then tease your appetite with soft rolls spread with green pepper paste. Don't neglect the soups, particularly the magnificent shrimp bisque. Then launch right into the potato variations. Peru has as many kinds of potato dishes as the Eastern Shore has crab recipes.

COSTA VERDE seems to host a continual round of Peruvian family reunions. No wonder everything is served on large platters. Wide, thin steaks vie for attention with that amazing conglomeration called *lomo saltado*: strips of juicy browned steak piled with french fries, tomatoes and onions, all drifting into the glossy white rice. It is simple, earthy and awfully good.

It's all basic. Meats are on the tough side, chicken is cooked until the juices have evaporated, and the fish dishes are unabashedly dry and chewy. But the flavors are irresistible. Refinements of texture are not the focus in this kitchen; hearty taste is.

Dessert is another matter. As you enter COSTA VERDE, you can't miss the tray of cookies. They are like the softest shortbread, cut into thin rounds and sandwiched with caramelly *dulce de leche*. One is just the right portion after this mountain-country food.

58

COTTONWOOD CAFE
4844 Cordell Ave., Bethesda, MD
(301) 656-4844

AMERICAN/SOUTHWESTERN

Lunch: M-Sat 11:30-2:30 **Entrees:** $6-$8
Siesta Menu: 2:30-5:30, $6-$8
Dinner: Sun-Th 5:30-10, F-Sat 5:30-11 **Entrees:** $12.65-$21
Credit Cards: All major, DC, CB
Reservations: Recommended **Dress:** Casual
Parking: Valet (fee) at dinner **Happy Hour:** M-F 4-7, $1 off
margaritas, select microbrews; half-price appetizers

The Southwestern feeding frenzy cooled down and left us with a few of the best chili-spiked restaurants, which by now are considered old favorites. COTTONWOOD CAFE has remained not just because of its consistently good food but because it also is one of our most comfortable Southwestern restaurants.

It's Tex-Mex for grownups. The booths are well cushioned, the sound level is condusive to conversation, and the appointments are handsome and lively without approaching garish. Even more important, the service is watchful but not intrusive. The great secret of COTTONWOOD CAFE

"The great secret of Cottonwood Cafe is that lunch prices are as little as half the dinner prices."

is that lunch prices are as little as half the dinner prices. True, the portions are smaller, and lunch doesn't offer such luxuries as shrimp-and-pinon pancakes, achiote duck or tenderloin with green chili corn pudding. But at midday you can still find greaseless incendiary "snake bites" (shrimp-and-cheese-stuffed fried jalapenos); fine Aztec chicken broth with avocado, cheese and grilled chicken; the enchiladas and tacos; fragrant and creamy chicken-and-shrimp Kachina pasta and several imaginative chicken and smoked turkey sandwiches. COTTON-WOOD CAFE'S food is more refined—and expensive—than its neighbor, Rio Grande Cafe, but its serenity is worth the money.

CRISP & JUICY
4540 Lee Highway, Arlington, VA
(703) 243-4222

LATIN AMERICAN/ROTISSERIE CHICKEN

Open: Sun-F 11 am-10 pm, Sat 11-9 **Entrees:** $4.50-$6
Credit Cards: No; cash only **Reservations:** No
Dress: Casual **Parking:** Free lot

You can take the name of this rotisserie-chicken carryout at face value, and the chicken is so aromatic you probably could close your eyes and find CRISP & JUICY from a block away. This is food that cries to be taken to the nearest picnic table for a succulent, messy feast.

The menu lists a few sandwiches, and maybe they're good. But why bother to try them when the alternative is the most wonderful rotisserie-cooked chicken? It's not only marinated, but it has been rubbed with spices under the skin so the flavor permeates the bird. It turns over a wood fire inside a bright orange cooker, and the finished meat—the white as well as the dark—is tender and juicy, not to mention impeccably crisp-skinned. With the chicken you get a choice of a clear, tart and peppery cilantro-spiced dipping sauce, a thick yolk-yellow mustard sauce or a creamy pink garlic sauce that tastes like France's *aioli* with a punch.

"This is food that cries to be taken to the nearest picnic table."

One of these birds probably could serve three people, but they are so good you'll probably not want to share between more than two. To fill in the meal, C&J sells tangy coleslaw, fragrant black beans with rice, an interesting potato salad and fried yucca, crunchy and greaseless. And before you leave with your dinner, consider tomorrow's lunch: The chicken is also sensational cold.

For the two Maryland branches of Crisp & Juicy: 1331-G Rockville Pike, Rockville, MD, (301) 251-8833, and Leisure World Plaza, 3800 International Dr., Silver Spring, MD, (301) 598-3333.

DAILY GRILL
1200 18th St. NW, Washington, DC
(202) 822-5282

AMERICAN	&#9855;

Lunch: M-Sat 10-3 **Entrees:** $7-$14
Dinner: M-Th 4-11, F-Sat 4-midnight, Sun 5-10 **Entrees:** $9-$23
Brunch: Sun 10-3 **Entrees:** $9-$16 **Credit Cards:** All major, DIS
Dress: Casual **Reservations:** Recommended (particularly for lunch)
Parking: Complimentary valet for dinner and brunch
Metro: Farragut North

This splashy chain restaurant is far more than just a pretty face. Its cooking has some solid character.

The menu, which features more than 40 entrees, is impossibly long. It tries to cover all the bases. And that's a problem: You have to do some editing and zero in on the dishes the DAILY GRILL does well. Here, the waiters can help. Since they are so intent on pleasing that they tend to hover, find out what they've tasted and liked. Or, if your tastes don't coincide, find out what dishes are most popular.

The DAILY GRILL offers up all the standards: Manhattan clam chowder, Caesar salad, Cobb salad, fried squid, popcorn shrimp. The soups are homey, the salads crisp and the fried seafood lightly battered and rarely greasy. Maybe they're not standouts, but they are only slightly awry.

Think meat when it comes to entrees. The DAILY GRILL makes a meatloaf to come home to, and it's served with really good mashed potatoes. An even greater treat is the short ribs. And liver is cooked just until it is pink in the center, delicate and luscious. When it comes to grilled beef, the DAILY GRILL can't compete with the neighboring steakhouses —or even a good burger joint. Fish has its good and bad days, too.

There's much to be said for dessert here. The cobbler of the day is an immense treat, packed with fruit under a fragile short crust and mounded with really good whipped cream. The brownie is also good, as is the rice pudding. If you're ending with coffee, try the espresso rather than the wimpy American coffee.

The DAILY GRILL tries too much. Yet what succeeds here is a reminder that chain restaurants can turn out dishes with distinctive personality.

A second location is in the Galleria at Tyson's II on Route 7 in McLean, VA, (703) 288-5100.

DC COAST
1401 K St. NW, Washington, DC
(202) 216-5988

AMERICAN/SEAFOOD

Lunch: M-F 11:30-2:30 **Entrees:** $12-$18
Dinner: M-Th 5:30-10:30, F-Sat 5:30-11 **Entrees:** $16-$23
Light Fare: M-F 2:30-5:30 **Entrees:** $6-$8
Credit Cards: All major, DIS, DC
Reservations: Recommended **Dress:** Casual
Parking: Valet (fee) after 5:30 **Metro:** McPherson Square

Chef Jeff Tunks left Washington a decade ago, and his fans sorely missed his Chinese-style smoked lobster with fried spinach. Now he's returned, having picked up some new tricks from Texas, California and New Orleans in his travels. He's showing them from the open kitchen of his new, mostly seafood restaurant, with its grand two-story dining room and glass-walled balcony, one of the most dramatic dining spaces in town.

His oysters dressed with frozen vodka and pickled ginger are sure to become a new signature, as are his tuna tartare served in half a coconut and his Hong Kong-style crispy whole fish, poised as if it's about to swim away. Those are the showpieces. But even his less dramatic dishes include some future classics: osso buco ravioli stuffed with veal and sauced with its *jus* and precision-diced vegetables, accompanied by a marrow bone; chile relleno in a crackle of batter with an earthy lava flow of mushrooms and goat cheese, or fillets of fish crusted with mushroom paste or grilled and set adrift on jalapeno grits. His crab cakes may unseat the Jockey Club's from their pedestal. And Tunks' pastry chef knows just how tart a lemon pie should be, just how buttery and crumbly its crust.

Tunks hasn't perfected his gumbo, and he has an unfortunate sweet tooth when it comes to meat dishes. But after all, he's just settling in. And it looks as if this time he'll stay awhile.

DEMERA ETHIOPIAN RESTAURANT
2325 S. Eads St., Arlington, VA
(703) 271-8663

ETHIOPIAN   ♿

Open: Daily 10 am-midnight   **Entrees:** $6-$13
Credit Cards: All major, DIS, DC   **Dress:** Casual
Parking: Free lot   **Metro:** Crystal City
Entertainment: Ethiopian music F-Sun 10-2 am

It was a cabdriver's tip that led me to DEMERA, a plain little restaurant half a block off the beaten track from Crystal City's 23rd Street dining strip. That gives it one advantage over its better-known Ethiopian competitors in Adams-Morgan: parking.

Dining in an Ethiopian restaurant is so simple. Rarely an appetizer, no desserts, neither forks nor knives. Just you and an Ethiopian-style beer or honey wine, a large tray covered with spongy, fermented pancakes—*injera*—and more folded on a plate to scoop up your food.

By now Washingtonians are so familiar with Ethiopian cooking that we recognize that injera as gray as DEMERA'S is made with authentic *tef* rather than American white flour, and that the chicken, lamb or beef can be stewed as a mild *wat* or a more spicy *alicha*, or cubed and sautéed as *tibs*. And we have already experienced those lentil or split pea purees that are smooth foils for the meat dishes.

DEMERA'S vegetables are wonderful, particularly the split pea purees. I'd be glad to skip meat altogether here and order just a combination of vegetables, being sure to include *timatim fitfit*, which is pieces of injera infused with a vinaigrette along with tomato, onion and jalapenos.

The meats tend to be chewy, their seasonings thin. Perhaps the kitchen tempers its spices for Americans; I've been unsuccessful in encouraging the chef to turn up the fire for my order.

What's intrigued me most at DEMERA is breakfast. It's served from about 10 until noon and includes five choices. The dish I like best is *injera firfir*, pieces of the pancake that have soaked up a spicy paprika-red sauce and been tossed with some of the crunchy, meaty tibs. There is also a soaked-bread variation called *fata*, made with large pieces of French bread. But I'm a traditionalist: I'll stick with injera for my breakfast.

DISTRICT CHOPHOUSE & BREWERY
509 7th St. NW, Washington, DC
(202) 347-3434

AMERICAN ♿

Lunch: M-F 11-4 **Entrees:** $6-$12
Dinner: Sun-M 4-10, T-Sat 4-11 **Entrees:** $10-$25
Credit Cards: All major, DC, CB **Dress:** Casual
Reservations: Recommended **Parking:** Street
Metro: Gallery Place/Chinatown
Happy Hour: M-F 4-7, various beer specials

The DISTRICT CHOPHOUSE & BREWERY, right down 7th Street from the arena, couldn't be more handy. Nor could this big, noisy brewpub better set the sports fan's mood. But be warned that the kitchen can be slow.

This is a jock kind of Big Food place, where even the Caesar salad warrants a steak knife. I only wish I could think of a way to fashion a balanced meal out of onion rings and cheddar mashed potatoes, for they are the highlights here by far. Try to capture a place at the bar for a one-course filler and a $2 happy-hour beer.

"This is a jock kind of Big Food place, where even the Caesar salad warrants a steak knife."

DOLCE VITA
10824 Lee Hwy., Fairfax, VA
(703) 385-1530

ITALIAN   ♿

Lunch: M-Sat 11:30-2:30 **Entrees:** $6-$7
Dinner: Sun-Th 4:30-10, F 4:30-10:30 **Entrees:** $9-$20
Credit Cards: All major, DIS, DC, CB
Reservations: Recommended for 4 or more only
Dress: No athletic wear **Parking:** Free lot
Entertainment: Guitar W, F 7-10; piano F 7-10

At first glance, this is a dream of a neighborhood Italian restaurant. The pizzas are baked in a wood-burning oven, and the bread is coarse and crusty. Often a live guitarist is playing. And the walls are covered with charicatures of famous Italians, right up to Pavoratti on the door leading to the restrooms.

The menu is more ambitious than the typical neighborhood restaurant, too, though it is not routinely more accomplished. Grilled calamari shows the kitchen at its best, and the pizza has a pleasant crust even when underbaked. Try it with an adventurous topping such as thinly sliced turkey and potatoes cemented together with gorgonzola.

Otherwise, the entrees are undistinguished, from the flabby veal to the gummy gnocchi and the canned artichokes with tired rockfish. You can liven your entree, though, by concentrating on the accompanying linguine with butter and crisped browned garlic. Add some grated cheese and salt if it needs it, and you'll feel well fed in the Italian style—especially if you top it off with a triple chocolate mousse cake, a heavy but appealing tiramisu or a lime tart.

DUANGRAT'S (AND NEARBY RABIENG)
5878 Leesburg Pike, Falls Church, VA
(703) 820-5775

THAI ♿

Lunch: Daily 11:30-2:30, Sat-Sun 11:30-3 **Entrees:** $7-$8
Dinner: M-Th 5-10:30, F 5-11, Sat 3-11, Sun 3-10:30
Entrees: $10-$21 **Credit Cards:** All major
Reservations: Recommended **Dress:** Casual **Parking:** Free lot
Entertainment: Thai classical dancing Sat evenings (winter only)

Back when Thai restaurants were rarely more than utilitarian-looking storefront eating places, DUANGRAT'S appeared as a soft-colored romantic dining room decorated like a museum of Thai treasures. Its waitresses wear long, gauzy gowns, and the menu is full of daring dishes as well as classics. Then DUANGRAT'S expanded to a country restaurant and a grocery around the corner called RABIENG. Since the Washington area now has several glamorous and dazzling Thai restaurants, I'm drawn to the simpler RABIENG (see notes below).

It's not a showpiece but a quietly attractive restaurant with tile tables and pale watercolors on the walls. Its service is professional and gracious, its menu an education in regional Thai cooking. Even more than DUANGRAT'S, it serves dishes that aren't found elsewhere around here. You can find an appetizer called *tidbit*, which is crisp squares of compressed sticky rice with a dip of minced pork in a spicy coconut sauce. Like DUANGRAT'S, it serves *bhram*, a subtle dish of chicken in a peanut-garlic sauce with crisped shallots on top. It has a fascinating roast pork permeated with a sweet-savory soy plum sauce with cilantro. And while its cooking is not better across-the-board than dozens of other very good Thai competitors, it pays special attention to the tenderness of its chili-lemon squid and to the chili fire of those dishes intended to be hot.

This is a restaurant confident of its clientele; it need not pull its punches. And it stocks quality ingredients so that you can trust the seafood to be fresh and plump, the vegetables to be bright and crisp. Thus, with these two Thai restaurants you can suit your mood and your level of dress, choose your price range and the extent to which you do or don't want to linger.

Rabieng is at 5982 Leesburg Pike, Falls Church, VA, (703) 359-5810. Lunch daily 11:30-5; entrees $6-$14. Dinner daily 5-10; entrees $9-$14. Credit cards: All major, DC. Dress is casual, no reservations are required, and there's a free parking lot.

DUBLINER
Phoenix Park Hotel
4 F St. NW, Washington, DC
(202) 737-3773

IRISH/AMERICAN   ♿

Breakfast: M-F 7-10 am, Sat-Sun 7:30-10:30 am
Breakfast Entrees: $5.50-$8.50
Lunch: Daily 11-3 **Entrees:** $6.50-$8.50
Dinner: Daily 3-11 **Entrees:** $8.50-$16.50
Late Night: M-Sat 11-1 am, Sun 11-midnight, $4-$8
Brunch: Sat-Sun 11-3, $3.75-$12 **Credit Cards:** All major, DC
Reservations: Accepted until 11:45 am only
Dress: Casual **Parking:** Street **Metro:** Union Station
Entertainment: Irish music M-Sat 9 pm-1 am, Sun 7:30-midnight

This place has an aura. That means the wood paneling has grown glossy and brown through the years, the dark wood tables are worn so that your elbows almost feel cradled, and the etched and stained-glass windows look as if they should have cracks (which they do). The DUBLINER is an old Irish pub, casual and easygoing, with food that's easy to define: mediocre. This is a restaurant for the I-don't-need-a-power-lunch crowd.

"The Dubliner is an old Irish pub . . . with food that's easy to define: mediocre."

The Auld Dubliner Amber Ale is a big draw. While the low prices and highly appealing atmosphere are components for a winning formula, there has to be more reason for lines to form at lunch. It's gotta be the beer. The barley mushroom soup tastes like an experiment in suspending grains in a salt solution, and the lamb is chewy enough to serve as your exercise for the day. The vegetables are tasteless, and the coffee is worse.

What to order? Burgers and grilled chicken sandwiches are probably the safest bets. Look for a cold plate special of roast duck salad with arborio rice atop a Caesar salad and surrounded by fresh fruit. It's a sleeper, utterly delicious.

EAT FIRST
728 7th St. NW, Washington, DC
(202) 347-0936

CHINESE

Open: Daily 10:30 am-11 pm **Entrees:** $7-$18
Lunch Special: M-F 11-3, $4
Credit Cards: All major, DC **Dress:** Casual
Reservations: Recommended **Parking:** Street
Metro: Gallery Place/Chinatown

Chinese restaurants seem timeless, but they, too, have their seasons to shine. These days EAT FIRST is Chinatown's most steadily excellent kitchen.

Its dining room looks promising, just a large plain room with food as its focus. The walls are laden with strips of colored paper announcing the specials, and these are the dishes to watch.

One of the most silken fish available is sable, and here you often can find the silken fish pan-fried or (my favorite) steamed with ginger and scallions. Shrimp are cooked many ways, but none better than shrimp cake—a kind of airy mousse, pan-fried and sliced on the diagonal—served with crunchy and faintly bitter Chinese broccoli. Ground shrimp is also stuffed in fried eggplant, irresistibly succulent and nearly melting as you eat it. There's also a long list of noodles, soups, *congees*, clay pot casseroles and oddities such as knuckles and innards. But above all, EAT FIRST is known for its barbecued meats, the roast duck, soy sauce chicken and barbecued pork that are a rich but marvelous way to start a meal.

Service is matter-of-fact and efficient, the kitchen feeds that busy dining room rapidly, and the prices are about what you'd pay for a soup and sandwich in most parts of town.

EL CATALAN
1319 F St. NW, Washington, DC
(202) 628-2299

SPANISH

Lunch: M-F 11:30-2:30 **Entrees:** $5-$26
Dinner: M-Th 5:30-10, F-Sat 5:30-10 **Entrees:** $6.25-$30
Credit Cards: All major, DC **Reservations:** Recommended
Parking: Complimentary valet **Metro:** Metro Center

First, chef Yannick Cam showed what a French chef could do in designing this Spanish kitchen. Now that he's left Provence and installed himself here, he's added some French touches to his Spanish creation. He showcases them from a large open kitchen in a vast, two-part dining room with vaulted ceiling and fieldstone walls.

Despite its erratic start, there are some wonderful dishes lurking on this menu. The kitchen's talents seem to lie in soups, in a few of the heartier seafood dishes and in meats with dark, rich sauces. Don't look for light and modern cooking; and if you want greenery with your dinner, you'll have to make a point of ordering a salad. Most entrees are unadorned.

In a Spanish restaurant I generally prefer to assemble a tableful of small plates—*tapas*—for my meal. Here I'd include octopus stew with potatoes and squid sautéed with chorizo, the mild squid cut as thin as spaghetti. Swordfish with mint, raisins and pine nuts is straightforward and very good. And nowadays you'll find some very French foie gras. To find these winning tapas, you have to wade through disappointments such as heavy duck-stuffed *canelon* (Spanish cannelloni).

When it comes to entrees, this is a meat kitchen. Beef rib stew is cooked so long that the meat is nearly caramelized and its orange-and-olive-flavored sauce is reduced to a powerful, almost black and syrupy intensity. Rabbit has a similar robust and midnight-dark sauce. If you're not prepared for such heavy richness, lamb is perhaps a safer bet.

Wintry meat dishes may not leave you yearning for dessert, but the sweets are the most consistent pleasures at EL CATALAN. Catalan cream is a silky flowing *crème brûlée*; sorbets are served in lacy ruffled nougatine cups. What reaches beyond familiarity is the dreary-sounding fried milk. Forget the name; it's a luscious slab of firm custard coated with crisped bread crumbs.

ELEVENTH HOUR
1520 14th St. NW, Washington, DC
(202) 234-0886

AMERICAN ♿

Dinner: Sun-Th 5-10, F-Sat 5-11 **Entrees:** $10-$22
Credit Cards: All major **Dress:** Casual
Reservations: 6 or more only **Parking:** Complimentary valet
Metro: Dupont Circle **Entertainment:** Dancing daily 11-3 am

ELEVENTH HOUR is a restaurant for the young—or at least those with young resiliant eardrums and larynxes. It's for people who are used to conducting a social life to high-decibel music, and it looks like a frat party. While the front is a conventional dining room—blonde wood tables and a wall of glass doors that open, French style, to the sidewalk cafe—most of ELEVENTH HOUR'S space is devoted to playground equipment for adults, with large puffy sofas and walls sculpted in bright colors. Service is slow, a little absentminded. As a restaurant, ELEVENTH HOUR seems like a joke, at least until you taste the food. It's unexpectedly professional. Decidedly French.

Whole squid are roasted with a delicate stuffing of chopped shrimp, scallops and oyster mushroms. North African lamb sausage, *merguez*, is covered with melted cheese and a light tomato sauce. Tempura shrimp are light, puffy and remarkably juicy in their thick, green parsley sauce.

Logic suggests that you should favor the fish entrees, but experience leads me to recommend otherwise. Instead, look for quail plumply stuffed with a smooth mousse of quail meat, chestnuts, eggplant and dried figs or lamb loin cut into quarter-inch slices and grilled crusty and rare, with a light-textured, hearty-flavored sauce. If the test of a restaurant is its sauces, ELEVENTH HOUR goes on the honor roll.

ELEVENTH HOUR is a restaurant that anyone not wearing something cool and black might approach with trepidation. One meal, though, is likely to make you want to try more.

ELLA'S BARBEQUE
1233 Brentwood Rd. NE, Washington, DC
(202) 635-3991

AMERICAN/BARBECUE   ♿

Open: M-Th 11-9, F-Sat 11-10, Sun 1-6 **Entrees:** $7-$9
Credit Cards: All major, DIS **Reservations:** Recommended **Dress:**
Casual **Parking:** Free lot **Metro:** Rhode Island Ave.

Until Levi and Gloria Durham set out to solve the problem, the only way to get real, eastern North Carolina barbecue in Washington was via Federal Express. Now, even though their Levi's barbecue is now known at ELLA'S, the pork is smoked on-site for 12 hours, overnight, so it's fresh for the lunchtime rush. Piled on a sesame-seed roll with a big dollop of coleslaw, ELLA'S barbecue is the kind of irresistible sandwich that makes you want to turn the car around and go back for another as soon as you're done.

ELLA'S serves more than barbecue. And it serves more varieties of barbecue than North Carolina chopped pork. It's a full-service, soul-food cafeteria. North Carolinians would shake their heads, but the steam table features pork ribs and beef ribs thickly slathered with tomatoey sauce that would be more familiar in Texas or Kansas than in the Carolinas. The steam table is also likely to be piled with such down-home necessities as baked or barbecued chicken, meatloaf, smothered pork chops, beef liver, Salisbury steak, pig's feet, chitterlings or fried seafood (whole fish, fillets, scallops, shrimp, oysters, crab cakes). And vegetables: greens fragrant with vinegar, potato salad enlivened with pickles and celery seeds, yams, butter beans, long-stewed cabbage and string beans. Unfortunately, the potatoes taste like instant and the hush puppies are heavy. The sleeper is the pork chop sandwich. The chop is half an inch thick and batter-fried; though it's reminiscent of chicken-fried steak, it's far more juicy and incomparably more delicious.

This is a big, bustling cafeteria that concentrates on carryout but has plenty of sit-down space. And eating-in has one major advantage: It's a short trip for that second sandwich.

ELLIS ISLAND
3908 12th St. NE, Washington, DC
(202) 832-6117

AMERICAN/IRISH   🚭

Lunch: M-Sat 11-4 **Entrees:** $6-$12
Dinner: Daily 4-11 **Entrees:** $10-$19
Brunch: Sun 11-3 **Entrees:** $7-$11
Credit Cards: All major, DIS, DC, CB **Reservations:** Recommended
Dress: Casual **Parking:** Free lot **Metro:** Brookland-CUA

Irish pubs aren't what they used to be. They're more ambitious, and this one's better. ELLIS ISLAND RESTAURANT & PUB, a spinoff of Capitol Hill's Irish Times, brings to the Catholic University area a restaurant priced low enough for students and nice enough for them to show off to their parents. Where else can you find Keats' poetry and a three-cheese pizza on the same menu?

The place has a scrubbed, blond-wood look, with seating at the bar, tables or booths (or in a small, bricked rear courtyard if the weather is nice). The beer list features local Wild Goose brews on tap. And the menu is small but cuts a wide swath. You can order anything from a basket of fresh-cut french fries to a proper dinner of, say, a lightly smoked and grilled fillet of salmon with rice and buttery fresh spinach. The current pub favorite, fried calamari, is one of

"Where else can you find Keats' poetry and a three-cheese pizza on the same menu?"

the kitchen's glories, tender under its crunchy cornmeal coating. The pizza crust, too, has a cornmeal graininess, plus an agreeable addition of sliced plum tomatoes. It's not great pizza, but it has an honest, handmade quality. The menu also features ribs and burgers, pastas and a grilled vegetable salad.

For such a small menu, desserts take up a lot of space. And given such choices as strawberry shortcake, coffeecake, chocolate sour cream cake and lemon poppy-seed cake (not to mention daily specials, perhaps apple pie or sweet potato pie), you might be tempted to skip right to the end.

ENRIQUETA'S
2811 M St. NW, Washington, DC
(202) 338-7772

MEXICAN   ♿

Lunch: Daily 11:30-2:30 **Entrees:** $6-$9.30
Dinner: Sun-Th 5:30-10:30, F-Sat 5:30-11 **Entrees:** $7-$12.50
Credit Cards: All major **Dress:** Casual
Reservations: Recommended for 6 or more **Parking:** Street

W hile other Mexican restaurants in town were serving just tacos and enchiladas, this colorful Georgetown spot was introducing Washington to real Mexican food. For years it's been a Georgetown landmark, with its pastel banners of paper lace and hand-painted chairs in primary colors. Space is tight and tables are close, but this is meant to be a sociable place.

The menu is still long and interesting, with regional dishes new to Washington. But the cooking has lost its luster. An appetizer of mussels is generous—a bargain—but the tangy herbed sauce has evolved into something mild and tomatoey. A squeeze of lemon is needed to bring it to life.

". . . a place to find an unusual menu and good value at lunch."

Tacos and enchiladas are certainly available, and so are *chiles rellenos*. But they're not just the standard red-sauce stuff. The stuffed peppers, with their fruit-meat filling, have long been a signature dish. And the menu lists several fish dishes that show the varied styles of Mexico's regions. Yet the glory of ENRIQUETA'S, its dark and intricate mole sauce, is nowadays too sweet and thick, not nearly as mysterious as it once was. The cooking can be careless. ENRIQUETA'S is no longer a marvel; it's a place to find an unusual menu and good value at lunch.

EVENING STAR CAFE
2000 Mt. Vernon Ave., Alexandria, VA
(703) 549-5051

AMERICAN   ♿

Lunch: Tu-Sat 11:30-2:30 **Entrees:** $6-$9
Dinner: Sun-W 5:30-10, Th-Sat 5:30-11 **Entrees:** $9-$17
Brunch: Sun 11:30-2:30 **Entrees:** $6-$11
Credit Cards: All major, DIS, DC **Dress:** Casual
Reservations: 5 or more only **Parking:** Free lot
Happy Hour: M-F 5:30-7:30, $2.50 drafts

Mount Vernon Avenue is beginning to look like Adams Morgan on a Friday night. New shops and cafes have opened, storefronts are sparkling with strings of tiny lights, and by 7 p.m. the crowd waiting for tables at the EVENING STAR CAFE is spilling out the door. That's in addition to the groups filling the sofas in the rear lounge and the standees roaming among the tables and greeting friends, glasses of wine or beer in their hands.

The cafe is as cute as a Fisher-Price toy box. Its walls are rain-slicker yellow, and the wooden booths are lit by lamps and chandeliers made of Erector set parts. One lamp sports a Mr. Peanut, another an old-fashioned spritz cookie press, a third a stove-top percolator. The chairs are blue velvet, a kind of '50s rendition of ice cream parlor chairs. And the tables are stenciled to look like kitchen tables of the '40s. Add the pressed-tin ceiling and the black-and-white board flooring and you have a little sampling of the entire century.

The menu pays homage to New Orleans with gumbo, *etouffe*, and often jambalaya, though the kitchen doesn't take the time to make a deeply browned roux and the sauces are more heat than flavor.

Entrees encompass a range of tastes, from a sandwich to a steak, but everybody's favorite dish is the rockfish. It's a thick and sweetly fresh fillet, sealed with a chopped-pecan crust that locks in the moisture. Its roasted-garlic sauce is hard to discern, and it's accompanied by a succotash that's prone to being dried out. Cajun popcorn—fried shrimp, catfish and crawfish—has a feathery crust, and crab cakes are high-quality seafood in a creamy mix—though excessively salty. The addition of a new chef has not noticeably improved the kitchen, but opening a wine store next door allows a grand choice of bottles to accompany your meal for a modest corkage fee. As a friendly neighborhood restaurant, it's a charmer.

FARYAB
4917 Cordell Ave., Bethesda, MD
(301) 951-3484

AFGHAN   🚻

Lunch: Tu-F 11:30-2   **Entrees:** $5.75-$6.75
Dinner: S, Tu-F 5-10, F-Sat 5-11   **Entrees:** $9-$15   **Closed:** M
Credit Cards: All major   **Dress:** Casual
Reservations: Recommended on weekends
Parking: Street   **Metro:** Bethesda

While the heyday of the area's Afghan restaurants is over, there has lately been a small resurgence. FARYAB is one of the new generation, a pretty little restaurant with stark white walls and lush red handmade carpets. Its service is more elegant than its exterior or its prices suggest, and it has a small but creditable wine list. It also serves some delicious food, particularly appetizers.

Aushak is an extraordinary creation that's the centerpiece of any Afghan menu, and here it is especially well made. Thinly rolled, slippery, hand-made noodles are stuffed with leeks and topped with tomato-meat sauce and sour cream, with peppery mint on the side. After you've tried it as an appetizer you might be tempted to order it as an entree, and it is even turned into a soup. Another appetizer, *bulanee*, is similar but fried and without the meat topping, and it's as crisp and greaseless a fried pastry as one can imagine. The dumpling theme continues with *Mandu*, fat little meat-stuffed noodles.

Entrees are mostly kebabs, served with fragrant rice and spongy Afghan bread. Lamb, lean and well marinated, is the best of them. Chicken and *kofta* have been dry, and other dishes—a lamb pilaf with carrots and raisins, and side dishes of eggplant, pumpkin or spinach—have suffered from blandness, excessive sweetness or both. Stray from the aushak, and you'll vow to be faithful to it on your next visit. For surely FARYAB will leave you eager for a next visit.

FASIKA'S ETHIOPIAN RESTAURANT
2447 18ᵗʰ St. NW, Washington, DC
(202) 797-7673

ETHIOPIAN   ♿

Open: M-F 5-midnight, Sat noon-1 am, Sun noon-midnight
Entrees: $8-$15   **Credit Cards:** All major, DC, CB
Dress: Casual   **Reservations:** Recommended   **Parking:** Street

Washington has many Ethiopian restaurants, all serving pretty much the same dishes: chicken, lamb or beef stews, either hot or mild, with an array of stewed vegetables. There are also a couple of lamb dishes either sautéed with onions and chiles or chopped with chiles and butter and served raw. They're all accompanied by *injera*, the large, spongy, thin, fermented pancakes that substitute for fork or spoon to scoop up bites of food.

Each Ethopian restaurant, though, has its subtle distinctions. FASIKA is hardly beautiful, unless you can get one of the basket-weave tables upstairs. And the service can be impatient. But it does a good job with the fried appetizers that are like India's *samosas*; here they're large and greaseless. There's a chickpea dip clearly related to hummus. And the menu offers more seafood dishes than most Ethiopian restaurants serve; be warned though, that the fish tends to be dry and chewy.

Here's a restaurant where the spicier dishes are the ones to be sought. Lamb wilderness style, for example, is grilled strips of chewy marinated meat with a crusty surface and powerful flavor. The vegetable dishes include wonderfully spicy lentils. Otherwise, FASIKA is just another Ethiopian restaurant—which is not a bad thing to be.

FELIX RESTAURANT & BAR
2406 18th St. NW, Washington, DC
(202) 483-3549

AMERICAN   ⟨♿⟩

Dinner: Daily 5:30-10:30 **Entrees:** $14-$23
Brunch: Sun 11-2:30 **Entrees:** $8-$14
Pre-Theater: $22, available upon request **Closed:** M
Credit Cards: All major **Reservations:** Recommended
Dress: Casual (no sneakers) **Parking:** Street **Entertainment:**
Dancing Tu 10-12, W 9-12:30, Th 10-1, F-Sat 11-3, Sun 9-11:30

F ELIX is a chameleon of a restaurant. It's hot, it's cool, it's modern
and it's nostalgic. And since chef David Scribner took over, on Fri-
days and Sundays it even serves the components of a traditional Jewish-
style Sabbath dinner. The house-baked bread those nights is a gorgeous
braided challah, and the specials are matzoh-ball soup and brisket.

I'd be glad to make a ritual of FELIX'S Friday and Sunday nights. The
matzoh-ball soup could move an atheist. Its broth is naturally golden,
and plenty of juicy strips of chicken as well as carrots, onions and parsley fill the bowl. The matzoh ball is so light and so oozing with flavor
that it could put an end to matzoh-ball jokes forever. The brisket is awfully good, too.

But you don't have to eat Jewish to enjoy FELIX. The clam chowder is
thick and richly infused with clam flavor. In fact, the soups are the best
ways to start a meal here. Like many other young, inventive American
chefs, Scribner is at his best with the most straightforward dishes. He
tends to add an ingredient or two too many. Grilled pork chop is everything you could hope it to be. One night's special of fettuccine with wild
mushrooms was, to its credit, simply a toss of shaved sharp cheese, fresh
tomatoes and fleshy mushrooms. A whole trout, on the other hand, was
drowned by a sun-dried tomato tapenade.

At dessert, the mood changes from New American sophistication to ice
cream parlor fun. The waiters are unanimous in urging you to give in to
something wildly gooey, either a huge warm brownie with ice cream,
whipped cream, walnuts, chocolate sauce and caramel, or a slightly more
restrained version with a grilled banana instead of the brownie. Dare I
mention that the chocolate sauce is a little wimpy? I'd trade it in for
double the caramel.

FIO'S
Woodner Apartments
3636 16th St. NW, Washington, DC
(202) 667-3040

ITALIAN   ♿

Dinner: Tu-Sun 5-10:45   **Entrees:** $5.50-$16   **Closed:** M
Credit Cards: All major, DIS, DC, CB
Reservations: Accepted for 6 or more   **Dress:** Casual
Parking: Free garage

This has to be the most hidden restaurant in Washington. With no sign on the street, it's tucked way back from the Woodner's vast apartment-building lobby. And this odd restaurant has room to waste, which it does with a jukebox in the empty lounge and various furnishings that look dropped off on their way to the attic.

So the decor is slapdash. That fits. The service is as homey as if you'd dropped in on friends unexpectedly, and the wine list is priced hardly above soft drinks. The menu seems far too long for a restaurant that's often near empty, and it is. So the specials are the dishes to order. Further advice: Concentrate on the appetizers. The list of specials is

> **"This has to be the most hidden restaurant in Washington."**

fascinating. Who else serves chickpeas with chestnuts? And when this chef makes fettuccine with smoked salmon and cream sauce, the sauce is light, the pasta is thin and supple and the smoked salmon is luscious, slightly crusty but not cooked so long that it turns strong.

With entrees, though, the highlight is often the side dish—the peppers and mushrooms. Swordfish might be beautifully complemented by lemon, capers, wine and sautéed onions, but the fish is overcooked. Lamb shank is meltingly tender but needs seasoning. Saltimbocca tastes of ham and cheese but not of veal. Yet the prices are so stunningly low that it seems churlish to complain. And if you're still hungry afterwards, all the better. It would be a shame to not have room for blackberry granita.

FOOD FACTORY
4221 N. Fairfax Dr., Arlington, VA
(703) 527-2279

PAKISTANI   ♿

Open: M-F 11 am-10 pm, Sat-Sun noon-10
Entrees: $5-$7 **Credit Cards:** V, MC
Reservations: No **Dress:** Casual
Parking: Free lot **Metro:** Ballston

The Washington area is now thickly studded with kebab places, and much of the credit is surely due to the FOOD FACTORY. Not only was it among the first, but it's still among the best, cheapest and most atmospheric.

Entered from an alley and sharing its space with an ethnic grocery, the FOOD FACTORY is self-service and strictly basic. You choose your kebab from the refrigerator case of raw, skewered meats or your curry dish from the steam table. You order at the counter and wait at a long bare table for your kebab to be charcoal-grilled. You pick up your plastic plate of food on a red plastic tray. And you fill yourself on well under $10.

The kebabs aren't quite as dazzling as they used to be, but they are still generous. Lamb's the best, vinegary from its marinade, though it's likely to be chewy. Chicken, rubbed with red spices, has lately tended to be dry. Kebabs are better than they sound, though, once you've spread them with the garlicky yogurt dressing and wrapped them in the house-made flat bread. The accompanying lettuce and tomato salad is tawdry, but you can end your meal on a grace note of house-made Afghan ice cream.

There is also a location at 8145 Baltimore Ave., College Park, MD, (301) 345-8888.

FRATELLI
5820 Landover Rd., Cheverly, MD
(301) 209-9006

ITALIAN   ♿

Lunch: M-Sat 11-4 **Entrees:** $6.75-$13
Dinner: M-F 4-10, Sat 2-11, Sun 2-9 **Entrees:** $8-$14
Brunch: Sun 11-3, $12 **Credit Cards:** All major
Reservations: Required **Dress:** Casual **Parking:** Free lot

C heverly has traded in an old Howard Johnson's in favor of an ambitious Italian restaurant. What's even better, the prices are still at HoJo's level.

FRATELLI is decorated with brick and faux columns, its spaciousness is emphasized by mirrors, and its tables are set with burgundy napkins and a couple of carnations. Its staff seems so happy to be here that the maitre d' is likely to sing as he comes to table, and the server turns the bread description into a ballad. Okay, so the cooking's not great. But no staff tries harder. And where else can you find a hot antipasto plate of crab-stuffed mushrooms, fried calamari, clams casino, grilled shrimp and steamed mussels for anywhere around $6? FRATELLI serves enormous, cheesy pizzas, though their toppings could use some zip, and the crust doesn't taste house-made.

> **"Where else can you find a hot antipasto plate of crab-stuffed mushrooms, fried calamari, clams casino, grilled shrimp and steamed mussels for anywhere around $6?"**

The tomato sauce is light and pleasant, so the pastas are good bets. Watch out for overcooked fish and oversalted sauces, press the waiter to tell you what's freshest, and look forward to homey, supersweet, hand-made cannoli for dessert.

FULL KEE
509 H St. NW, Washington, DC
(202) 371-2233

CHINESE

Lunch: M-F 11-3 **Entrees:** $4.50-$5.75
Dinner: M-Th 3-1 am, F 3-3 am, Sat 11 am-3 am, Sun 11 am-1 am
Dinner Entrees: $5.50-$15 **Credit Cards:** Cash only
Reservations: Accepted for 5 or more **Dress:** Casual
Parking: Street **Metro:** Gallery Place-Chinatown

You can't get more plain than the dining rooms of FULL KEE, which look like a workers' dining hall in the People's Republic of China.

The full view of the soup-making and dumpling operation hints at what to order here: shrimp dumplings in soup. The broth is richly flavorful, and the dumplings, with the sheerest of skins, are fat with a filling of small whole shrimp and little else. They beat any fast food I can think of, in price as well as quality.

"The city's chefs come to dine . . . after their own kitchens close." The whole fish—usually flounder—steamed with ginger and scallions, is such an expert preparation that the city's chefs come to dine on it after their own kitchens close. The rest of the menu is more serviceable than distinguished, though I do particularly crave the tart and gingery green sauce that accompanies the steamed chicken. Payment is in cash only—but it would be hard to spend more than the contents of your wallet.

For the Virginia location: 6400 Horsepen Rd., Richmond, VA., (804) 673-2233.

GABRIEL

Radisson Barcelo Hotel
2121 P St. NW, Washington, DC
(202) 956-6690

SPANISH/LATIN AMERICAN/MEDITERRANEAN   🏛

Breakfast: M-F 6:30-11, Sat 7-11, Sun 7-10:30
Breakfast Entrees: $7-$9.25, $9.25 buffet
Lunch: M-F 11:30-2:30 **Entrees:** $5.50-$12.25, $10.75 buffet
Dinner: M-Th 6-10, F-Sat 6-10:30, Sun 6-9:30 **Entrees:** $16.50-$22
Brunch: Sun 11-3, buffet $19.75
Happy Hour: W-F 5:30-8, $7.50 tapas buffet
Credit Cards: All major, DIS, DC **Reservations:** Recommended
Dress: Casual **Parking:** Complimentary valet **Metro:** Dupont Circle

Venturing well beyond the usual hotel fare, GABRIEL serves Spanish and Latin American inventions with a few Mediterranean sidelights, and it has a full tapas menu of creative little tidbits. It's hotel dining with personality. The rooms are plush and comfortable (though the low banquettes might require a pillow), and the service is sweetly thoughtful. Chef Greggory Hill buys the best Spanish cheeses and never-frozen shrimp, and knows his way around Latino cooking from *pupusas* to a whole suckling pig, which is the centerpiece of Sunday brunch. His dishes are complex; even a steak is made of bison, topped with green mole and accompanied by potato gratin and kale with bacon. But while the vegetables tend to exceed expectations, the sauces falter—too strong, too salty, or in some other way overwhelming.

The trick is to come for Sunday brunch, where you can sample all and concentrate on what suits your taste. It's crowded, and you'll need a reservation. Furthermore, the most familiar dishes include undercooked bacon, chewy sausage and dried-out breakfast breads. Adventurous tastes are better served. The salads are a colorful bunch, with wild rice or wheatberries, chickpeas or sardines, glorious olives or Tex-Mex salsas. Quesadillas are made to order, the hand carved lamb and roast beef are as rare as you like, and here's the only routine chance you'll have around here to sample suckling pig. If that's beyond your ken, you can fill up agreeably on paella, some intriguing stew or even nicely moist scrambled eggs.

The sumptuous array of cakes, tarts and pies compensates for many a shortcoming, and after having your fill of mimosas, you probably wouldn't have noticed them anyway.

GALILEO
1110 21st St. NW, Washington, DC
(202) 293-7191

ITALIAN   ♿

Lunch: M-F 11:30-2 **Entrees:** $11-$17
Dinner: M-Th 5:30-10, F-Sat 5:30-10:30, Sun 5-10
Dinner Entrees: $22-$30 **Credit Cards:** All major, DIS, DC, CB
Reservations: Required for dinner **Dress:** Nice casual
Parking: Complimentary valet M-Sat at 6 **Metro:** Foggy Bottom

Washington's premier Italian restaurant has been playing to full houses for so long, it seems to expect them no matter what. Can it hope no one will notice that GALILEO is known as much for overbooking tables as for its exquisite pastas, risottos, fish and meats? Chef-owner Roberto Donna is a genius, but a very busy one.

Even so, I can't help loving GALILEO. I keep expecting my entire dinner will be at the level of such treasures as the fresh scampi with morels, the creamy green-pea risotto, the rustic little veal ravioli strewn with chunks of sweetbreads and fava beans.

"Galileo is a great restaurant. But not always."

The dining room is overcrowded, and the pasta prices are outrageous, none under $21.95, but I just might cut out the expensive excess and make pasta my meal one of these days. Or maybe I'll opt merely to share the whole bursting-with-juices roasted farm chicken with potato puree and truffles, $46 for two. I'll certainly remember to ask for it plain, rather than spoil it with the strong, salty and overwhelming wine sauce. I'll insist that Michael, the maitre d', find a luscious wine in the moderate range rather than accept the $75 suggestion of my waiter. And I'll request that my veal chop be served unsliced, lest it dry out on the way from the kitchen to my table.

Galileo is a great restaurant. But not always.

GENEROUS GEORGE
3006 Duke St., Alexandria, VA
(703) 370-4303

ITALIAN   🔲

Lunch: Daily 11-4   **Entrees:** $5-$12
Dinner: Sun-M 4-10, Tu-Th 4-11, F-Sat 4-midnight   **Entrees:** $5-$14
Winter Hours: M-Th closed at 10
Pre-Theater: M-F 3-6, $2-$3 off select entrees   **Dress:** Casual
Credit Cards: MC, V, DIS **Reservations:** No   **Parking:** Free lot
Entertainment: Bluegrass music/clown performance Tu 6:30-9:30,
jazz W 6:30-9:30, karaoke Th 7-11

GENEROUS GEORGE is a high-volume, much-loved pizza fun house strewn with '50s kitsch where everything is turned into a pizza. Even the pastas are served on a pizza crust. This restaurant knows what it's about, because the pizza crust is its strongest suit. It's puffy and crispy, yeasty and chewy, a dreamboat pizza crust. And if you are looking to enjoy it at rock-bottom prices, go at lunch on a weekday. That's when personal-size pizzas are available.

A "much-loved pizza fun house strewn with '50s kitsch."

I like the combo with everything—fennel-spiked sausage, pepperoni, black olives, Canadian bacon, peppers, Genoa salami, quartered fresh mushrooms, slices of fresh tomato (and, I confess, anchovies). It's like an open-face pizza sandwich, so thick are the fillings. And it's enough for 1 1/2 people. So I'd bring a couple of friends, order two combos and three bathtub-size iced teas. I'd skip the pastas and the salad, which is overpriced for iceberg lettuce and bottled dressing. Maybe the regular pizza is as good a bargain or better, but the personal pizza serves more crust per portion, and that's the point of this pizza, after all.

For the two other Virginia branches of Generous George, which have mostly similar hours, menus and prices and a $5.95 buffet M-F 11 am-2 pm: 7031 Little River Tpk., Annandale, VA, (703) 941-9600, and 6131 Backlick Rd., Springfield, VA, (703) 451-7111.

GEORGIA BROWN'S
950 15th St. NW, Washington, DC
(202) 393-4499

AMERICAN/SOUTHERN

Open: M-Th 11:30-11, F 11:30-midnight, Sat 5:30-midnight,
Sun 11:30-10:30 **Entrees:** $11-$19 **Brunch:** Sun 11:30-3, $22
Dress: Business casual **Credit Cards:** All major, DIS, DC
Reservations: Recommended **Parking:** Valet (fee) at 6
Metro: McPherson Square **Entertainment:** Sun brunch jazz group

It took a Southern theme to bring black and white together in a Washington restaurant. GEORGIA BROWN'S is a gathering place that, more than any other upscale restaurant here, mingles races, political parties, GS-levels and office hierarchies. It's a beautiful and busy hive of curved wood walls and open kitchen, a place for table-hopping and plate-sharing. Its warmth borders on effusion.

One of the draws is the Southern menu of she-crab soup, gumbo, fried catfish, fried chicken, shrimp and grits, and such low country seafood conglomerations as Charleston perlau and frogmore stew. Southern classics are even adapted to vegetarian diets.

Georgia Brown's "mingles races, political parties, GS levels and office hierarchies."

This is big food, rich food, piled on the plate, modestly priced yet as glamorous as a mess of greens can be. Some of it is great stuff: creamy grits, skin-on mashed potatoes, rich she-crab soup and those greens laced with the pepper vinegar from the table. The frying is crisp and greaseless, whether of chicken livers, catfish, oysters, green tomatoes or chicken. But this kitchen has a penchant for overcooking and underseasoning, the quality of the seafood isn't as awesomely fresh as it once was, and the gumbo tastes disconcertingly Italian. Not so the pecan pie, which is all the more Southern for its dousing of bourbon.

GEORGETOWN SEAFOOD GRILL
1200 19th St. NW, Washington, DC
(202) 530-4430

AMERICAN/SEAFOOD   ♿

Lunch: M-F 11:30-5 **Entrees:** $5-$22
Dinner: M-Th 5-10, F 5-11, Sat 5:30-11, Sun 5:30-10 **Entrees:** $10-$24
Credit Cards: All major, DIS, DC, CB
Reservations: Recommended **Dress:** Casual
Parking: Complimentary valet M-Sat after 5:15 **Metro:** Dupont Circle
Happy Hour: M-F 4-7, Sat-Sun open-close; drink and seafood specials

Now that oysters are collected from waters known to be safe, I've been celebrating with oysters as first course, oysters as main course, oysters as my whole dinner. I've had perfectly scrumptious ones everywhere. But I remain eager to return to our own homegrown GEORGETOWN SEAFOOD GRILL, which doesn't happen to be in Georgetown. Besides, if you want to go on to a crab cake sandwich, there's no contest. On its good days it's as close to ideal as a Washington crab cake gets. Another nice thing about the GEORGETOWN SEAFOOD GRILL is that it looks like a seafood restaurant rather than a fancy private club or a college *Bierstube*.

Chances are you'll love the service. The manager not only greets and chats with diners, but he pays quiet attention to what is going on. However, on occasion you can be smothered by an overbearing waiter who thinks he's the star of your evening.

The interesting—and dismaying—thing about seafood restaurants is that they can do some things gloriously, and on the next plate serve something so dreadful you might think it had been delivered from some other restaurant. You can't go far wrong with clams casino here; on the other hand, oysters Rockefeller is a mess. Clam chowder is thick and institutional, and marinated seafood tastes as if the marinade were tap water.

Usually the safest route at an inconsistent seafood restaurant is the plain grilled fish. Here you can order the day's catch grilled, broiled, sautéed, blackened or poached, and it comes with an assortment of half a dozen sauces on the side. Desserts look super-rich, super-sweet and gummy, and they taste much the same. After a couple of disappointments, I learned my lesson: I ordered more oysters for dessert.

GERARD'S PLACE
915 15th St. NW, Washington, DC
(202) 737-4445

FRENCH   ♿

Lunch: M-F noon-3 **Entrees:** $16.50-$20.50
Dinner: M-F 5:30-10, F-Sat 5:30-10:30 **Entrees:** $16.50-$32.50
Closed: Sun **Reservations:** Recommended
Credit Cards: All major, DC **Dress:** Nice casual
Parking: Street **Metro:** McPherson Square

This is a French star-worthy restaurant hiding in a plain wrapper. The dining room is small and modestly decorated. The mood is quiet, the service unobtrusive. And the kitchen is run (though sometimes at a distance) by Gerard Pangaud, who was indeed a two-star chef in France.

If the food sounds simple, it's the kind of simplicity that masks considerable expertise. What is "marinated salmon cooked at a low temperature"? It turns out to be particularly soft and delicate, almost raw fish with a lovely relish. Pangaud's appetizer of scallops is just shellfish and parsley, but it tastes intensely green and rich. As for entrees, he wraps lamb in filmy layers of eggplant, poaches lobster with ginger, lime and Sauternes, and buries a thick veal chop in a savory thicket of julienned prosciutto, artichokes and mushrooms. Sometimes he gets too simple: The lamb's accompanying napoleon of zucchini and tomato tastes of just that. Boring.

Order your dessert ahead so you can try a creative soufflé, perhaps with pistachios and fresh cherries in season. Or an impossibly rich, foamy, melting chocolate cake baked to order. Ice cream, too, is made to order, but the only thing impressive about it is its hefty price. Yes, price can be a problem at GERARD'S, unless the fine points of the cuisine are the ones you care about. Simplicity here is a costly enterprise.

GOLDEN PALACE
720-724 7th St. NW, Washington, DC
(202) 783-1225

CHINESE   🔲

Lunch: M-F 11-3   **Entrees:** $6.50-$9
Dinner: M-Tu 3-10, W-Sat 3-12, Sun 3-12   **Entrees:** $7.50-$14
Credit Cards: All major, DC   **Dress:** Casual
Reservations: Recommended   **Parking:** Street
Metro: Gallery Place-Chinatown   **Dim Sum:** Daily 11-3, $2-$6.50

The GOLDEN PALACE has revived. It's been spruced up so that the dining rooms throb with red lacquer and gold-painted, carved woodwork. It's an ocean of white-clothed tables with polished wood chairs, and its entrance boasts large fish tanks, though sometimes with only one giant grouper as a lonely neighbor to the somnolent lobsters.

The menu covers all bases, with a low-fat, low-sodium healthy section, a vegetarian category and plentiful chef's specials. A large selection of dim sum is served all day. The lunch menu was described by one waitress as "tourist stuff," but the more exotic dinner menu is always available if you ask.

Clearly the kitchen attempts too much. I've found slapdash bon bon chicken and tired dumplings with chewy fillings that tasted reheated, if not frozen first. Seafood has been tough; much of the cooking seems thoughtless. Then there have been isolated and unexpected hits such as shrimp with candied walnuts and broccoli marinated in, of all things, mayonnaise. Who'd have expected it to be delicious? It spurs one on to keep trying to find more gold amidst the dross of this extensive menu.

GOLDONI
1120 20th St. NW, Washington, DC
(202) 293-1511

ITALIAN   ♿

Lunch: M-F 11:30-2 **Entrees:** $12-$22
Dinner: M-Th 5:30-10, F-Sat 5-11, Sun 5-10:30
Dinner Entrees: $16-$28 **Credit Cards:** All major, DIS, DC
Reservations: Recommended **Dress:** Nice casual
Parking: Complimentary valet at dinner
Metro: Farragut North, Farragut West, Foggy Bottom

Being Venetian, chef Fabrizio Aielli serves the most elaborate Italian dishes in the city—and changes his menu every day. Think of Venetian glass, with its swirling tendrils in candy colors, and you'll have a hint of his style. Appetizers are layered, pastas contrast tinted dough with vivid fillings and sauces, and entrees often look like models for the pavilions at some world's fair.

Sometimes the dishes fall flat. But Aielli's fans—and I am one—willingly take such risks. His rack of lamb, poised on intricate vegetables and balancing a lacy potato cake, looks like a fanfare, and the chops themselves are meltingly tender, infused with herbs. As for fish, simple is best; the salmon wrapped in prosciutto with a salty mushroom-shallot sauce tastes overdressed compared with the barely adorned grilled rockfish or snapper.

The pastas are more numerous than the entrees, and include familiarity (linguine with agreeably spicy tomato sauce and shellfish) as well as fantasy (if you can believe it, a luscious rabbit ragu over chocolate fettuccine actually works. Carrot and shrimp tortelli doesn't). Luck runs better with fantasy desserts such as a chocolate and nut napoleon.

The service is like the food: effusive, sometimes dramatic and sometimes overextended. If you can catch the attention of the wine steward, you'll be expertly advised; otherwise you can make an expensive mistake. GOLDONI is the kind of restaurant that takes an investment of time and money to find the best it has to offer, but then you're likely to be hooked.

GOLDONI has now moved to 20th Street, a few blocks from its original West End dining room. Who knows what a new kitchen will inspire?

GREENWOOD AT CLEVELAND PARK
3529 Connecticut Ave. NW, Washington, DC
(202) 833-6572

AMERICAN   ♿

Dinner: Sun, Tu 6-10, W-Sat 6-11   **Entrees:** $14-$27
Closed: M   **Credit Cards:** All major
Reservations: Preferred   **Dress:** Jacket preferred
Parking: Street   **Metro:** Cleveland Park

GREENWOOD AT CLEVELAND PARK has a determined understatement that suits its neighborhood, where the diners talk about the food and critique each bite as if they were awarding a final score with their credit card. It is also the restaurant that won my unofficial award its opening year for the most complaints about service.

The menu changes daily but usually includes a vegetarian entree. Most entrees are seafood, but the steak—a Summerfield Farm sirloin—is one of the best in town. It comes with classy mashed potatoes, fat and spicy onion rings and plump asparagus.

Chef-owner Carole Wagner Greenwood is at her best devising appetizers. I'd make a meal—frequently—of the house-smoked salmon stack, an ethereal pyramid of herbed phyllo layered with salmon and avocado under a cascade of roe. One of the salads, though, is perhaps a more sensible beginning.

A thick tuna steak served rare is the safe bet among fish entrees. And it's a pleasure to discover plain old mussels blossoming in a broth that tingles with lemon and garlic, with whole potatoes an ingenious device for absorbing those flavors. The controversial chicken is brined and then roasted, so sometimes its salt is excessive.

Then there's Happiness, a $12.50 dessert that has everyone pestering the waiters for an explanation. It's an assortment of all the desserts. Given their richness, you might conclude it's a misnomer.

GREENWOOD is eccentric, unpredictable, alternately delightful and frustrating. It tempts me to join the dialogue, to warn my neighboring diners to proceed cautiously among the fish dishes, to encourage them to spring for the steak or the mussels with potatoes. GREENWOOD is a quirky restaurant, and it deserves its opinionated public.

THE GRILL FROM IPANEMA
1858 Columbia Rd. NW, Washington, DC
(202) 986-0757

BRAZILIAN   ♿

Dinner: M-Th 5-11, F 5-midnight, Sat 4-midnight, Sun 4-10
Dinner Entrees: $9-$18 **Brunch:** Sat-Sun noon-4, $14
Credit Cards: All major, DIS, DC **Reservations:** Recommended
Dress: Casual **Parking:** Street

The name alone should be enough to make the restaurant, but the GRILL FROM IPANEMA has a lot more going for it. This Brazilian restaurant sizzles, from its incendiary spiced shrimp to its pulsating late-night music.

If you're looking for an Adams Morgan scene, hit the GRILL after 11 p.m. If you're looking for good Brazilian food in a quieter mode, go earlier. No matter the hour, though, the restaurant is witty and chic, with gauzy, man-made palm leaves waving from matte black tree trunks and tropical colors undulating across the dining room.

The *caipirinhas*—extra-strength clear liquor barely diluted with fresh limes—make you feel young and beautiful and on vacation. The menu offers plenty to choose from among the seafood stews with palm oil and coconut milk, the marinated grilled fish, the steaks well seasoned and seared, and chicken imbued with garlic and pepper. But there is one standout here. It's *feijoada*, the black bean stew filled with a mysterious conglomeration of sausages and pork parts, to be spooned over rice and complemented with orange wedges, shredded collards and grainy *farofa*. It's only served Wednesdays, Saturdays and Sundays; on the off days you'll have to make do with the elegant black bean soup. But that's like watching Black Orpheus on a small screen—or Dona Flor with only one husband.

"This Brazilian restaurant sizzles, from its incendiary spiced sprimp to its pulsating late-night music."

HAAD THAI
1100 New York Ave. NW, Washington, DC
(Entrance on 11th Street)
(202) 682-1111

THAI   ♿

Lunch: M-F 11:30-2:30   **Entrees:** $6.25-$8.25
Dinner: M-F 5-10:30, Sat noon-10:30, Sun 5-10   **Entrees:** $7.50-$23
Credit Cards: All major, DC   **Reservations:** Recommended
Dress: Casual   **Parking:** Street   **Metro:** Metro Center

Thai restaurants are no longer considered exotic. They've become our everyday restaurants, much as Chinese restaurants used to be. And the Washington area has so many terrific Thai restaurants that I probably could include a couple dozen among my favorites. So why single out HAAD THAI? Many Thai restaurants have food this good. And if there is one near you, you may want to substitute it for this.

What HAAD THAI has going for it is a downtown location—most Thai restaurants are in the suburbs, and few restaurants this good are within a short walk of the D.C. Convention Center. But that's not all. It also has an imaginatively decorated dining room, circled by a pink and black mural of the Thai coast. The service is solicitous, too.

None of which would be important if the food weren't good. It is fairly simple—no lavish ingredients, just standard shrimp, scallops, beef, pork, chicken breast that's a little dry and vegetables that don't go much beyond carrots and snow peas. Yet it is seasoned with care, in light-textured sauces with plenty of fragrance and flavor. It shows refinement and delicacy. The hot dishes are boldly peppered but not macho-searing. The sweet sauces are a little too much so, but still compelling. These aren't dishes that teach you about the breadth and heights of Thai cooking; they merely remind you how delicious standard Thai food can be.

Another location was scheduled to open in Alexandria in March.

HEE BEEN
6231 Little River Turnpike, Alexandria, VA
(703) 941-3737

KOREAN/JAPANESE

Dinner: Sun-Th 11 am-11 pm, F-Sat 11 am-midnight
Entrees: $9-$30 **Lunch Special:** M-F 11:30-2 (buffet $7)
Credit Cards: All major, DIS
Reservations: Recommended for large parties **Dress:** Casual
Parking: Free lot

While this large, bustling Korean restaurant has been crowded by more competition each year, it is still a fine and popular all-purpose restaurant.

Its long menu covers a variety of tastes, and its customer base ranges from diners raised on Korean food to *kalbi* novices. The dining room is pleasant, and there are Asian-style private rooms for dinner parties, but it is the waitresses who make the place. Dressed in silk gowns in confectionery colors, they guide newcomers through the menu, show them how to wrap and dip, and supervise the tabletop grilling. All this takes calm and efficiency—which the waitresses have always displayed, but in recent years they've also grown more adept at English.

A meal is accompanied by miso soup and a dozen or so tiny dishes of condiments, from *kimchi* to spinach to dried fish. Appetizers range from Japanese sushi to Korean meat dumplings. Nearly everyone goes on to meats—tame soy-marinated short ribs or thinly sliced beef *bulgogi*, spicy marinated pork and more—grilled at the table and then wrapped in lettuce leaves for eating by hand.

If you have room, you can then have noodles—as a hot soup or chilled and dipped in vinegar, perhaps. There are also fish stews, casseroles of tofu and seafood, thick chewy seafood pancakes and rice dishes—*bibimbop*—to be tossed at the table with bits of meat or shellfish, vegetables and pepper sauce. A meal can be familiar and mildly seasoned or full of new tastes and wildly peppered, perhaps washed down by Korean firewater called *soju*. At the end, peace is restored by a cup of chilled buckwheat-and-ginger tea—delicious, I assure you—floating a few pine nuts. HEE BEEN is always an adventure and routinely comes to a happy ending.

HIBISCUS CAFE
3401 K St. NW, Washington, DC
(202) 965-7170

CARIBBEAN	🏄

Dinner: Tu-Th 6-11, F-Sat 6-midnight, Sun 5-10
Entrees: $9.50-$18.50 **Closed:** M
Credit Cards: All major **Dress:** Casual
Reservations: Strongly recommended
Parking: Street

You'd never guess that the Caribbean can be found under the Whitehurst Freeway. There, practically beneath the Key Bridge, is HIBISCUS. It's a summery sizzle, a tropical palette. It's three small rooms crammed with a bar, a balcony and an open kitchen. It's noise and color and scintillating food. And, wonder of wonders, it's a Georgetown restaurant with plenty of street parking.

HIBISCUS is no standard Caribbean eating place; it's Jamaica by way of South Beach. The bright, funky furnishings were designed by owner Jimmie Banks, and the lush, original cooking is the work of his wife, Sharon. She starts with Caribbean familiars—jerk chicken, creoles and curries—and reinterprets them so they are flowery and fragrant, their heat a pleasure rather than a pain.

Hibiscus "is Jamaica by way of South Beach."

Begin your meal with shark and bake, wedges of crusty flat bread stuffed with succulent fish and accompanied by pineapple relish. Or peppa shrimp, made with huge and fresh-tasting crustaceans. Spinach and crab soup is a kind of northern callaloo and deeply flavored.

Entrees include seafood such as blackened fish, lobster and shrimp with coconut or salmon with gingered black beans. Meats are less emphasized; there's filet mignon, crab-stuffed chicken, and jerk quail, plus the hit of the menu, smoked rack of lamb. It's elegant, tender meat with an earthy smokiness, accompanied by a perfumed and airy sweet potato mousse.

HOLLYWOOD EAST
2312 Price Ave., Wheaton, MD
(301) 942-8282

CHINESE   ♿

Dinner: Sun-Th 11 pm-1 am, F-Sat 11 am-2 am **Entrees:** $5.50-$18
Lunch Specials: M-F 11-3, $4-$5.75 **Credit Cards:** All major, DIS
Dress: Casual **Reservations:** Recommended for large groups
Parking: Street **Metro:** Wheaton

HOLLYWOOD EAST should really be named Guangzhou West. It's a Chinese restaurant. Even more astonishing, it's one of the area's best, with a menu ranging from little-known classics listed in Chinese characters on the wall to new inventions chalked on an electric blackboard.

To settle the question of the name, the staff offers a couple of answers. The owner's father apparently organized performances in America for Chinese singers. Second, the intention was to make this an entertaining sort of place, with a karaoke bar next door and a specialty in tropical nonalcoholic drinks (an allusion to Schwab's?).

Like many Chinese restaurants, this plain-Jane Wheaton storefront one devotes a window alcove to barbecue, with ducks, pork and chickens hanging from hooks. Few others prepare them nearly so well. The duck is supple and juicy, with a veneer of crisp skin. And while the barbecued pork can be too intense and dry, the crispy roasted pork is a revelation. Though its quality varies, on its best days it brings to mind sugar-glazed ham crossed with foie gras. Then there's the leaner and equally luscious baked salted chicken with a dip of ginger and scallion oil.

Narrowing down the countless entrees is hopeless, so I'll just suggest a few highlights. You may have had crispy fish at other restaurants, but certainly not better. I've been less enamored of the shellfish dishes, even when the crustaceans are fetched live from tanks. The best dishes here tend to be the richest pork dishes—made with sweet-spicy roast pork or fragrant cured bacon. Also look for seasonal Chinese vegetables—probably listed on the wall. And noodle dishes are satisfying here.

Dinner ends with the usual orange wedges and fortune cookies, plus a dilemma: Next time around, do I want to try all the dishes I missed, or taste those I loved once again?

HOUSTON'S
1065 Wisconsin Ave. NW, Washington, DC
(202) 338-7760

AMERICAN/SOUTHWESTERN   ♿

Open: M-Th 11:30-11, F 11:30-midnight, Sat 12-midnight, Sun 12-10
Entrees: $10-$25 **Credit Cards:** All major
Reservations: No **Dress:** Casual **Parking:** Street

There must be a huge shredder assigned its own quarters in the rear of HOUSTON'S so it can, without deafening anybody, just churn out endless julienned vegetables for countless salads.

Salads are big sellers here. And HOUSTON'S serves big salads, the kind that without a doubt make a meal. There's a chef salad—called the Sunbelt—with bacon, chicken and croutons added to the usual ham and cheese. There's the Club salad, with fried chicken, bacon, egg and avocado instead of the usual turkey, bacon and ham. And there's a Caesar salad made with no egg. The most popular salad is said to be the grilled chicken salad. I can understand why. It's a big bowl piled with a mountain of ice-cold shredded greens—iceberg, romaine, red cabbage and spinach—and plentiful strips of chicken, with julienned carrots and tortilla strips for crunch. It's no doubt one of the most user-friendly salads you'll encounter: Everything is bite-size and well tossed, so with a single stab of the fork you can get a cross section of tastes and textures.

> **"There must be a huge shredder assigned its own quarters in the rear of Houston's . . ."**

And this being HOUSTON'S, the salads and other dishes are presented by cheerful and thoughtful servers, in a clubby wood-and-leather dining room. HOUSTON'S is easy to like. Of course, that's its problem. It gets too crowded and noisy, and no chicken salad, bowl of chili or even a top-notch burger is worth a long wait. That's why I like HOUSTON'S in the middle of the afternoon for a late lunch, when this high-quality chain restaurant is nearly mine alone to enjoy.

---

*For the two other branches of Houston's: 7715 Woodmont Ave.,
Bethesda, MD, (301) 656-9755, and 12256 Rockville Pike, Rockville,
MD, (301) 468-3535.*

HUONG QUE RESTAURANT
(Also known as Four Sisters Restaurant)
6769 Wilson Blvd., Falls Church, VA
(703) 538-6717

VIETNAMESE   ♿

Open: Sun-Th 10:30-10, F-Sat 10-10   **Entrees:** $5-$10
Credit Cards: MC, V   **Dress:** Casual
Reservations: Recommended (especially weekends)
Parking: Free lot   **Metro:** Falls Church

You could spend a week at the Eden Center, Northern Virginia's Vietnamese shopping mall, and never eat at the same restaurant twice. Among the most recent additions, HUONG QUE has the strongest claim to elegance. Still, no matter how thoroughly you feast among the more than 200 dishes, you would be unlikely to spend more than $20 per person.

HUONG QUE tames the bewilderment of choices by offering fixed-price family dinners for two, four or six people. Further help comes from the waitresses, who are forthright about recommending dishes and explaining their intricacies.

The soup list is the most daunting. There are 26 noodle soups, ranging from the familiar *pho* variations to braised duck leg in egg noodle soup.

What could be new with won tons? At HUONG QUE they are refined, with crisp wrappers so light they are nearly bubbly. Spring rolls and cold garden rolls are ordinary at best, tired at worst. Watch instead for special appetizers such as fritters of chopped pork and shrimp paste wrapped around whole shrimp or enclosed in crisp bean curd skin.

If the sauces and seasonings are often no more than ordinary, the basic ingredients tend to be high quality. And nearly every dish has a vegetarian alternative.

It's not a single dish that makes HUONG QUE stand out from the crowd. Instead, it's the bountiful choices. And with most things priced at $5 to $8, sampling those hundreds of dishes would not be an impossible goal.

I MATTI
2436 18th St. NW, Washington, DC
(202) 462-8844

ITALIAN   ♿

Lunch: M-Sat noon-2 **Dinner:** Sun-Th 5:30-10, F-Sat 5:30-11
Entrees: $10-$17 **Credit Cards:** All major, DC
Reservations: Preferred **Dress:** Nice casual
Parking: Valet (fee) dinner
Entertainment: Dancing (house, acid jazz) F-Sat 11:30-2

This Italian trattoria has mellowed over the years. Its plain wood tables, its clean and airy look suggest a lack of fussiness that is a large part of its appeal. The service can get harried on a busy evening, but the staff is seasoned enough to keep things moving comfortably. And on a quiet night, the place feels restorative.

The stickier problem is the food. One season it's wonderful, the long menu offering interesting homestyle dishes nobody else serves. Another season it's dreary, with limp pasta and chewy meats. At those times, a retreat to plain fish dishes is the safest tack. Or when in doubt, stick to the thin-crusted, yeasty and understated pizzas.

"One season [the food] is wonderful ... Another season it's dreary."

How can you tell before you order whether it's a good season or a bad one? The bread basket is as accurate an indicator as you'll find, short of examining your neighbors' plates or their expressions. Sometimes I MATTI serves savory and nicely chewy *foccaccia*, other times it's spongy and tasteless. Take a bite and consider carefully. The rest of the meal is likely to follow suit.

I RICCHI
1220 19th St. NW, Washington, DC
(202) 835-0459

ITALIAN

Lunch: M-Fri 11:30-2 **Entrees:** $12-$22
Dinner: M-Sat 5:30-10:30 **Entrees:** $16-$28
Closed: Sun **Credit Cards:** All major, DC, CB **Dress:** Nice casual
Reservations: Required **Parking:** Complimentary valet at dinner
Metro: Dupont Circle

I RICCHI watchers take readings on this Tuscan restaurant and com- plain that the tomato- or herb-topped *focaccia* is spongy these days (it is). They say that the place has gone downhill (it has) and that the prices are outrageous (some are). And I, too, waver, grousing that the specials and such extras as coffee steeply escalate the bills. But two practices particularly irritate me. The hosts refuse to seat a diner until the whole party is there, and waiters shamelessly push expensive wines. (Can it be true that none of the chiantis, even the 10-year-old ones, is ready to drink? If so, why have them on the list?)

Even so, I find both the pastas and the dining room often satisfying and refreshing. The room has that simple, Tuscan, earth-toned dignity. And I love the down-to-earth pastas such as tortelloni stuffed with ricotta and spinach in just a wash of sage butter, the *pappardelle* with rabbit sauce and the spaghettini in a thick, coarse and wonderful tomato sauce with mushrooms and lightly cooked shrimp.

As for entrees, everybody here seems to order seafood, but I'd proceed with caution. It's cooked on a wood-burning grill, and the fish is lightly crumbed and bursting with juices, perhaps topped with a bit of herbed tomato puree or with lemon and herbs. Shrimp are sometimes wonder- ful, sometimes iodiney and dry. Among the meats, rabbit and sausage are the stars. While the accompaniments hardly vary—crusty fried polenta and the same vegetables, such as green beans, on every dish—I can't resist that polenta.

For dessert, a little sorbet or just that overpriced but properly thick espresso leaves me feeling deliciously virtuous.

IL RADICCHIO
1509 17th St. NW, Washington, DC
(202) 986-2627

ITALIAN   ♿

Open: M-Sat 11:30 am-11, Sun 5-10:30
Entrees: $8-$17 **Credit Cards:** All major, DC, CB
Dress: Casual **Reservations:** No
Parking: Street **Metro:** Dupont Circle

I like the formula here: an endless bowl of spaghetti with the sauce or sauces of your choice bought à la carte from a long list, nicely wood-baked pizzas with a wide variety of toppings, a few sandwiches and specials from the rotisserie. I like the prices: modest. I like the environment: sweet colors and whimsical murals of barnyard animals and outsize vegetables. And now that the lines have abated and reason can reign, I like the service: breezy and efficient.

IL RADICCHIO is Roberto Donna's down-market restaurant chain. Nobody would compare it with his Galileo or I Matti. The chairs are flimsy, the floors are bare. The tomato sauces are likely to run thin, the rotisserie lamb (Thursday's special) is dreary, and the pasta is neither homemade nor exotically shaped—it's just plain old spaghetti. The point is that this is Italian almost-fast food—quick, easy and cheap, yet still authentic and good. For less than $10 you can eat admirable, yeasty, puffy pizza with respectable ingredients, or have as much pasta as you can eat, topped with seasonal sauces

"The point is that this is Italian almost-fast food."

containing fresh herbs, in-the-shell seafood and reliably virginal olive oil. And the bread is as good as at Galileo.

For the other branches of Il Radicchio: 1211 Wisconsin Ave. NW, Washington, DC, (202) 337-2627; 223 Pennsylvania Ave. SE, Washington, DC, (202) 547-5114; 1801 Clarendon Blvd., Arlington, VA, (703) 276-2627, and 4009 Chain Bridge Rd., Fairfax, VA, (703) 934-1007.

INN AT LITTLE WASHINGTON
Middle and Main streets, Washington, VA
(540) 675-3800

AMERICAN

Dinner: M, W-F 6-9:30, Sat 5:30-9:30, Sun 4-9
Fixed-Price: $88 (M, W-Th), $98 (F, Sun), $118 (Sat)
Closed: Tu (except October, May) **Credit Cards:** MC, V
Reservations: Required **Dress:** Jacket, tie **Parking:** Street, church lot

The INN AT LITTLE WASHINGTON is hardly just a restaurant. It's an event. It's the region's most famous dining place, having won just about every award but the Oscar. It's a 90-minute drive from the city, and its Saturday night fixed-price dinners run $118—without wine, tax or tip.

Why would anybody go to such expense and trouble? The answer is that while the Inn is not perfect, it probably is as close as any restaurant on this continent. In a tiny rural Virginia town, chef Patrick O'Connell and maitre d' Reinhardt Lynch have created the American equivalent of the best English country house inns, where even the fresh flowers in the rest rooms are magnificent. The dining room is lush and intimate, the garden has a dreamlike beauty, and you mustn't leave without seeing the new kitchen: truly manorial.

Nevertheless, you're there for the food. Dinner begins with tiny tartlets and canapés, followed by a demitasse of some haunting and subtle soup. Then come the appetizers. They're the challenge as far as I'm concerned: They're all irresistible, and I'd gladly trade any entree for a couple of appetizers. Next comes a salad of unrivaled freshness or a stunning sorbet. For entrees, O'Connell seeks out pale ivory king salmon and the season's first sorrel, or American-raised Kobe beef. He rubs duck with Asian spices and cooks it thrice for tenderness and crispness. He plays with local corn, peas, wild mushrooms, peaches, berries, greens—whatever it is we've been waiting all year to ripen. Vegetarians are fed like emperors. His food seems uncomplicated, much as the Inn's faux marble and wood might at first glance seem plain.

Desserts, though, are unmistakably wild. My favorites play on tartness: glazed grapefruit on orange shortbread with lemon curd, numerous vivid sorbets arranged on a glass painter's palette. Then there's the world's best caramel sundae. If your heaven requires chocolate, it is served molten, frozen, rolled, white, dark, four ways or included among the combination called Seven Deadly Sins. Dinner is served by an angelic staff, and accompanied by a wine list that, in itself, is worth the trip.

ISABELLA
809 15th St. NW, Washington, DC
(202) 408-9500

MEDITERRANEAN   👪

Lunch: M-F 11:30-5:30 **Entrees:** $9-$18
Dinner: M-Th 5:30-10:30, F-Sat 5:30-11 **Entrees:** $9-$20
Pre-Theater: M-Sat 5-6:30, $20 **Closed:** Sun
Credit Cards: All major, DIS, DC **Dress:** Casual
Reservations: Recommended **Metro:** McPherson Square
Parking: Complimentary valet for F-Sat dinner

I SABELLA is a Mediterranean restaurant that was designed with a kind of Arabian Nights grandiosity, and if you are seated in one of the spacious banquettes, the restaurant looks slightly mysterious. If, however, you're squeezed next to a column or along a wall, dinner might seem as appealing as a trek across the desert.

So it might if you stray from the few excellent dishes on the menu. ISABELLA is one of those restaurants to remember for specific dishes, like a cookbook that has one page lovingly stained and the rest pristinely unused.

Start with the mussels in white wine, garlic and shallots, their zesty sauce delivering a one-two punch of garlic and pepper. A more unusual seafood starter is oyster and brie stew, a brew of haunting, cheesy earthiness with the sparkle of chives.

ISABELLA might sound Italian, but its food doesn't taste so. The pizza is flabby and soggy. Fettuccine is thick and mired in cream. That's the trouble with a menu that is a little of this (pasta or pizza), a little of that (grilled chicken or fish). The kitchen is too often the master of none.

What can you count on when it comes to entrees? The magnificent lamb shank, without a doubt. It's cooked until its lean surface is darkly caramelized and the meat falls off the bone at the touch of a fork. It is irresistible. If the ample lamb shank has left you too full for dessert, that's no great loss.

Sit in a comfortable banquette and order with care, and you'll probably consider ISABELLA a reasonably priced restaurant. Every misstep, though, makes it seem more expensive.

JALEO
480 7th St. NW, Washington, DC
(202) 628-7949

SPANISH

Lunch: M-Sat 11:30-3 **Entrees:** $8-$13
Dinner: Sun-M 5:30-10, Tu-Th 5:30-11:30, F-Sat 5:30-midnight
Dinner Entrees: $13-$15.50
Brunch: Sun 11:30-3 **Entrees:** $3.75-$6.25 (brunch tapas)
Credit Cards: All major, DIS, DC **Reservations:** Recommended
Dress: Casual **Parking:** Valet (fee) at dinner
Metro: Archives-Navy Memorial, Gallery Place-Chinatown
Happy Hour: M-F 4:30-6:30, $3 sangria, house wines and select
beers; tapas menu **Entertainment:** Flamenco dancers W at 8 & 9

The freshest news on 7th Street is not the new restaurants but the revival of JALEO'S kitchen under the close attention of chef Jose Andres, who also oversees Cafe Atlantico. In this energetic and noisy restaurant, the entree list has been pared back and the main event—tapas—has been elaborated. Three pages are filled with these appetizer-size offerings, and the most interesting are those that change with the seasons.

"Jaleo reminds you that eating well is just plain fun." Order a tableful, and you can vary from cold to hot, light to rich, delicate to spicy, meat to seafood to vegetarian. On the simple side, JALEO offers excellent Spanish cheeses and cold cuts, including imported ham on bread rubbed with fresh tomato. Hearty traditional plates star tiny chorizo sausages on sensational mashed potatoes, crusty grilled chicken with a green herb sauce, ham croquettes or blood sausage.

Among seafood, paprika-spiked octopus, garlic shrimp and calamari either fried or stewed in its ink are classics. But don't miss modern adventures such as raw Belon oysters bedded on chopped green olives, raw tuna with anchovy oil and pine nuts or, in season, fresh morels with blue cheese. And the modest-sounding fried potatoes with spicy tomato sauce and garlicky *alioli* or grilled asparagus with romescu sauce are revelations.

A long list of sherries, a few good Spanish wines and beers or sangria fill out the evening. JALEO reminds you that eating well is just plain fun.

JEFFERSON RESTAURANT
Jefferson Hotel
1200 16ᵗʰ St. NW, Washington, DC
(202) 833-6206

AMERICAN

Breakfast: Daily 6:30-11 **Entrees:** $8.50-$12
Lunch: Daily 11:30-2:30 **Entrees:** $14-$20, $18 (prix fixe)
Dinner: Daily 6-10:30 **Entrees:** $23-$28
Brunch: Sun 11:30-2 **Entrees:** $18.50-$25 **Tea:** Daily 3-5, $15
Credit Cards: All major, DIS, DC **Reservations:** Preferred
Parking: Valet available **Metro:** Farragut North

This handsome little hotel restaurant has become a bit obscure in recent years, so it's a surprise to find it so ambitious. The L-shaped dining room has the look of burled wood, as if it were the interior of a cigar humidor. It's luxurious and sedate. The service is formal, if a bit awkward, but tradition stops at the kitchen door. The food takes off in adventurous directions.

Expect the dishes to be complicated weavings of ingredients—star anise and New Orleans' tasso ham electrify a butternut squash soup. Sumptuous pan-roasted sturgeon rests on a ragout of two kinds of beans, but the chef has them a bit backwards: the fish is overcooked, the beans are undercooked.

When it is more carefully timed, this chef's high-wire act has been impressive. I'd never have expected a melange of Chilean sea bass, mushroom puree, smoked tomato, ricotta gnocchi and wilted pea shoots to work in harmony, but so they did. There's promise in this kitchen. Roasted banana ice cream? Against all expectation, it won my heart.

JOCKEY CLUB
Weston Fairfax
2100 Massachusetts Ave. NW, Washington, DC
(202) 835-2100

FRENCH/AMERICAN   ♿

Breakfast: M-F 6:30-11, Sat-Sun 7-11:30
Breakfast Entrees: $4.50-$12.25, $16 (continental)
Lunch: Daily noon-2:30   **Entrees:** $10.50-$23
Dinner: Daily 6-10:30   **Entrees:** $24.50-$34
Credit Cards: All major, DIS, DC
Dress: Jacket & tie for lunch & dinner   **Reservations:** Recommended
Parking: Complimentary valet   **Metro:** Dupont Circle

In the JOCKEY CLUB'S 30-plus years here, the more it has changed, the more it has stayed the same. The hunt-club knickknacks and horsy artwork are unwavering. The homey red-and-white tablecloths are still dressed with a single red rose. The yellow glass lanterns continue to throw a warm light against the cave-dark wood. This is the look of relaxed money, the restaurant version of silk cravats and tweed. Not that anyone would wear tweed at the JOCKEY CLUB. No, it's definitely dark suits. And handed-down pearls for the wives, gold lame blouses for the girlfriends. The waiters, too, are among the most formal in town.

The management wouldn't dare do away with the Traditional Baked French Onion Soup, the Caesar salad or the crab cakes that became famous three decades ago. "Our traditional *Pommes Soufflés* are available," boasts the menu, and it invites you "to order any of our JOCKEY CLUB tableside specialties."

The grand-hotel standby, Dover sole, is the real thing here. Another mainstay is rack of lamb. The list of entrees continues with gently updated luxuries: lobster with *beurre blanc*, beef with *perigourdine* sauce and foie gras; steak with roasted garlic puree. At lunch there are also a couple of pastas, plus several salads that are warm or cold edible still lifes.

All this comes at a hefty price, just as you'd expect in a grand hotel dining room where you can count on a proper Caesar salad or order the finest *pommes soufflés*—potato chips puffed into balloons—outside of New Orleans, and where there's an entire cart of dessert choices, plus endearing little petits fours, with your coffee. Year after year.

KINKEAD'S
2000 Pennsylvania Ave. NW, Washington, DC
(202) 296-7700

AMERICAN/SEAFOOD

Lunch: M-Sat 11:30-2:30 **Entrees:** $12-$19
Dinner: Sun-Th 5:30-10, F-Sat 5:30-10:30 **Entrees:** $21-$24
Brunch: Sun 11:30-2:30 **Entrees:** $9-$16, $22 (prix fixe)
Credit Cards: All major, DIS, DC
Light Fare: Daily 2:30-5:30 **Entrees:** $4-$18
Raw Bar: Sun-Th 10 pm-11 pm, F-Sat 10:30 pm-11 pm
Reservations: Recommended **Entertainment:** Jazz at dinner
Dress: Nice casual **Parking:** Complimentary valet at dinner
Metro: Foggy Bottom

Bob Kinkead is a master. What's more, his namesake seafood restaurant (with a few meat dishes, of course) has developed a warm supper-club feel, particularly if you're in a booth, surrounded by etched glass so you can watch the kitchen and feel the bustle without listening to your neighbors' conversation.

Given that this can be the best restaurant in town, the prices are moderate. The waiters are intelligently professional and the wine list is a treasure of reds as well as whites, in a range to appeal to novices and connoisseurs.

Under KINKEAD'S hand, this kitchen can be a revelation. The seafood ravioli rivals the finest Italian pasta or Chinese dim sum. The char-edged grilled squid is the tenderest and most flavorful version you are ever likely to encounter; its polenta with tomato fondue and pesto tastes as if squid and polenta were meant for each other. The classics—tempura soft-shells, crab cakes, fried clams, tuna tartare—are as good as they get anywhere.

And those are just the appetizers. The signature entree, pepita-crusted salmon with shellfish and chile ragout, still tastes like a fresh and brilliant invention. Grilled whole fish—pompano if you're lucky—can be ideal. Seafood stews, plain grilled fish, elaborately crusted and roasted fillets are usually flawless.

For dessert, the lemon *crème brûlée* is astonishingly and wonderfully tart and, in season, rhubarb desserts are its equal. This kitchen can be superlative.

L'AUBERGE CHEZ FRANCOIS
332 Springvale Rd., Great Falls, VA
(703) 759-3800

FRENCH

Dinner: Tu-Sat 5:30-9:30, Sun 1:30-8 **Full Dinner:** $36-$44
Closed: M **Reservations:** Inside, required 4 weeks in advance
Credit Cards: All major, DIS, DC
Dress: Jacket & tie **Parking:** Free lot

It's more than a restaurant. It's a tradition. It's a phenomenon. It's a vast French restaurant way off in the country that needs two people just to answer its ceaselessly ringing phones.

What has kept L'AUBERGE CHEZ FRANCOIS incomparably popular over three decades is its air of festivity. It has a rustic charm rather than grandeur, and its servers are friendly as well as professional. The dining room runs beautifully.

The menu is immense, and dinners run to six courses plus garlic bread with herbed cottage cheese, and tuiles at the end. The French classics are still honored here, from brains and tongue with browned butter or mushroom crepes as appetizers, to Dover sole in lobster sauce or salmon in a pastry crust as entrees. The restaurant's Alsatian roots show in the *choucroute*—with fish as an appetizer or with sausages, pheasant, ham and foie gras as an entree—as well as in frogs' legs with garlic and parsley, the fish stew called *matelote*, and for dessert, plum tart or *kugelhopf*. More universal traditions such as châteaubriand and rack of lamb also find space here.

It's the forest more than the trees that counts at CHEZ FRANCOIS. Few of the dishes are standouts, but the dinner seems so generous that the evening is nevertheless glorious. A wine list with an interesting selection of Alsatian labels helps, as do such aperitifs as champagne with framboise.

The experience comes together best on an evening when the garden is open. On a slate terrace, surrounded by meadows and trees, abundant with flowers, dinner becomes magical. And the best trick is that you don't have to reserve weeks ahead for the garden as you do for indoor dining. Just come early, because tables are first-come, first-served.

LA BERGERIE
218 N. Lee St., Alexandria, VA
(703) 683-1007

FRENCH   ♿

Lunch: M-Sat 11:30-2:30 **Entrees:** $7.50-$14
Dinner: M-Sat 6-10:30 **Entrees:** $15-$25
Closed: Sun **Credit Cards:** All major, DIS, DC, CB
Reservations: Preferred weekdays, required on weekends
Dress: Casual **Parking:** Pay lot across street

What a civilized restaurant. One has the sense that it has been here forever and that it will be here forever more, neither changing nor falling behind the times. The dining room is a calm space, traditional but not stuffy, festive but not flashy. The tables are arranged for privacy, and the chairs are designed for comfort. The brick walls are softened by paisley draperies and tapestries, and crystal chandeliers provide flattering light. Most important, the waiters operate as a team, familiar with their work and their customers.

The menu celebrates French traditions in such dishes as *garbure*—a soup of vegetables and white beans—along with a long list of fish in classic sauces, a real coq au vin and a few Basque specialties, including an almond-filled pastry among the sparkling, perfect tarts. The preparation is sure-handed and professional without being showy, though it carries on that traditional French failing of oversalted broth.

"This is not newsworthy food, or food to draw raves; rather, it's consistently agreeable, year after year."

The vegetables are particularly nice— diced potatoes sautéed with mushrooms, perhaps, and a mix of buttery fresh cauliflower, broccoli and carrots. Simple and just right. This is not newsworthy food, or food to draw raves; rather, it's consistently agreeable, year after year.

108

LA CHAUMIERE
2813 M St. NW, Washington, DC
(202) 338-1784

FRENCH   ♿

Lunch: M-F 11:45-2:15 **Entrees:** $10-$14
Dinner: M-Th 6-10:30, Sat-Sun 5:30-10:30 **Entrees:** $14-$20
Credit Cards: All major, DC, CB **Dress:** Casual
Reservations: Preferred **Parking:** Validated for 2 hours at Four
Seasons, dinner **Metro:** Foggy Bottom

This Georgetown French restaurant, two decades old, is best enjoyed on a wintry day when you crave coziness. Ask for a table near the stone fireplace; since it is in the center of the room, your request should be easy to accommodate. And order something richly old-fashioned.

On Wednesday that could be couscous, on Thursday cassoulet. And every day it could be snails with garlic butter or puffy, airy *quenelles de brochet* in dark, lobster-enriched sauce. There's a sort of bouillabaisse, though sharper and more peppery than is traditional. Some days you'll find delicate *boudin blanc*; other days

"Ask for a table near the stone fireplace ... And order something richly old-fashioned."

the special might be dark blood sausage. Here's a menu that regularly features tripe or rabbit or brains, and often serves dishes that require braising or stewing, the long cooking methods that have been upstaged by grilling.

That said, it must be added that the food can be lackluster, sometimes stodgy and less exciting than it sounds. This is a restaurant whose creative energy has settled into a cozy somnambulance. Still, LA CHAUMIERE has always been known for a wine list that's intelligently chosen and fairly priced; even the wines by the glass are high-quality bargains. The service is thoughtful and the dining room is comforting, especially in sight of the blazing fire.

LA COLLINE
400 N. Capitol St. NW, Washington, DC
(202) 737-0400

FRENCH   ♿

Breakfast: M-F 7-10 **Entrees:** $5-$8.75
Lunch: M-F 11:30-3 **Entrees:** $8.75-$16.25
Dinner: M-Sat 6-10 **Entrees:** $18.75-$21
Closed: Sun **Credit Cards:** All major, DC
Dress: Casual **Reservations:** Recommended
Parking: Free garage after 5 **Metro:** Union Station

No other French restaurant gives you such stylish and expert cooking at such modest prices. For a start, LA COLLINE'S sauces are impeccable. On the seafood fricassee, the sauce *homard* tastes deeply of lobster and slides lightly along the tongue. On the sweetbreads, a complex and mellow brown sauce is Americanized only by its touch of bourbon; otherwise it tastes like a classic.

The pâtés and terrine of foie gras are made in-house, as are the smoked salmon and trout. And the French repertoire dips into North Africa for a marvelous appetizer of spicy lamb sausage and grilled vegetables wrapped in phyllo—here called brick dough. Entrees include the predictable duck *à l'orange*, *escalope de veau*, rack of lamb and châteaubriand, but unlike many more expensive restaurants nowadays, LA COLLINE garnishes them all with seasonal vegetables. And it goes beyond those standby entrees to local fish—grilled with fennel or topped with bearnaise and fresh mint, for example—and modern American touches such as blackening the fish or flavoring the *beurre blanc* with cilantro.

> **"No other French restaurant gives you such stylish and expert cooking at such modest prices."**

LA COLLINE doesn't manage to overcome its office-building anonymity. Still, it is comfortable if not handsome, the service is highly professional, and the prices are far less ambitious than the cooking.

LA COTE D'OR
6876 Lee Highway, Arlington, VA
(703) 538-3033

FRENCH   🖖

Lunch: M-Sat 11:30-3 **Entrees:** $7-$12
Dinner: M-Th 5-10, F-Sat 5:30-10, Sun 5-9 **Entrees:** $18-$25
Brunch: Sun 11-3 **Entrees:** $8-$11.50
Pre-Theater: M-Th 5-6:30, $15 **Credit Cards:** All major, DC
Dress: Casual **Reservations:** Preferred
Parking: Free lot **Metro:** East Falls Church

It is the *vrai* French-restaurant-in-an-American-suburb. It retains an Alpine look from its predecessor, but the half-timber and stucco walls look sufficiently French and certainly cozy. Most important, the owner is constantly in evidence, infusing the place with his ebullience.

LA COTE D'OR charms more with its dining room and its personality than with its cooking, even if dinner starts with a tiny spinach flan or some such delicacy. Probably the best dish in the house is the fish soup, saffron-tinted and served with a powerfully garlicky *rouille*. It's also a rare treat to find *quenelles de brochet* on a menu today, and though they tend to be too stiff and doughy, their fish flavor is honest and fresh.

The recurrent problem is timidity, underseasoning, flavors too faint. Even *confit de canard* is undercured, though its fat deliciously flavors its bedding of a potato pancake. LA COTE D'OR retains more the memory than the full flavor of its old-fashioned French cooking. But the dining room keeps up all the nuances of the country restaurant tradition.

LA FERME
7101 Brookville Rd., Chevy Chase, MD
(301) 986-5255

FRENCH

Lunch: Tu-F 12-2 **Entrees:** $7-$12
Dinner: Tu-Sat 6-10, Sun 5-9 **Entrees:** $16-$23 **Closed:** M
Dress: Jacket & tie suggested **Reservations:** Required
Entertainment: Piano at dinner, Tu-Sun **Parking:** Free lot

When you want to get out of town but not too far, LA FERME fills
the bill. Even though it's on the edge of the city, it's a spacious,
slightly countrified, comfortable and dignified dining room with a vine-
covered terrace, in a quiet spot along Chevy Chase's pretty Brookville
Road. And it's immensely popular for leisurely suburban lunches. The
service is polished, and the food is sedately French. Here's a place to
take a visiting aunt or to have a family reunion. It has something for
everyone, plenty of panache, and moderate prices for its level of luxury.

You can count on LA FERME for gently grilled, absolutely fresh fish—
say, swordfish or Dover sole. Along with the expected meat offerings, it
also lists venison and chateaubriand. Its veal is sauced with calvados and
mushroom cream, its duck with cider and turnips, its liver with port wine
and truffles. And the plates are garnished with a colorful bouquet of vegetables—though they are sometimes less luscious than picturesque. LA
FERME serves the classics —onion soup, lobster bisque, even a refined
variation of bouillabaisse. And it ventures tentatively into new tastes,
creating a deliciously
rich lunchtime pasta
with duck *confit* and a
touch of Southwestern
chili heat.

"Here's a place to take a visiting aunt or to have a family reunion."

Even so, there are no bold breakthroughs here. This is nice food, consid-
erately served, reliable if not dazzling. No wonder LA FERME has thrived
through the decades.

LA FOURCHETTE
2429 18th St. NW, Washington, DC
(202) 332-3077

FRENCH

Lunch: M-F 11:30-4 **Entrees:** $6.75-$22
Dinner: M-Th 4-10:30, F-Sat 4-11, Sun 4-10 **Entrees:** $9-$22
Credit Cards: All major, DC, CB **Dress:** Casual
Reservations: Recommended **Parking:** Street

When a restaurant lasts this long, in a neighborhood that's constantly changing, it's clearly doing something right. In this chef-owned, family-run place, what's right is the reliable traditional French cooking at moderate prices.

That might not seem so hard until you consider that this is a French restaurant, with the full complement of sauces and a long list of specials based on seasonal ingredients and classical methods. At LA FOURCHETTE you'll find such old-world appetizers as pâtés, escargots, onion soup and homey, hearty French garlic sausage with potatoes in a creamy vinaigrette. Main courses are led by a close-to-authentic bouillabaisse, innards such as tongue, liver and sweetbreads, and mainstream rack of lamb or steak Bercy.

Specials emphasize seafood, from imported Dover sole to local rockfish, soft-shell crabs, shrimp or fresh sardines. And if this year's fashion dictates ostrich, that's what you'll find on the menu. The vegetables won't vary much—usually long-cooked haricots verts and crumb-topped tomato halves. Desserts run to custards, a small assortment of pastries and refreshing liqueur-spiked orange wedges.

The food and the friendly service are what you'd expect in a French country bistro, and the decor furthers the illusion. Dining beneath a mural of just this kind of restaurant on its home ground, you almost feel you're joining the crowd.

LA TOMATE
1701 Connecticut Ave. NW, Washington, DC
(202) 667-5505

ITALIAN   ♿

Lunch: Daily 11:30-4 **Entrees:** $10-$13
Dinner: M-Th 4-10:30, F-Sat 4-11, Sun 4-10 **Entrees:** $13-$22
Credit Cards: All major, DC, CB **Reservations:** Recommended
Dress: Casual **Parking:** Complimentary valet Tu-Sun, dinner
Metro: Dupont Circle **Entertainment:** Piano W-Sat 7-11

In spring, tulips bloom in front of this glass-walled, wedge-shaped restaurant. It becomes the most visible dining spot on Connecticut Avenue. Inside, flowered vinyl tablecloths suggest spring even in winter. Vinyl? Yes, but dressed up with cloth napkins.

LA TOMATE is light, bright and lively. It has all the activity and bustle of a trattoria, with tables so small and close that you'll have no trouble seeing a preview of your possibilities on your neighbors' plates. But it's not so noisy you'd have trouble conversing. If you seek a little less noise, ask for a table upstairs. Service is quick and unobtrusive.

The menu is Italian despite the restaurant's French name, and the dishes are largely familiar standards. Regulars praise the chicken-vegetable soup and the pastas. But zucchini croquettes are so heavy as to threaten to gum up the conversation. Tomato sauces and spinach dishes are good bets. Seek also the simple

" . . . a basic, modestly priced trattoria despite a few gastronomic pretensions."

dishes such as butterflied trout, smoked on the premises, with lemon and herbs. Vegetables are stodgy, and anything fancy is risky. This is a basic, modestly priced trattoria despite a few gastronomic pretensions.

LAURIOL PLAZA
1801 18th St. NW, Washington, DC
(202) 387-0035

MEXICAN/SPANISH

Open: Sun-Th 11:30-11, F-Sat 11:30-midnight **Entrees:** $8-$16
Brunch: Sun 11-3, $5-$9
Credit Cards: All major **Dress:** Casual
Parking: Lot (18th & California)
Reservations: Accepted until 7 pm only

S uccess definitely has hit LAURIOL PLAZA. It's expanding and moving from its corner, abandoning one of the most lively open-air cafes
in the city. Through many years and seasons, I've appreciated the urban
scene to the accompaniment of ultra-thin, crisp chips with a tart margarita
or pisco sour.

Along the way, the once-Spanish menu has grown increasingly Tex-Mex,
with fajitas upstaging the Spanish dishes. Those fajitas are actually very
good. Amend that: The fajita meat is excellent, smoky and rare. But the
guacamole is bland, the *pico de gallo* more so. And the formerly wonderful *chile relleno*, as well as ordinary tacos, haven't the zest they once
had.

What does that leave? *Masitas de puerco* are still pungent and tender,
sometimes crunchy. And I retain hope for the other Spanish dishes. While
most of the crowd goes for enchiladas, tacos and fajitas, I'm more interested in roast pork or garlicky chicken. I'll just have to learn to love
them in LAURIOL PLAZA'S new setting.

---

*In March 1999, Lauriol Plaza will be moving to 1835 18th St. NW. The
telephone number will remain the same.*

LAVANDOU
3321 Connecticut Ave. NW, Washington, DC
(202) 966-3002

FRENCH   ♿

Lunch: M-F 10-5   **Entrees:** $9-$13
Dinner: Sun-Th 5-10, F-Sat 5-11   **Entrees:** $13-$17
Pre-Theater: Daily 5-6:30, $15   **Credit Cards:** All major, DC
Dress: Casual   **Reservations:** Recommended
Parking: Validated   **Metro:** Cleveland Park

This Provençal restaurant is so small you might have to squeeze past diners to reach your table, and when it is crowded, the close quarters and low ceiling turn it into an oven. So why is it continually popular? Its Cleveland Park neighbors love its countrified French look, its menu of little-known Provençal dishes and its gentle prices. Regulars find the service friendly. And those who know their way around the menu find some very appealing food.

Newcomers, on the other hand, have to put up with erratic service—sometimes the waiters are jolly, but it can be difficult to flag them when you need a drink, a fork or the check. And the cooking is no more consistent than the service. An appetizer of chickpea crepe is topped with zesty, well-dressed crabmeat and capers, while an entree of lentil pancake with grilled sweetbreads tastes as if the sweetbreads had been boiled rather than grilled, then served without seasoning.

The choices are adventurous, with fish dishes such as grilled tuna in a feisty aged vinegar sauce on a bed of white-bean puree, or bouillabaisse of cod, and old-fashioned meat preparations such as daube of beef, lamb stew with artichokes and bacon-wrapped pork tenderloin cooked in Provençe's bandol wine.

"Your second visit is likely to be better than the first."

So LAVANDOU can be worth the inconveniences, and your second visit is likely to be better than the first. And with its new renovation, some of those inconvieniences may have disappeared.

LAYALINA RESTAURANT
5216 Wilson Blvd., Arlington, VA
(703) 525-1170

SYRIAN   [&]

Lunch: Tu-Sun 11:30-3:30 **Entrees:** $4.25-$4.75
Dinner: Tu-Th 3:30-10, F-Sat 3:30-11, Sun 3:30-10 **Entrees:** $10-$15
Closed: M **Credit Cards:** All major, DIS, DC **Dress:** Casual
Reservations: Recommended **Parking:** Free lot

LAYALINA is a kind of cultural crossroads, run by a Syrian family and filled with such disparate elements as gilded swords, a hookah and an inlaid push-button telephone. Diners feast in this heartwarming spot while the staff circulates with inquiries, suggestions, encouragement and guidance.

You wonder what the difference is between the meat and the vegetarian *kibbeh*? You'll not only be informed—you'll find it nearly impossible to order any but the vegetarian version invented by the mother, Rima Kodsi. When Souheil, the father, pours two glasses from a full bottle of Lebanese wine, he practically empties it. LAYALINA specializes in generosity.

That spirit is best captured by ordering a *mezze*—a tableful of appetizers. Hummus is just hummus, right? Not after you've tasted it here. Rima's stuffed grape leaves are flavored with lemon for a refined sweet-and-sour tang. Souheil is exceedingly proud of the okra, but I think his pride is perhaps bolstered by nostalgia. *Soujok*, the hotter of the sausages offered, is wildly delicious; *ma'anek* is milder but still zingy. I'd order them both. To lighten the load, include the *fattoush* salad. LAYALINA makes it easy to order an assortment. There's a $24 mezze combination large enough for a group, or a vegetarian sampler for $12 among the entrees.

Otherwise, the entrees fill me with "if only." If only the Cornish hen were cooked about half the time it would be dazzling. Chicken kebab and *shawarma* are also cooked until dry, and grilled salmon has spent too much time on the fire. Beef entrees stand up better to this penchant for overcooking. As long as the meat is going to be overcooked, you might as well turn the problem into an asset and order it braised. Lamb shank is straightforward and succulent.

Desserts depend on what Rima's been doing. They're sweet and aromatic, all small and homey. Then comes Turkish coffee. But the more memorable ending is social, not culinary: a warm goodbye, a wish for your return and a sense that you'll be remembered when you do.

LE GAULOIS
1106 King St., Alexandria, VA
(703) 739-9494

FRENCH   ⟨&⟩

Lunch: M-Sat 11:30-5 **Entrees:** $5.75-$13.75
Dinner: M-Th 5-10:30, F-Sat 5-11 **Entrees:** $6.50-$22.50
Closed: Sun **Credit Cards:** All major, DIS, DC, CB
Reservations: Recommended **Dress:** Nice casual
Parking: Free after 6 **Metro:** King St.

Once a cozy French restaurant downtown, LE GAULOIS is large and anonymous in Alexandria, with lots of wood, plenty of bustle and no particular charm. It hardly matters, though, because its menu is well loved.

Those who know their way around start with a modestly priced and well-chosen wine from France or Virginia, and they pick their dinner not from the printed menu but from the long typed list of specials. There might be six seasonal soups in addition to the three regulars. Appetizers are likely to include such seldom encountered and very French dishes as brains in vinaigrette. Entrees follow in seasons, and in winter tend to be rich and homey concoctions such as bouillabaisse, cassoulet or puff pastry filled with seafood and perhaps sweetbreads in a creamy, aromatic wine sauce. In summer, a myriad of meat and seafood salads appear, though richness is not totally left behind: Amid the updated composed salads you'll also find rich and nostalgic dishes such as airy, creamy quenelles. Desserts are home-style French classics.

Perfect? No. I've had tired pâtés and pastries. And LE GAULOIS is too busy a place for the welcome to exhibit much warmth. Still, it is efficient, and often enough the real welcome is in the cooking.

LE RIVAGE
1000 Water St. SW, Washington, DC
(202) 488-8111

FRENCH

Lunch: M-F 11:30-2:30 **Entrees:** $7.50-$12
Dinner: M-Sat 5:30-10:30, Sun 5-9 **Entrees:** $14-$21
Pre-Theater: Daily 5:30-6:30, $18
Credit Cards: All major, DIS, DC, CB **Reservations:** Preferred
Dress: Casual **Parking:** Valet (fee) **Metro:** L'Enfant Plaza

Waterfront restaurants are largely big-business, tour-bus dining factories, but right next door to the typical Phillips Flagship is a French restaurant so nice it wouldn't even need a water view to recommend it. LE RIVAGE is Gallic to the core, spacious and comfortable without being particularly beautiful. That's fine, since its decor is the Potomac, right out the window. It has a large deck overlooking the water, the boat dock and the Maine Avenue seafood market. And it has a menu filled with appealing French food, much of it seafood.

While most waterfront seafood restaurants simply defrost, heat and serve the likes of Alaskan crab legs or frozen breaded seafood dinners, LE RIVAGE goes so far as to smoke its own salmon. Its fish is not only fresh, but it's prepared with obvious care. Its crab bisque is a spicy, earthy, house-made broth that's just a variation on the classic lobster bisque, and there's also a Riviera-style fish chowder.

The standing menu lists the typically French mussels in white wine, lobster in *beurre blanc*, gratin of seafood and meat dishes from duck breast with cassis to beef stew with mushrooms. The most interesting items on the menu, however, are the daily specials. That's where you'll find the fresh catch—the usual farmed salmon fillets, to be sure, but offered in a modern French manner with seasonings like lemon grass or sometimes blackened with Cajun spices. The vegetable accompaniments are bright and firm (there's a Provençal vegetable stew for vegetarians), the salads are tangy and crisp, and LE RIVAGE makes all its desserts, from the sorbets to the tarts of seasonal fruits. You can sample the full range of desserts on a whimsical mock palette with nearly a dozen little dishes arranged along the rim, enough for two or even more. Just the thing for after the theater at Arena Stage down the street.

LEBANESE TAVERNA
2641 Connecticut Ave. NW, Washington, DC
(202) 265-8681

LEBANESE   ♿

Lunch: M-F 11:30-2:30, Sat 11:30-3 **Entrees:** $5.50-$12
Dinner: M-Th 5:30-10:30, F-Sat 5:30-11, Sun 5-10
Entrees: $10.50-$15.50 **Credit Cards:** All major, DIS, DC, CB
Reservations: Accepted until 6:30 **Dress:** Casual
Parking: Complimentary valet **Metro:** Woodley Park-Zoo

The walls are the color of sand, and arches suggest a courtyard. Potted trees hint of gardens, etchings and photos of old Lebanon establish the cultural setting, and the open kitchen is as lively as an open-air market. On a weekend evening the hubbub is loud, the mood exuberant. So if you are looking for quiet, you'll need to find another time or place.

A Lebanese dinner is at its best a group activity, because with a tableful of people you can order a proper *mezze*—an array of appetizers that can be a prelude to dinner or dinner itself—mostly served in charming, handmade pottery bowls. The menu lists almost two dozen appetizer possibilities. I'd focus on pastry-wrapped cheese or spinach pies. The meat choices are also special—tiny spicy sausages called *maanek*, milder beef patties called *sujok*, the raw lamb and cracked wheat paste called *kibbeh nayeh*, or the oval cooked *kibbeh*, its thin, even, beef-wheat shell stuffed with ground lamb and nuts.

Note the wood-burning oven that produces LEBANESE TAVERNA'S breads. A *falafel* sandwich is wrapped in a house-made pita, and a huge, paper-thin, pale bread comes wrapped around the *kafta mechwi* and the rotisserie chicken. That chicken is the best main dish I've tried, its skin crisp and fairly tingling with spices. Chicken is also handled with respect in a kebab, *shish taouk*, lemony from its marinade. I'd choose chicken over lamb and beef here. Peppered red snapper is succulent in its soft, walnut-lemon sauce, and shrimp kebabs offer large shrimp, smoky from the grill, yet still juicy. In all, the food tastes better in a conglomeration of dishes than dish by dish. The combinations enhance each— mild, spicy, tart, crisp, oozing, hot, cold—by their contrasts. And they add up to a festive meal.

For the Virginia branch of Lebanese Taverna: 5900 Washington Blvd., Arlington, VA, (703) 241-8681.

LEDO
2420 University Blvd. E., Adelphi, MD
(301) 422-8622

ITALIAN   ♿

Open: M-Th 9 am-11 pm, F-Sat 9 am-midnight, Sun 9 am-10 pm
Entrees: $4-$14   **Lunch Specials:** M-F 11-4, $3-$7
Pre-Theater: M-F 3-6, 10% off   **Credit Cards:** MC, V
Reservations: Accepted   **Dress:** Casual   **Parking:** Free lot

After decades of going to LEDO, I finally ventured beyond the pizza, fried ravioli and eggplant Parmesan, since the waitress recommended the fried chicken. Actually, the chicken was crisp and juicy, very good stuff. And there are probably other good things on the vast Italian and American menu. But I can't see any reason to tear myself away from the pizza (even though LEDO'S pizza is now sold everywhere from our Virginia suburbs to Ocean City). This is square pizza, its dough a cross between piecrust and bread, and the thick tomato sauce is rather sweet but also nicely spicy. The toppings are plentiful, the favorite being bacon.

It's a tradition here to start with fried ravioli, which are a kind of glorified convenience food in that they taste like canned ravioli breaded and deep-fried. Mainly they are a vehicle for eating that thick and aromatic tomato sauce by the bowlful. And then you go on to pizza.

LEDO is always busy, inevitably crowded and noisy, more a dining hall than a dining room. Considering the circumstances, the service is terrific. After doing duty at LEDO, those waitresses could meet any task with aplomb. At breakneck speed, they serve, clear, bring you another beer just as you're emptying your last bottle and wrap your leftover pizza even before you've made a move to go. LEDO is an institution. Every institution should feed us so well.

"I can't see any reason to tear myself away from the pizza."

LEGAL SEA FOODS
2020 K St. NW, Washington, DC
(202) 496-1111

AMERICAN/SEAFOOD   ♿

Lunch: M-F 11-5 **Entrees:** $8-$14
Dinner: M-Th 5-10, F-Sat 5-10:30, Sun 4-9 **Entrees:** $12-$20
Credit Cards: All major, DIS, DC **Dress:** Casual
Reservations: Recommended
Parking: Complimentary valet at dinner **Metro:** Farragut West
Happy Hour: M-F 4-7, $2 off drafts, half-price appetizers

LEGAL SEA FOODS, in its nearly half a century, has grown from a small Boston-area grocery into a chain of restaurants, retail markets and a mail-order operation. The restaurants have hundreds of seats. Their menus list well over three dozen entrees. LEGAL SEA FOODS is such a vast operation now that every seafood item—even the Maryland crab, they say—must be sent to its New England processing plant for inspection before it arrives on your plate.

Actually, that's its strength. I'm afraid to eat raw oysters most places, but I feel safe at LEGAL. I have no hesitation here to order my tuna rare or my clams on the half shell. LEGAL'S policy is to inspect all its shellfish for bacteria. It buys fish directly at the docks, demands the last-day catch and monitors its temperature every 30 seconds along the way to the restaurant. That's the secret to appreciating LEGAL SEA FOODS: Its buying and handling are brilliant; its cooking and service are institutional.

Order a piece of fish—scrod or swordfish if you're a nostalgic New Englander, bluefish or haddock if you are a real fish lover, tuna if you prefer swimming in the mainstream, salmon or char if you like mild, pink, farm-raised fish. Have your fish grilled, or if you want to be a little bolder, order your fish Cajun style. Of course LEGAL serves wonderful lobsters, pearly and tender, appropriately steamed or—a bow to the South—baked and stuffed with crab. A more modest option is a lobster salad roll, the traditional, flat-sided hot dog roll buttered and toasted, packed with an extraordinary amount of succulent lobster in a minimum of mayonnaise. Don't forget the fabulous fried onion "strings" and the terrific fried soft-shell clams. In general, keep your order simple, and think New England. Stray at your peril.

Legal also has branches at 2001 International Dr., McLean, VA, (703) 827-8900, and National Airport, New North Terminal, (703) 413-9810.

LES HALLES
1201 Pennsylvania Ave. NW, Washington, DC
(202) 347-6848

FRENCH/STEAKHOUSE   ♿

Lunch: Daily 11:30-4   **Entrees:** $12.50-$22.50
Dinner: Sun-W 4-midnight, Th-Sat 4-2 am   **Entrees:** $14-$22.50
Credit Cards: All major, DC, CB   **Reservations:** Preferred
Dress: Casual   **Parking:** Complimentary valet after 6:30
Metro: Metro Center, Federal Triangle
Happy Hour: Daily 11:30-6 pm (at tables), 6 pm-midnight (at bar); special appetizer menu

Steakhouses are generally burly, masculine places where size counts above all. LES HALLES is a French steakhouse, however, and that makes all the difference.

"In recent years, Les Halles has slipped badly . . . I would no longer venture beyond the steak and fries."

This large, bustling, slightly art-nouveau bistro is casual—the servers wear jeans—and its steaks are cut and served French style: sirloin with red wine shallot butter, skirt steak *bordelaise*, rib-eye entrecote, steak *au poivre*, steak tartare and the flavorful little grainy-textured cut called hangar steak. The traditional French plate of steak, *frites*, *salade* is a particularly good value.

LES HALLES also offers other French bistro classics such as a house-made onion soup, frisee salad with bacon and roquefort, pork *rillettes*, duck *confit*, blood sausage and pigs feet. There's fish, too, of course, with *moules* and *frites* as a bistro standby. All this and an outdoor cafe too.

It once was Paris on Pennsylvania Avenue. In recent years, though, LES HALLES has slipped badly. Quail has tasted reheated, cassoulet reeked of vinegar and risotto was soupy. Service has grown vague and distracted. The hangar steak has so far held its own, but I would no longer venture beyond the steak and fries.

LESPINASSE

Sheraton-Carlton Hotel
923 16th St. NW, Washington, DC
(202) 879-6900

FRENCH

Breakfast: M-F 7-10, Sat-Sun 7-11 **Entrees:** $8-$19
Lunch: M-F noon-2 **Entrees:** $36 (prix fixe)
Dinner: M-Sat 6-10 **Entrees:** $23-$32, $48-$85 (prix fixe)
Tea: Th-Sun 3-5:30 (later in winter), $19
Dress: Jacket **Credit cards:** All major, DIS, DC, CB
Reservations: Preferred **Parking:** Complimentary valet
Metro: Farragut North **Entertainment:** Harpist at tea

LESPINASSE has been reborn as a grand French restaurant with sky-high ambitions—and more humane prices. As from its first days, the dining room is a breathtaking assemblage of silk, velvet, silver and crystal. The service flows so smoothly and gracefully it could go on stage. The wine list is enough to bring tears of joy to an oenophile—though you'll need to enlist Vincent, the sommelier, to find the few glories under $50.

Now, with the import of a young chef, Sandro Gamba, who has trained in France's finest kitchens, the food has a new and dashing style. If his early promise is realized, Gamba could be making local gastronomic history by the time he's 30. He still needs to adjust to American ingredients and expectations (more vegetables with the entrees), but his startup showed exciting ideas and impressive finesse. Among the appetizers, his shellfish ragout and cream of chestnut soup with truffles display an alchemy of familiar ingredients transformed into new experiences. Among entrees, risotto is creamy and silken, with a garden of asparagus and tiny white mushrooms with gauzy curls of Parmesan. Salmon and tuna need work: They are combined in a ying-yang that looks beautiful but tastes contorted. Lamb is presented in four tiny and delicious variations on one plate—very good, if not magical. The menu is not extensive, but it balances tradition with creativity. And desserts, from pastry chef Jill Rose, are worthy of framing, yet even more beautiful to taste.

LESPINASSE is a work in progress, but it starts out high on the ladder. Equally good news for diners is that it's tempered its prices. Sure, you can pay as much for an appetizer of foie gras as for an entree—and even more for caviar. But you can find a three-course, fixed-price menu for $48 as well as a six-course chef's menu for $85. These prices will seem like bargains as Gamba's stock goes up.

124

LUIGINO
1100 New York Ave. NW, Washington, DC
(Entrance on 12th and H streets)
(202) 371-0595

ITALIAN

Lunch: M-F 11:30-2:30 **Entrees:** $7.50-$14.50
Dinner: M-Th 5:30-10:30, F-Sat 5:30-11:30, Sun 5-10
Entrees: $13.50-$21.50 **Pre-Theater:** Daily 5:30-7, $23.50
Credit Cards: All major, DC, CB **Reservations:** Preferred
Dress: Casual **Parking:** Validated for dinner **Metro:** Metro Center

Washington once had hardly any good Italian restaurants. Now it has wonderful ones of all sorts: expensive and inexpensive, traditional and modern, Milanese and Tuscan. LUIGINO, a handsome, contemporary, art deco revival dining room in an authentic art-deco ex-bus station, is an Italian restaurant with a long menu of dishes that might be at home in France as much as Italy.

It's a restaurant full of energy, with flames crackling in the wood-burning stove and cooks working at full tilt in an open kitchen. Cheerful waiters in brightly patterned vests serve with considerable zest. And in addition to the printed menu, there's a two-page list of daily specials and a wine list that has an endearing Italian selection at prices that make you breathe a sigh of relief.

" . . . dishes that might be at home in France as much as Italy."

It's not a restaurant, however, where I would concentrate on the pasta. The menu is heavy on ravioli, and those ravioli have a stolid thickness and meager filling. The dishes that tempt me arc the light and adventurous ones. An appetizer of frittata wedges—thin omelets of onion and artichoke—is piled on shredded arugula with a tomato salad that's even delicious out of season. And salmon breaks away from boring, repetitious, grilled fillets to be served here in crisp-edged, sautéed chunks, with other chunks of carrots offering a teasingly close contrast of color and texture, on a pool of dark green spinach sauce so vivid it takes your breath away. Even the everyday menu explores more than the usual veal and chicken: goat stew, duck in garlic sauce and, instead of the usual sausage, one made from chicken. Or you can order grilled fish, the usual and unusual pizzas, even the inevitable veal Milanese and tiramisu.

LUNA GRILL & DINER
1301 Connecticut Ave. NW, Washington, DC
(202) 835-2280

AMERICAN   ⓑ

Breakfast: All day, 8 & on (10 weekends), $3-$7
Lunch and Dinner: M-Th 11:30-11, F-Sat 11:30-midnight, Sun 3-10
Entrees: $8-$14 **Brunch:** Sat-Sun 10-3, $3-$8
Pre-Theater: M-F 4:30-7, $11 **Credit Cards:** All major, DIS, DC
Reservations: No **Dress:** Casual
Parking: Street **Metro:** Dupont Circle

Newcomers will discover at LUNA GRILL & DINER the whimsy of painted sunbursts and lunar ceramics, the prices of a small-town luncheonette and the homey cooking of a diner where the kitchen has learned modern lessons about cutting the fat. The dining room staff still needs a few lessons, though. What kind of diner never offers to refill your coffee cup at breakfast?

You won't find balsamic vinegar on this menu. It's a diner. Think plain food. You can find a grilled cheese sandwich or chicken salad three ways: as a side dish, a salad or a sandwich. The pastas don't stretch beyond vegetarian lasagna, stuffed shells and spaghetti with the usual half a dozen sauces, none of them memorable. Order something brown and meaty, preferably with potatoes. Skip the turkey, which tastes like a thoroughly salted sponge. And don't risk breakfast, which tastes as if the cook is still asleep.

> **"Don't risk the breakfast, which tastes as if the cook is still asleep."**

Unlike most diners, LUNA serves grilled vegetables, aromatic and oil-glossed; and the french fries here are soft, thick and greaseless—just wonderful. Fried sweet potatoes are plump and moist, with crunchy charred edges. But who could pass up the mashed potatoes, so rough and lumpy, with a crater of gravy? On my first visit to LUNA GRILL, the woman at the next table ordered a bowl of mashed potatoes for dessert. She was a woman who knows what's what. I bet she had the fries as an appetizer.

There is another Luna Grill & Diner at 1424 South 28th St., Arlington, VA, (703) 379-7173.

MAGGIANO'S LITTLE ITALY
1790 M International Dr., McLean, VA
(703) 356-9000

ITALIAN   ♿

Lunch: M-F 11:30-3 **Entrees:** $6-$12
Dinner: M-Th 3-10, F 3-11, Sat 11:30-11, Sun noon-9
Entrees: $12-$28 **Credit Cards:** All major, DIS, DC, CB
Dress: Casual **Reservations:** Preferred
Parking: Complimentary valet at dinner

Dinner family-style is back. And it's drenched in red sauce at MAGGIANO'S LITTLE ITALY.

MAGGIANO'S looks like a little piece of the Bronx, even though it's wedged between Neiman Marcus and Saks Fifth Avenue. The front room houses a bakery and a self-service cafe with a dazzling selection of pastas, salads and pizzas. Top-notch bread, too. The main dining room is in back, and it's almost always full.

While the lunch menu offers single portions, at dinner everything's sized for group dining. The steaks are upwards of 16 ounces, and pastas are meant to feed at least four. Some half portions are available, so dinner for two is at least a possibility. If there are four or more in your group, you can order an all-you-can-eat family dinner for a moderate price.

MAGGIANO'S is not for the fainthearted. It can get loud, and it's not unusual to wait 45 minutes for a table—even with a reservation. In fact, you can wait that long just for appetizers. And they're not worth the trouble. The thin, crisp onion strings are the most satisfying.

Service can get bogged down, but steak *contadina* can save the evening. It's a marvel, measuring well over an inch thick, crusty and juicy. Its flavor hardly matters, buried as it is in peppers, mushrooms, potatocs and a river of pan juices. And it's definitely a bargain. Not so with the eggplant Parmesan or the veal marsala. Among the pastas, rigatoni country style is delicious. And dessert here is as good as the bread.

MAGGIANO'S can be pleasant if you hit a quiet moment, perhaps on a snowy Tuesday night or at lunch. Still, I'd just as soon eat my next meal at the cafe out front. At MAGGIANO'S, there's no service like self-service.

Maggiano's is also at 5333 Wisconsin Ave. NW, Washington, DC, (202) 966-5500.

MAINE AVENUE WHARF
1100 Maine Ave. SW, Washington, DC

SEAFOOD   ♿

Open: Daily 9 am-9 pm **Service:** Carry-out only
Entrees: $5.25-$13 **Credit Cards:** All major
Parking: Street

Next time you want to show off authentic local seafood, head for the MAINE AVENUE WHARF, which now sells not just raw ingredients but fried, boiled, steamed and spiced stuff ready to eat. It's one of those colorful corners that makes cities great.

All day and long into the evening, crowds come to gather the makings of an urban picnic. You can buy just-shucked clams and oysters, steamed crabs practically buried in dangerous-looking, red seafood seasoning, and soulful crab cakes. There are mountains of pink, steamed shrimp, with or without spicing. Or you can buy the less local but perennially popular steamed snow or Dungeness crabs, crayfish or lobsters.

Blue crabs are the best bet here. They are, after all, what has made mid-Atlantic waterfronts famous in food circles. But if you stopped at crabs, you'd be missing a lot. The stalls serve fish sandwiches with moistly fresh fillets—or whole fish on the bone—dredged in spiced cornmeal, then fried to lacy crispness. You can choose what you like of the season's catch: flounder, trout, whiting, catfish, porgies, rockfish or—the crown jewel of local seafood—soft-shell

"All day and long into the evening, crowds come to gather the makings of an urban picnic."

crabs. All are slapped between two slices of flabby white bread and accompanied by a plastic pouch of tartar or cocktail sauce. There's no place to sit, but for such a great slab of fried fish and an invigorating look at teeming urban life, a few discomforts are a small price.

128

MAKOTO
4822 MacArthur Blvd. NW, Washington, DC
(202) 298-6866

JAPANESE

Lunch: Tu-Sat noon-2 **Dinner:** Tu-Sun 6-10 **Entrees:** $9-$23
Multi-Course Meal: $38 **Closed:** M
Credit Cards: V, MC **Reservations:** Recommended
Dress: Casual; socks required **Parking:** Street

This is a truly Japanese restaurant, with meticulous, bowing service and a row of slippers inside the door. Space is so tight that in winter you store your coat in the bin under your backless seat. But the dinner that awaits is big—eight or 10 courses if you opt for the fixed-price meal.

It's not as daunting as it sounds, since the courses are utterly delicate. You might not even feel full, much less stuffed, at the end.

Raw fish shows up as sushi or sashimi, but otherwise the meal is a parade of surprises. There might be a single large mussel buried in steamy white turnip purée, or a tomato-onion salad with a couple of slivers of fish. In summer, the tempura is likely to be soft-shell crab, and year-round the main-dish course is a choice of beef tenderloin or fish such as yellowtail or salmon, the portion just a thin slice deliciously grilled. Then come buckwheat noodles in broth, and for a dessert a slush of frozen fruit, just a few spoonfuls.

This is more than a dinner, it's an event, though now at dinnertime you can also opt to order à la carte from MAKOTO'S long list of sushi, sashimi and exotic skewered meats. Lunchtime is all à la carte, a time to concentrate more closely on some of the most flavorful sushi in town.

MALAYSIAN SATAY HOUSE
2666 University Blvd., Wheaton, MD
(301) 946-3232

MALAYSIAN   ♿

Open: Daily noon-midnight   **Entrees:** $9-$15
Lunch: M-F noon-3, $4.50   **Credit Cards:** All major, DIS, DC
Dress: Casual   **Reservations:** Accepted for 5 or more only
Parking: Street   **Metro:** Wheaton

I've long craved the chance to sample the hawkers' stalls of Southeast Asia. At MALAYSIAN SATAY HOUSE I almost feel I've succeeded.

The menu is not only mysterious, it is long, with at least 15 appetizers and nearly four dozen entrees, plus variations. Fortunately, proprietor Leslie Phoon is a talented guide. Eventually, most everything turns out to be vaguely familiar—a little Chinese, Indian and Thai. Still, the undercurrents of dried shrimp, sesame, tamarind and cinnamon, the signature garnishings and the sweetness remind you that these dishes have detoured through Malaysia on their way here.

The best dishes are appetizers. An obvious hint is the restaurant's name: The various *satays* are perfectly succulent and fragrant. Fried appetizers are greaseless, crisp and flavorful, from the curry puff to stuffed fritter. One appetizer that seems more like a self-contained meal is *roti canai*, the flaky, chewy, rough-hewn Indian pancake meant to be dipped in the accompanying bowl of curry. The most complex appetizer is an array of stuffed vegetables in a broth of your choice (for me it's curry). And an appetizer not to miss is the crispy squid salad.

If there's a consistent disappointment here, it's the overpowering sweetness of many dishes. Indian *rojak* is like a combination of dessert and salad. The *Nonya* sauce is a fascinating interplay of ingredients, but it tastes drowned in sugar. Even the *tow foo* and *ikan bilis*, an unexpected pairing of fried tofu with fried anchovies and thousand-year eggs, is drenched in a syrupy glaze.

Most of the entrees are noodle dishes; they're homey preparations, soft and mild. An entree of more complex character is *asam* shrimp, large crustaceans coated with a spice paste and tossed with tomato and onion. If there is one reliable path among the entrees, it's the curries—with chicken, with noodles, in soup.

THE MARK RESTAURANT
401 7ᵗʰ St. NW, Washington, DC
(202) 783-3133

AMERICAN   🔲

Lunch: M-Sat 11:30-3   **Entrees:** $8.50-$14
Dinner: Sun-Th 5-10:30, Sat 5-11   **Entrees:** $15-$25
Brunch: Sun 11-3   **Entrees:** $9-$14
Pre-Theater: $25 (Shakespeare Theater nights only)
Credit Cards: All major, DIS, DC   **Dress:** Casual
Reservations: Preferred   **Parking:** Valet (fee) at dinner
Metro: Archives-Navy Memorial   **Happy Hour:** M-F 4:30-7, $2.50
beers, $5 special cocktails; menu: $4.25-$6.75

These are glory days for the blocks near the MCI Center. Pubs have been springing up, old restaurants have been revamping. Now comes the MARK, an eclectic American restaurant, bringing chef Alison Swope back from stints in Alexandria.

Her cooking has always been adventurous but perhaps too trendy; even now her dishes often sound heavenly yet taste earthbound. But she returns with a new measure of restraint and maturity. Swope goes to great efforts to muster resources that make a difference. The wine list is inspired. The ever-changing menu features Copper River salmon and fiddlehead ferns in season and Summerfield Farm beef. Swope roams a whole world of flavors but has a particular affinity for Southwestern accents. Here and there she slips into a Southern vernacular.

She's at her best when the tone is down-home. She's invented a marvelous appetizer baklava of sliced portobellos and feta. Her lamb sausage is leaner than most. Her corn chowder with *andouille* is mild and pleasant, and the repertoire of two daily soups includes more homey offerings. Other appetizers—fried calamari, smoked salmon with an agreeable but oil-soaked, orange-fennel salad—are predictable. The buttery, oily excess is a theme that continues through to dessert. Like an overhyped movie, the MARK'S menu encourages high expectations. The lamb chops are good, but the promising *pinot noir* glaze is a letdown. The best accompaniment is the potato puffs sparked with *Asiago* cheese.

If the rice pudding were drained of butter, desserts would be the most consistent stars here. A mocha *pot de creme* is dark velvet. Chocolate hazelnut tart is crunchy through and through. Simple strawberries are royalty with a drift of lemon *mascarpone* cream. Whatever you do, don't fill up before dessert.

MARKET LUNCH

225 7th St. SE, Washington, DC
(In Eastern Market)
(202) 547-8444

AMERICAN//SEAFOOD/BARBECUE

Breakfast: Tu-F 7:30-11, 7:30-noon **Entrees:** $2-$7
Lunch: Tu-Sat 11-3, Sun 11-3:30 **Entrees:** $4-$12 **Closed:** M
Credit Cards: No; cash only **Dress:** Casual **Reservations:** No
Parking: Free lot **Metro:** Eastern Market

Walking through markets makes me hungry, and MARKET LUNCH serves just what a stroll through Eastern Market makes me crave. At breakfast time it has ham and eggs and grits and pancakes. At lunch it serves two grades of crab cakes—a good, spicy, shredded-crab version and a better all-lump luxury version—along with fried fish and shrimp. Here's one of the rare opportunities to order fried perch—small fish having fallen out of favor these days—and fried shrimp that's hand-breaded and long on flavor.

In season you'll find soft-shell crabs and corn on the cob, while year round there's terrific creamy potato salad and slaw and decently tangy cucumber salad. But all is not seafood here. MARKET LUNCH is one of the best in-town sources for authentic, North Carolina barbecue, smoky and vinegary, piled thickly on a huge soft bun with a layer of cole slaw. It's strong, sloppy and wonderful.

> **"Market Lunch is one of the best in-town sources for authentic, North Carolina barbecue."**

Service is friendly, but the lines run long, so you're expected to rattle off your order without hesitation, eat quickly at one of the tables or counters and relinquish your seat for the next customer. MARKET LUNCH isn't for lingering. It's for a quick hit of old-time atmosphere and down-home food.

MARRAKESH
617 New York Ave. NW, Washington, DC
(202) 393-9393

MOROCCAN   ♿

Dinner: M-F 6-11, Sat 5:30-11, Sun 5-11 **Full-Course Dinner:** $24
Credit Cards: Cash or check only **Dress:** Casual
Reservations: Preferred **Parking:** Valet (fee)
Metro: Gallery Place/Chinatown
Entertainment: Belly dancer nightly

Even Chuck E. Cheese couldn't host many more birthday parties than
MARRAKESH. This Moroccan pleasure palace is a warehouse-size
space converted into one of the city's most ornate dining rooms. Sofas
are arranged in clusters around low brass tables, so it makes sense to go
with a group.

The festivity starts well before you're seated. A valet parks your car—at
a price—then you knock on a wooden door that's opened by a costumed
host, who ushers you through a curtain to the dining room. The place
vibrates with color, from the intricately painted ceiling to complex pat-
terns on the sofas and pillows. All waiters are in costume, and they begin
their service by washing your hands from an etched metal ewer.

The meal is seven courses, served communally and eaten with the hands
(spoons are served only with the couscous). Three salads begin the parade, with bread for scooping them. Next comes *bastilla*, the chicken-
egg-almond pie wrapped in phyllo and dusted with powdered sugar.
Chicken—cooked whole and drenched in lemon and green olives—follows. For the meat course you must make a communal choice among
lamb with honey and almonds, lamb with chickpeas and onions or beef
kebabs. Vegetarian couscous follows, then a bowl of fruit and, finally,
small, nut-filled phyllo turnovers and mint tea. Somewhere in the middle
a belly dancer provides a change of pace. The wine flows (budget watchers should exercise caution about that). The music plays.

Like the decor, the food is a barrage of ornate tastes. This is rich food,
heavy perhaps, and no dish is outstanding. But it is all good. Maybe
MARRAKESH makes you feel like a tourist. Maybe this is a Moroccan
version of fast food. But with a seven-course interplay of lemon, olives,
cumin, onions and honey, what could be bad

MARTIN'S TAVERN
1264 Wisconsin Ave. NW, Washington, DC
(202) 333-7370

AMERICAN   ♿

Breakfast and Lunch: M-F 8-4:30 **Entrees:** $4-$9
Dinner: Sun-Th 5:30-11, F-Sat 5:30-1 am **Entrees:** $13-$18
Brunch: Sat-Sun 8-5 **Entrees:** $6-$10
Credit Cards: All major, DIS, DC, CB **Dress:** Casual
Reservations: Recommended
Parking: Validated 1 hr. (8-5), 1½ hrs. (5-close)

If you want to know what the old Georgetown was like, drop into MARTIN'S TAVERN. It still displays green plaid upholstery on its oddly narrow, scarred, near-black wooden booths. Its waiters still wear suspenders. The long bar is still a gathering place for students, faculty, visiting scholars, conventioneers and townies. And MARTIN'S is one of the last restaurants that honors spring by serving shad—the fish as well as the roe.

Four generations of Martins have run the place, since 1933, and they still know how to do the old stuff well.

If you think back to the '30s, you'll know to order beef. It's Angus, and a bargain. The Caesar salad is a misnomer—vinaigrette-dressed rather than creamy with egg. But it's better than the other bottled-dressing combos. Clams casino are purely clam, chopped red and green peppers and bacon, no more than should be there. The crab cakes aren't worthy of national acclaim, but they are thick and moist and credible.

> **"Everything here tastes all the better for being seasoned with more than six decades of history."**

On a sandwich with onion, tomato and lettuce, they'll seem great. The french fries might sometimes be soggy, but they are freshly made, as is the creamed spinach. Everything here tastes all the better for being seasoned with more than six decades of history.

MATUBA
2915 Columbia Pike, Arlington, VA
(703) 521-2811

JAPANESE   ♿

Lunch: M-F 11:30-2 **Entrees:** $5-$11
Dinner: Sun-Th 5:30-10, F-Sat 5:30-10:30 **Entrees:** $8.25-$15
Credit Cards: All major **Reservations:** 5 or more only
Dress: Casual **Parking:** Free lot **Metro:** Rosslyn

In both Maryland and Virginia, you're in range of excellent, modestly priced sushi, thanks to the two branches of MATUBA. These busy, efficient little restaurants are almost sushi bargain-basements, considering the variety of specials their menus offer. A small sampler? A large sampler? A box lunch? A tray large enough for a party? Sushi with sashimi? Or tempura? Even if you order à la carte, you can fill yourself without crushing your budget.

There is, of course, more than sushi here. You can find traditional Japanese noodle dishes, grilled meat or fish, and sesame-scented salads. And if you like, you can have raw fish for a first course, before your sushi. That's my choice, since the chopped raw tuna salad, studded with shreds of black seaweed, is one of the spiciest and most scrumptious versions of tuna tartare anywhere.

Then check the daily specials for sushi treats: diced raw scallops, soft-shell crabs or fried shrimp formed into a sushi roll, pale pink tuna belly, red clams. And every day there are such rare choices as yellowtail cup, its fish minced and seasoned, then piled on rice and wrapped in seaweed; or rolls of spiced tuna, spiced cod with radish sprouts or raw asparagus with smoked salmon.

The greatest treat, though, is a rainbow roll, with diagonal stripes of salmon, yellowtail, tuna and avocado waiting to blend and meld on the tongue. You eyes will love it, too.

For the Maryland branch of Matuba, which has similar dishes, prices and hours: 4918 Cordell Ave., Bethesda, MD, (301) 652-7449.

MAX'S OF WASHINGTON
1725 F St. NW, Washington, DC
(202) 842-0070

AMERICAN/STEAKHOUSE   🚹

Lunch: M-F 11:45-2:30   **Entrees:** $9-$25
Dinner: M-Sat 6-10   **Entrees:** $18-$32
Light Fare: M-F 2:30-6   **Entrees:** $5-$10
Closed: Sun   **Credit Cards:** All major, DIS, DC
Dress: Business attire preferred   **Reservations:** Required
Parking: Complimentary valet at dinner
Metro: Farragut West/Farragut North
Happy Hour: M-F 4:30-6:30, 2-for-1 drinks

The old Maison Blanche was the kind of place where a spy would gladly trade his cellar of Bollinger for any briefcase that came through the door. Now it's been rechristened as MAX'S and has gone from serving mediocre French food to the staples of an American steakhouse. Given that most of the decor of the old Maison Blanche is still intact, from the acres of red carpeting to a parade of tufted banquettes, the effect is of Maurice Chevalier in a 10-gallon hat and bolo tie.

Anyone in his right mind would expect the food to be awful, but he'd be wrong. MAX'S has some good solid cooking, and its desserts are better than the more established steakhouses'. The cold appetizers are right out of the standard steakhouse manual—smoked salmon and steak tartare—but it's the crab cakes that won me over. They're creamy and crisp-edged, with the lump crabmeat left to dominate.

Of course, the point here is steaks, and MAX'S are as thick and weighty as any $30 hunk should be. But they don't have the deep meaty flavor of the best in town. The burger at lunch, however, is everything you'd demand from a $9 hamburger. And unlike most of its steakhouse competitors, MAX'S steaks come with side dishes. The creamed spinach is sensational, as are the *latkes*.

After an inch-thick steak and a platter of potatoes, dessert is surely not a necessity. And when the waiter promoted the profiteroles, I was highly skeptical. I felt like apologizing to the pastry chef after I tried them: They were light, crisp puffs, obviously freshly made. The apple tart was also a surprise; it was far more sophisticated than I'd expect in an American steakhouse. It reminded me that under this restaurant's hearty red-meat exterior, MAX'S was born speaking French.

McCORMICK & SCHMICK SEAFOOD RESTAURANT
1652 K St. NW, Washington, DC
(202) 861-2233

AMERICAN/SEAFOOD   ♿

Open: M-F 11am-11pm, F-Sat 11-midnight, Sun 5-11 **Entrees:** $11-$24 **Credit Cards:** All major, DIS, DC, CB **Dress:** Casual
Reservations: Preferred **Parking:** Valet (fee) after 5 pm
Metro: Farragut West/Farragut North **Happy Hour:** M-F 3:30-6:30, M-Sat 10:30-midnight; with drink, $1.95 food specials

MCCORMICK & SCHMICK has put considerable design effort into this, its 21st restaurant. The dining room seats 250, but it is so cleverly outfitted that its scale feels human. The service is friendly yet dignified. Where chain restaurants falter is in the kitchen, and fish restaurants are particularly vulnerable. When ownership is spread among several sites, the first impression is often far better than the last bite.

But a plate of pristine raw oysters and a glass of sauvignon blanc could convince me that MCCORMICK & SCHMICK is just what I need three blocks from my office. Those fine oysters also appear gently pan-fried in a batter that's a tad flabby but not greasy. An appetizer of seared rare tuna is cooked exactly as promised. And, most unexpectedly, the chicken and dumpling soup has an endearing flavor even if the dumplings are leaden.

If you're just looking for a decent grilled or baked fish with a touch of vinaigrette, you'll find it here. Unfortunately, it won't have much intrinsic flavor. The fancier the dishes, the further the kitchen slips. Crab cakes taste like generic fish cakes. A New Orleans seafood stew turns out to be the chicken soup with dry chunks seafood and moderately spicy sausage. The "lunch and light entrees" section of the menu is the secret to good value here. It's available all day, and the dishes tend to be under $10.

Remember the Pacific Northwest, the chain's home ground, when it comes to dessert. Its apples are put to delicious use in a crisp. And the berry cobbler, made with marionberries, also has a welcome fruity tartness. Oysters and dessert: Now that sounds worth a visit.

Another local branch in the Reston Town Center, 11920 Democracy Dr., Reston, VA, (703) 481-6600, serves lunch on Saturdays and Sundays, beginning at 11:30 a.m.

MELROSE
Park Hyatt Hotel
1201 24th St. NW, Washington, DC
(202) 955-3899

AMERICAN

Breakfast: Daily 6:30-11 **Entrees:** $14-$22
Lunch: M-Sat 11:30-2:30 **Entrees:** $14-$24
Dinner: Daily 5:30-10:30 **Entrees:** $24-$29
Pre-Theater: Daily 5:30-7, $27 **Brunch:** Sun 11:30-2:30, $33-$36
Tea: Th-Sun 3-5, $16-$19 **Light Fare:** Daily 2:30-5:30
Credit Cards: All major, DIS, DC **Reservations:** Preferred
Dress: Casual **Parking:** Complimentary valet **Metro:** Foggy Bottom
Entertainment: Dancing (Big Band) Sat 7-11, pianist at teas, brunch

For a quiet place to talk, with space between tables for privacy and carpeting to muffle noise, chairs soft enough to encourage lingering and tables large enough to conduct business, hotel dining rooms are ideal. MELROSE has the further amenity of an inviting shaded terrace with a cooling fountain, not to mention smooth, thoughtful and unintrusive service. But often such hotel assets are accompanied by institutional cooking.

Not so at MELROSE, which serves food that far outshines that at most chain hotels, even competes with fine chef-owned, free-standing restaurants. Chef Brian McBride has a special way with pastas, such as his nearly weightless ravioli filled with shrimp and sauced with corn and tomato in *beurre blanc*. At lunch he emphasizes seafood and light entrees, and plates them with an abundance of bright fresh vegetables. At night his house-made gravlax keeps company on the appetizer list with regal smoked salmon from Petrossian, crawfish purses and a pretty green-flecked calamari salad with lemon grass and mint. Entrees also emphasize seafood—*goujonettes* of sole, pepper-crusted rare tuna, lobster with angel hair and plump, full-flavored, lightly bound crab cakes, along with such exotic meats as venison or lamb.

McBride's food is lush and colorful, and while he may occasionally over-sweeten a squash puree or underseason his peppered tuna, he heightens his fresh, seasonal cooking with Asian spices, Mediterranean olives and house-dried tomatoes, wild mushrooms and cheeses—Parmesan, *mascarpone*, goat. He excels with pastries; don't miss any vegetable tart you might find, and save room for dessert. Fruit crisps are lovely—all perfume and crunch—and the chocolate bread pudding is upstaged only by the astonishingly good chocolate sorbet that comes with it. For a business lunch particularly—indoors or out—MELROSE is well worth its hotel prices.

MENDOCINO GRILLE AND WINE BAR
2917 M St. NW, Washington, DC
(202) 333-2912

AMERICAN   ⬚

Lunch: M-Sat 11:30-3 **Entrees:** $7-$13
Dinner: Sun-Th 5:30-10, F-Sat 5:30-11 **Entrees:** $13-$25
Credit Cards: All major, DIS, DC **Dress:** Nice casual
Reservations: Recommended **Parking:** Valet (fee) after 6:30
Metro: Foggy Bottom

G eppetto, one of the oldest restaurants in Georgetown, turned its space into MENDOCINO GRILLE AND WINE BAR, named after the county in California. Now it's serving pizzas with paper-thin crusts and toppings of porcini or fresh tomatoes. Its pastas are not red-sauced but multi-hued and exotically flavored. Veal Parmesan has given way to rare grilled tuna. The wine selection is all-California, listed with ratings from *Wine Spectator* and *Wine Advocate* magazines.

A gust of fresh air has swept through the dining room, leaving a serene mingling of bare wood floors and walls of smooth stone, lit by sconces that look like slabs of ice. MENDOCINO makes remarkable use of mirrors, set at just the right angle so that you get a secret view of another part of the dining room.

There's certainly a California friendliness here. The greeting at the door is effusive. The music weaves classics with Sinatra for a lilting mood.

MENDOCINO is a restaurant on a mission to impress. But factor in the prices, and I'd say the mission is not accomplished, at least in the kitchen. The crab-stuffed shrimp illustrate what's wrong. At lunch they're priced like dinner, for four shrimp topped with slightly acrid crab on a pool of tomato sauce that drowns out any of the seafood's subtlety. Black linguine smothers it further. Each dish seems to have its assets and its flaws (though the fruit *crostata* for dessert is all assets). As soon as a dish comes out right, though, you're reminded of the price, and you're likely to conclude that it's not *that* right.

MESKEREM
2434 18th St. NW, Washington, DC
(202) 462-4100

ETHIOPIAN   ♿

Open: Sun-Th noon-midnight, F-Sat noon-1 am
Lunch Entrees: $5-$10.50 **Dinner Entrees:** $7-$12
Credit Cards: All major, DIS, DC **Reservations:** Recommended
Dress: Casual **Parking:** Street
Entertainment: Ethiopian band F-Sat 12-3 am (no kitchen after 1)

Washington has no Scandinavian restaurants, and almost no Eastern European restaurants, yet it has more Ethiopian restaurants than any other city in the nation. Ethiopian food clearly is enormously popular here. It's spicy, it's cheap and you eat it with your hands. But there's even more to appreciate, as one can tell at our prettiest and most ambitious Ethiopian restaurant, MESKEREM.

On two of its three floors it serves on basket-tables. A table-size tray of *injera*—tangy, fermented pancakes that look like thick napkins—is set atop the basket, and various stewed meats, seafood and vegetables are spooned onto the layer of pancakes. You can order chicken, beef, lamb, shrimp or vegetable stews, hot or mild, but don't shy away from the hot. They're not fiercely hot, and they feature the dis-

" . . . our prettiest and most ambitious Ethiopian restaurant."

tinctive flavor of *berbere,* a haunting red pepper paste. There are also sautéed, diced meats with onions (*tibbs*) and spicy, buttery, raw meat (*kitfo*). A plate of folded injera is served alongside, and you eat communally, tearing off pieces of injera to use as scoops for the stews. It's kind of a soft variation on chips and dip and equally hard to stop eating. Dollops of lentils, cabbage, collards and green-bean stews provide variety.

Unlike most Ethiopian restaurants here, MESKEREM offers a list of appetizers, including an exceptional shrimp cocktail with a tart, red-pepper dipping sauce, delicate *samosas* and refreshing salads of beets or potatoes. Its list of entrees is more extensive than any other's. And its cooking is lively and not greasy. Like its competitors, it serves locally made honey wine and a flavorful Ethiopian beer, brewed in Northern Virginia by Old Dominion.

MEZZA 9
Rosslyn Hyatt
1325 Wilson Blvd., Arlington, VA
(703) 276-8999

MEDITERRANEAN   🖔

Breakfast: M-F 6:30-11:30, Sat-Sun 7-12   **Entrees:** $6-$13
Lunch: M-F 11:30-2   **Entrees:** $6-$21
Dinner: Daily 5:30-10   **Entrees:** $13-$26
Credit Cards: All major, DC, DIS   **Dress:** Casual
Reservations: Recommended
Parking: Valet compl. at dinner; validated lunch & dinner   **Metro:** Rosslyn

The Hyatt in Rosslyn has created a bold restaurant theme revolving around the Mediterranean's "small plates." It's even hired a rather good chef to carry out the concept. It is still, however, a pricey hotel restaurant with all the drawbacks of institutional service.

The room is determinedly and cheerfully modern, which means it has that slightly depressing undertone of an empty shopping mall. The service is attentive to a fault, overbearing and pretentious. The view from the wraparound windows is of office buildings. And waiters are prone to gossip loudly with the inevitably noisy groups of visiting businessmen.

On the other hand, the appetizers displayed in glass-fronted cases taste even better than they look. Your order of cumin-spiked lentil salad with crisp prosciutto, or roasted peppers with nicely browned almonds, arrives dramatically on a tiered tray. The more expensive first courses—in-season tomatoes with a shimmery goat-cheese custard, delicately cured salmon cleverly matched with designer potatoes, avocado, lime and cilantro—are conventionally served. As are the entrees of superbly cooked fish and roast chicken or duds such as tomatoey seafood stew that is oily and overbearing. Vegetable side dishes are ambitious constructions of gratins and hashes, but they're all too likely to taste old and tired.

MEZZA 9 specializes in cleverness. Pricing all wines at $23 is an idea that works. The tabletop furniture—a conical wire bread basket, a metal arch for presenting ice creams in what look like votive candle glasses, a tiered tray of complementary sweets (sugared dried fruits, strawberries on the stem and chunks of waxy white and dark chocolate)—seems all show. The contents don't live up to the promise. It all makes one wish to enjoy the generally good food in less fussy surroundings.

MICHEL RICHARD'S CITRONELLE
Latham Hotel
3000 M St. NW, Washington, DC
(202) 625-2150

AMERICAN/FRENCH

Breakfast: Daily 6:30-10:30 **Entrees:** $3.75-$14 (buffet $12.50)
Lunch: M-F noon-2 **Entrees:** $8-$16
Dinner: Sun-Th 5:30-10, F-Sat 5:30-10:30 **Entrees:** $24-$32
Credit Cards: All major, DC **Reservations:** Recommended
Parking: Complimentary valet **Metro:** Foggy Bottom
Dress: Jacket & tie (dinner), business attire (lunch)

Los Angeles' loss is Washington's gain. One of the country's most extraordinary French chefs, Michel Richard, has relocated here to make CITRONELLE the headquarters of his restaurant empire. His California sensibility must be responsible for the new mood wall, a glowing expanse that changes colors by the minute. But otherwise the room is sedately luxurious, an homage to food (the chef and his cadre cooking in full view) and wine (a breathtaking collection stored behind glass).

As described on the menu, the dishes are deceptively simple. But Richard goes beyond seasoning to employ geometry and texture to enhance their taste. On the plate, they are inventive shapes, and in the mouth, they are often sublime. For example, filaments of dough—Middle Eastern *kadaif*—encase fried langoustines, shrimp or soft-shell crabs. The explosion of crackly bits on the tongue highlights the silken shellfish. He compacts sweetbreads into thick disks so that when they are sautéed, the surface is crisp yet the whole interior stays uniformly velvety. Lamb fillets and chicken breast are rolled into logs that allow such control in the cooking that every bit of the lamb can remain pink, every part of the chicken smoothly tender. Thin haricots verts are cut into small bits to play against baby peas and kernels of corn—the shapes of these vegetables are used to remarkable advantage.

While Richard doesn't avoid the richness of *foie gras*, lobster or duck, his sauces are wispy and light, his use of fresh vegetables refreshing, his seasonings deft and delicate. His are dishes that unfold as you eat them, revealing his mastery gradually. While MICHEL RICHARD'S CITRONELLE is one of the most expensive restaurants in town, few would argue with its right to that position.

MIKE BAKER'S 10TH STREET GRILL
518 10th St. NW, Washington, DC
(202) 347-6333

AMERICAN   🦽

Lunch: M-Sat 11:30-4 **Entrees:** $6-$11
Dinner: M-Th 4-11, F-Sat 4-3 am **Entrees:** $7-$15
Credit Cards: All major, DIS **Dress:** Casual **Closed:** Sun
Reservations: Recommended **Parking:** Garage (fee) across street
Metro: Metro Center

Think of MIKE BAKER'S as an antidote to the Hard Rock Cafe. The infamous Hard Rock, just down the block, inevitably has a line in front. MIKE BAKER'S is where the tour buses tend to park, and the people bound for the Hard Rock don't seem to notice it. But Mike Baker himself doesn't look disappointed that the buses bypass his little joint. He's been running bars in the area for at least 20 years. He's a perennial.

The downstairs is just what you'd expect of a Mike Baker grill: talkative, opinionated waitresses and leathery booths. The upstairs dining rooms make a brave attempt at formality.

MIKE BAKER'S is not a place that's comfortable with niceties. It's more suited to jeans than jackets, a burger and a heap of fries than an Asian-fusion halibut with a flag of thyme stuck in an oversize *gaufrette* potato. ("Just think, a potato died for this," quipped one astonished recipient.) Those fries may be the best thing on the menu. Maybe that's the lesson here: The less tidy the dish, the better it's going to taste.

Let's test that theory on the appetizers. The white bean and cheddar soup is grayish and perfunctorily garnished with scallions. It's delicious. Defying my theory, the cute little curried-lamb spring rolls are quite nice.

As for entrees, I could happily skip the main event and eat the accompaniments: the mashed potatoes, those great fries and a scallion potato salad with bacon. The most appealing match between mainstay and side dish is grilled salmon with a plateful of shiitake fried rice.

Kindergartners might have invented the banana split. It's a swamp of bananas with coconut ice cream, fudge sauce, red berry sauce and a drizzle of something orange. The *crème brûlée* has no more flavor than pudding mix. Of course: It's just too tidy to be the right thing to order here.

MR. YUNG'S
740 6th St. NW, Washington, DC
(202) 628-1098

CHINESE   🦽

Lunch: M-F 11-3 **Entrees:** $5-$9
Dinner: M-Th 3-10:30, F 3 pm-11 pm, Sat-Sun 11 am-11 pm
Entrees: $7-$16 **Credit Cards:** All major, DIS, DC
Reservations: Accepted **Dress:** Casual **Parking:** Street
Metro: Gallery Place-Chinatown **Dim Sum:** Daily 11-3, $2.30-$4

Despite the MCI bringing new life to 7th Street, Chinatown has fallen into the doldroms. Few of its restaurants are as reliable as they once were. MR. YUNG'S is an example. It was the best restaurant in Chinatown, and it still has what is perhaps the most wide-ranging and exciting menu. But its cooking has become unreliable.

There's much to like here. The dining room is spacious and well kept, with several round tables (and lazy susans) to accommodate groups. The service is probably the nicest, most helpful and pleasant of any restaurant within several blocks. And a few dishes are outstanding.

If you call ahead and are willing to splurge, you'll find a whole boneless steamed chicken with ham and black mushrooms, beautifully arranged and layered in an elegant banquet style. The Peking duck is excellent. The choice of seafood, noodles, vegetables and more is extensive. But too many of the dishes are heavy, thickly sauced, murky. Watch for seasonal specials and try to ferret out what's freshest in the kitchen. And hope that MR. YUNG'S gets back on track.

MORRISON-CLARK INN
1015 L St. NW, Washington, DC
(202) 898-1200

AMERICAN/SOUTHERN

Lunch: M-F 11:30-2 **Entrees:** $12.75-$15.75
Dinner: M-Th 6-9:30, F-Sat 6-10, Sun 6-9 **Entrees:** $17.50-$22
Brunch: Sun 11-2, $27.50 **Credit Cards:** All major, DIS, DC
Reservations: Preferred **Dress:** Business attire suggested
Parking: Complimentary valet **Metro:** Metro Center

Some restaurants make you feel that life is so good it never should change. That's the serene and lovely MORRISON-CLARK INN, with its Victorian dining room, exquisite service and faintly Southern cooking that gently surpasses all its other assets.

You enter through a tiny and distinguished lobby to settle into the dining room, furnished with flowered, circular sofas and immense pier mirrors, lace curtains covering the windows. The eating begins with a tray of good breads and proceeds to seasonal dishes abundant with color and flavor, many of them lightened versions of classics.

Chef Susan McCreight Lindeborg takes grits and spoonbread in new directions: A grits soufflé is smothered with crayfish and *etouffee* sauce as an appetizer; spoonbread sops up the pecan-bourbon sauce that comes with the grilled rabbit entree. In the summer she mingles tomato and potato salad, tomato and leeks in a soup. Her soft-shell crabs are perfect, teamed Southern-style

"Lindeborg's cooking . . . has the maturity of tradition, leavened by wit."

with hush puppies and coleslaw. Her scallops are sweet and juicy, elevated by tomatoes and peppers applied with a light hand. Lindeborg's cooking, from meats to fish, salads to desserts, has the maturity of tradition, leavened by wit. And while I wouldn't want to ignore her seasonal cobblers or her upside-down cake, or her chocolate-nut creations, if anyone has ever made a better lemon chess pie, I'd be surprised.

Above all, the MORRISON-CLARK INN has a quiet and relaxing quality that isn't often found under the same roof with such creative modern cooking. It's like an English country house with the kitchen of a small French inn.

MORTON'S OF CHICAGO
1050 Connecticut Ave. NW, Washington, DC
(202) 955-5997

AMERICAN/STEAKHOUSE   ♿

Lunch: M-F 11:30-2:30   **Entrees:** $10-$20
Dinner: M-Sat 5:30-11, Sun 5-10   **Entrees:** $19-$30
Credit Cards: All major, DC   **Reservations:** Recommended
Dress: Business attire   **Parking:** Complimentary valet at dinner
Metro: Farragut North, Farragut West
Happy Hour: M-F 5:30-7, complimentary steak sandwiches

You've got to get there early if you're to get the best of MORTON'S. In addition to offering the finest porterhouse in town, this chain of dark, clubby and spacious he-man restaurants serves the most flavorful, juicy, taste-of-yesteryear prime rib I've found anywhere. But only one is prepared each evening, at least at the Connecticut Avenue MORTON'S, which is my favorite, so it runs out early. This prime rib is cut so thick that it looks like what you might serve to a whole dinner party. It is food for which the doggie bag was invented.

MORTON'S greatness is all about beef. The steak I covet is cooked on the bone, preferably seared black-and-blue so it comes deliciously charred and rare. It doesn't need much adornment to add up to a grand meal. The potatoes—crisp and buttery hash browns or crusty potato skins—are terrific, and spinach is an excellent grassy contrast. When I stray to other vegetables or salads, I generally wish I hadn't bothered. The veal chops, lamb chops, chicken, fish and lobsters are nice enough, but I'm here for beef. Such a meal hardly needs a first course, though scallops wrapped in bacon are about as good as that preparation can get. Desserts glory in richness, but once again I'd rather concentrate on the steak and roast beef—washed down by a fine red wine, which MORTON'S provides with considerable expertise.

"The prime rib is cut so thick that it looks like what you might serve to a whole dinner party."

There are other Morton's at: 3251 Prospect St. NW, Washington, DC, (202) 342-6258; 8075 Leesburg Pike, Vienna, VA, (703) 883-0800, and 300 S. Charles St. (Inner Harbor), Baltimore, MD, (410) 547-8255.

MUSIC CITY ROADHOUSE
1050 30th St. NW, Washington, DC
(202) 337-4444

AMERICAN/SOUTHERN   🔲

Dinner: Tu-Sat 4:30-10, Sun 2-10   **Entrees:** $8-$13
Family-Style Meal: $13   **Brunch:** Sun 10:30-2, $13
Late Night: Th 10-midnight, F-Sat 10-1 am, $3-$7.50
Closed: M   **Credit Cards:** All major, DC, CB, DIS   **Dress:** Casual
Reservations: Recommended   **Parking:** Validated garage
Happy Hour: M-F 4:30-close, various beer specials
Entertainment: Blues Sat 7-10, gospel at Sun brunch

MUSIC CITY ROADHOUSE is a magnetic restaurant, not only because of the music—ranging from blues to gospel—and the outdoor tables lining the C&O Canal. People go just for the food.

Surely nobody expects to go to a down-home Southern restaurant for a
vegetable plate, but that's what I'm tempted to order at MUSIC CITY
ROADHOUSE. This big, sprawling barn of a place, with a decor that
runs to cat caps and barbecue signs, serves family-style, fixed-price
lunches and dinners (and sensational brunches, as well as à la carte salads and sandwiches) that allow you to order all you can eat of three
different meats (say, fried chicken, pot roast, barbecued chicken or ribs)
or fish (fried catfish, broiled trout). And with them you get all you can
eat of three different vegetables, plus some of the best, richest, creamiest
skillet corn bread this side of Georgia. Who could complain?

My problem, though, is that the great greasy fried chicken, the carrot-
laden pot roast and the meaty ribs don't leave me enough room for the
vegetables. And I can never happily pick only three from the list of six.
So one of these days I'm going to order just the vegetable plate (not
vegetarian, mind you, since the greens are flavored with pork). Then I
can have all of them, and concentrate on those spicy, just-vinegary-enough
and truly wonderful cooked greens, the slightly lumpy mashed potatoes
with chicken-flavored cream gravy, the sweet potatoes that are light and
airy and so delicately sweetened that for once I don't think they should
be served as dessert, the sometimes-available black-eyed peas, the slaw
and whatever else happens to be on the menu.

MYKONOS
1875 K St. NW, Washington, DC
(202) 331-0370

GREEK   ♿

Lunch: M-F 11:30-3:30 **Entrees:** $6-$14
Dinner: M-F 5:30-10:30, Sat 5-11 **Entrees:** $10-$20
Closed: Sun **Credit Cards:** All major, DIS, DC, CB
Reservations: Recommended **Dress:** Casual
Parking: Complimentary valet at dinner **Metro:** Farragut West

A t this lively, casual Greek restaurant, first look to the daily specials—especially when they involve stewed or roast lamb. Next consider the Greek Taverna Salad, cut-up romaine combined with tomato, cucumber, onion and black olives, then—this is the important part—tossed with vinaigrette and crumbled feta cheese, so that the dressing and cheese permeate it all. Add a couple of dollars and you can get it topped with tuna or chicken.

Or forget the standard Greek salads altogether and make a comforting lunch from a combination plate of cold appetizers (the menu prices it for two, but you can order a single portion). This one looks as if the kitchen went to considerable effort, and it tastes worthy of it. To spread on your crusty Greek bread there's a mound of *tzatziki* (cucumber with yogurt), another of smoky eggplant puree, and my favorite, the tangy *tarama* (coral-tinged fish roe whipped with bread, lemon, onion and olive oil). A hillock of white beans with onion and a chunk of eggplant buried under diced tomatoes, onions and pine nuts, along with garnishes of tomatoes, purple olives and feta cheese, complete the plate.

For the Maryland location, which is open on Sunday: 121 Congressional Lane, Rockville, MD, (301) 770-5999.

NAM VIET
3419 Connecticut Ave. NW, Washington, DC
(202) 237-1015

VIETNAMESE	♿

Lunch: M-Th 11-3, F-Sun 11-3:30 **Entrees:** $7-$12
Dinner: M-Th 5-10, F-Sat 11am-11pm, Sun 3:30-10 **Entrees:** $8-$14
Credit Cards: All major, DIS, DC **Dress:** Casual
Reservations: Recommended for 4 or more **Parking:** Street
Metro: Cleveland Park

While most of the area's early Vietnamese restaurants have remained static and grown a little shabby, losing ground in the increasing competition, NAM VIET has only improved. That's what shows in its big, bright, new in-town branch: a matter-of-fact excellence. It's a sea of green tables with fresh flowers on each and paintings on the walls that are art as well as decoration. While the atmosphere is hardly cozy or personal, and the service seems harried, every dish shows care. The meats and fish are plump and juicy, the vegetables bright and crisp, and the sauces—most with a touch of sweetness and some with curry fire—are light-textured and highly perfumed.

The long menu is too much to explore on one visit, but you can safely put yourself in the hands of your waiter. The shrimp toast is unusual, with a crisp layer of rice paper on the bottom and a haunting flavor. *Cha gio*—spring rolls—are crunchy and fragrant. Grilled pork and beef dishes are crusty and fetchingly marinated. But the restaurant's unique quality shows in its fish dishes—grilled, curried or braised in a sweet-salty caramel and black pepper sauce. Seek them out to be reminded of how light and delicate yet intriguing Vietnamese cooking can be.

For the Virginia branch: 1127 N. Hudson St., Arlington, VA, (703) 522-7110.

THE NARROWS
3023 Kent Narrows Way South, Kent Island, MD
(410) 827-8113

AMERICAN/SEAFOOD

Lunch: M-Sat 11-4 **Entrees:** $7-$15
Dinner: Sun-Th 4-9:30 **Entrees:** $15-$28
Brunch: Sun 11-2 **Entrees:** $8-$14
Dress: Casual **Reservations:** Recommended
Parking: Free lot

C an you really get great seafood among the bland, plastic miles of restaurants on the way to the beach? Yes, but it's not easy. You have to know which of these prefabricated-looking restaurants is deep-down real.

THE NARROWS. That's what you need to know. It's right on the water at Kent Island (down the street from the Angler's, which serves a top-notch soft-shell sandwich in season), and it has a deck where you can watch the boats and jet skis. It looks like a chain restaurant decorated by Hallmark, yet it serves world-class crab cakes that could hardly be improved.

"It serves world-class crab cakes that could hardly be improved."

They're expensive, but worth it for every back-fin morsel. Broiled, barely shaped almost a blob rather than a cake, NARROWS' version is close to crab imperial, and crabmeat itself is stunning.

And there's more. Fried green tomatoes are as good as any in Georgia: lemon-tart in a firm, crunchy batter. The Caesar salad, too, is as tangy as you'd hope, and it is regal when topped with fried oysters that, like the crab, taste right out of the water. Fried onion strings are worth whatever dietary agony they cost. Then again, you might want to save your sin quotient for dessert. Where else can you find fried chocolate truffles?

NATHANS
3150 M St. NW, Washington, DC
(202) 338-2000

AMERICAN   🔯

Lunch: M-F noon-3 **Entrees:** $10-$12 **Dinner:** M-F 6-10, F-Sat 6-11
Entrees: $18-$22 **Brunch:** Sat-Sun 11-3 **Entrees:** $10-$12
Light Fare: Daily 3-6 **Entrees:** $5-$12 **Credit Cards:** All major, DC
Dress: Casual **Reservations:** Recommended **Parking:** Validated at
dinner for Georgetown Park **Entertainment:** Dancing (DJ) F-Sat 11-3

Restaurants, too, have life stories. NATHANS was born in 1969, back
when Georgetown was Georgetown. Its owner, Howard Joynt, wasn't
yet 30, but he was able to turn this bar, dance spot and dining room into
a success that's outlasted most of the competition. He hired the infamous
Giuseppina, and for a time her sublime pasta was the best in town. When
Howard Joynt died, his wife Carol hired a new chef, Paul Wahlberg (who
until now has been better known as Marky Mark's brother). She did a
little redecorating. And she's kept up her late husband's convivially rich
wine list.

Pastas remain a large part of the menu, but Giuseppina's legacy does not
prevail. Wahlberg's sauces are all too likely to be cream-based—and
bland. Among appetizers, the duck *confit* spring roll is the standout. Inevitably, there's Caesar salad, and while its dressing is heavy, it's also
zesty. In contrast, the old NATHANS standby, fried calamari, is a little
bland and soggy. A smoked salmon "club" rests in the middle ground.

Among entrees, the homiest is usually the best. Meatloaf is two immense
slabs wrapped in bacon. You can also get a thick, juicy cheeseburger. Or,
moving up the scale, there are steaks, including a grilled tenderloin that's
more satisfying than the rack of lamb. To their credit, the desserts don't
try to be too fashionable. If you're not tired of *crème brûlée*, NATHANS
version is a winner.

NATHANS is a work in progress. Still, it's one of the few places in town
where you can have a burger at dinner time or dance on the weekend,
with champagne to suit any occasion.

NEW HEIGHTS RESTAURANT
2317 Calvert St. NW, Washington, DC
(202) 234-4110

AMERICAN/INTERNATIONAL

Dinner: Sun-Th 5:30-10, F-Sat 5:30-11 **Entrees:** $16.50-$25
Brunch: Sun 11-2:30 **Entrees:** $7-$15 **Credit Cards:** All major,
DC **Reservations:** Recommended **Dress:** Casual
Parking: Complimentary valet **Metro:** Woodley Park-Zoo

NEW HEIGHTS is unwaveringly lovely on the surface: urbane, contemporary, quietly stylish. It's a second-floor restaurant that makes an asset of its big windows, and a neighborhood landmark for a very demanding group of neighbors. It's always been known for its discreetly excellent, never stuffy service. And though chefs have come and gone, its New American menu has always featured a few dishes so beloved that they are available as entrees as well as appetizers. Thus, no matter who is in the kitchen, you can count on the crunchy buttermilk-fried oysters, with corn, chiles and lime; a deconstructed version of Indian-style spinach with fresh cheese cubes—*palak paneer*—that is elegantly presented in a *pappadum* shell and hauntingly delicious, and beautifully constructed crab cakes.

Underneath, though, NEW HEIGHTS has been the victim and the beneficiary of a succession of chefs. Now the chef is John Wabeck, young and fresh out of the kitchen at Restaurant Nora. Under his hand, the menu is better than ever. There are some missteps, but they're far outweighed by such appetizers as scallops with eggplant-curry emulsion or *foie gras* with mango salsa and pumpkin seeds, and entrees of sizzlingly spiced lamb chops, crisp-surfaced fish with meltingly delicious spinach or quinoa-corn salad, or duck with *hoisin* glaze. Even his filet mignon—with pickled fennel and blue cheese—is just fine.

Wabeck cooks like a seasoned chef. His colors are vivid, his flavors are penetrating yet balanced, and he lets each ingredient stand out rather than get lost in the crowd. To show his food to advantage, there's an impressive and thoughtfully priced wine list. And classic desserts, from *crème brûlée* to chocolate extravaganzas to lush sorbets, add the final flourish to a most satisfying restaurant.

NIZAM'S
523 Maple Ave. W., Vienna, VA
(703) 938-8948

TURKISH/MEDITERRANEAN   ♿

Lunch: Tu-F 11-2:30 **Entrees:** $7.50-$14.50
Dinner: Tu-Th 5-10, F-Sat 5-11, Sun 4-9 **Entrees:** $13-$17.50
Closed: M **Credit Cards:** All major, DIS, DC **Dress:** Casual
Reservations: Recommended **Parking:** Free lot

Even Istanbul has no better *doner* kebab than NIZAM'S (unfortunately, it's not served every night). And if you have only tasted doner kebab elsewhere in Washington, you are probably in for a surprise. Most of the restaurants, carryouts and fast-food stands that serve doner kebab —or gyros, as it is often called—buy it as a big frozen loaf of ground meat. It is cooked on a vertical spit and thinly sliced as the surface browns. But it still tastes like frozen hamburger meat. NIZAM'S starts from scratch, marinating paper-thin slices of lamb and stacking them on the spit to form a giant loaf. As it is served, each portion is a cross section of the thin slices of lamb that have melded together into a juicy, gently herbed and spiced web. It is luscious meat, with crisp edges and juicy texture. And at NIZAM'S you can have it plain or spread over chunks of sautéed pita bread with a bit of thick tomato sauce and dense, rich, tangy yogurt.

"For a moderate price you can get a meal that's both simple and exotic."

If you hit NIZAM'S when it's not doner kebab night, you can compensate with *yogurtlu* kebab, the same mix of bread and sauces with sautéed tenderloin.

The menu goes on to kebabs of swordfish, shrimp, cubed or ground lamb, plus the usual Turkish casseroles. Grilled meat is carefully cooked, but my favorite remains the doner kebab. I'd start dinner with the fine grape leaves stuffed with currants and pine nuts, or the highly peppered *baba ghanouj*; the *borek* here are heavy. And I'd look into the listing of Turkish wines. Platters are preceded by a salad and accompanied by pilaf— nothing exciting but rather nice. The black-tie service is a little shy and certainly efficient; the dining room is quiet and agreeable, with a few reminders of Turkey. In sum, for a moderate price you can get a meal that's both simple and exotic.

OBELISK
2029 P St. NW, Washington, DC
(202) 872-1180

ITALIAN

Dinner: Tu-Sat 6-10 **Full Dinner:** $45 (prix fixe) **Closed:** Sun-M
Credit Cards: MC, V, DC **Reservations:** Recommended
Dress: Casual **Parking:** Street **Metro:** Dupont Circle

R estaurants change from day to day, dish to dish. Thus the challenge is not only to choose the right restaurant but to cull its menu for the best things to order. Once you choose OBELISK, though, the possibility of error is slim. Of all the finest restaurants in the Washington area, it has the smallest menu, the narrowest choices—and the greatest consistency.

You're always going to get a simply beautiful meal at OBELISK. Despite its American name, OBELISK is Italian. It has the unfussy look of a trattoria, and like most trattorias, its tables are close enough that you can smell your neighors' entrees and listen to their conversation. It's likely to be about the food.

The menu is fixed-price, and there are only three or four choices for each of the three savory courses, which are followed by cheese and your pick of about

". . . the kind [of place] you'd love to keep a secret . . ."

half a dozen desserts. Even with the menu's limitations, though, it's hard to choose. I've seen beet disdainers and tongue haters scrape up the last bits of the beet-and-tongue antipasto. For the second course, the soups are luscious, but nobody should miss the pasta. The barely sauced fettuccine is the best in town, and alternatives are the likes of ravioli filled with heavenly eggplant. Entrees are small and at first seem plain; I challenge anyone to find a veal medallion with more flavor or a duck breast more perfectly seasoned. And the bits of sauce must be swiped up with bread, since the house-made bread is as crusty and flavorful as bread gets.

Add to these assets a wine list that is lovingly assembled and fairly priced, waiters who are as knowledgeable as if they'd done the cooking themselves, and desserts that are always interesting even if they're not as wonderful as they sound. The sum is an extraordinarily satisfying little restaurant, the kind you'd love to keep a secret so there'd always be a table available for you and your friends.

OLD ANGLER'S INN
10801 MacArthur Blvd., Potomac, MD
(301) 365-2425

AMERICAN

Lunch: Tu-Sat noon-2:30 **Entrees:** $14-$15.50
Dinner: Tu-F 6-10:30, Sat 5:30-10:30, Sun 5:30-9:30
Entrees: $21-$29 **Brunch:** Sun noon-2:30 **Entrees:** $23-$25
Closed: M **Credit Cards:** All major, DC **Dress:** Jacket preferred
Reservations: Recommended weekdays, required weekends
Parking: Free lot

OLD ANGLER'S INN is a near-legendary restaurant. Its setting, hidden above the C&O Canal with a large terrace embraced by trees, lends itself to romantic description. Inside or out, it's exactly the place to propose—just about anything. Be careful, though, in considering OLD ANGLER'S as a site for true romance. Dining here involves climbing a narrow iron spiral staircase, and on busy evenings as many as 40 extra seats are packed in too little space.

". . . exactly the place to propose —just about anything." If you can ignore the prices and set aside the staff's—and the dining rooms'—insufficiencies, you're likely to find that chef Tom Power's food is sturdy, recognizable and generally satisfying. He's not breaking new ground but revisiting a pleasant, well-trodden landscape.

Lobster tail is the last shellfish I'd order in most places, but here it's redeemed. But while you'd think that tuna tartare would be a cinch for such a chef, Power's version is desperate for some zip. For the entrees, too, stick to the classics. Veal strip loin, a special, is a satisfying piece of well-browned prime veal. Rack of lamb is also good. Power repeatedly overcooks his fish, which is too bad, since the salmon comes with an evocative potato and shiitake ragout. I'd prefer a plate of just the vegetables.

The crispy milk chocolate bar is unforgettable, but there's nothing special about the other desserts (although they're improved by being served in the lounge before a roaring fire). Of course, timing is everything. On a busy Saturday night, OLD ANGLER'S seems like high-priced subway dining. But on an evening when everyone else has stayed home, the food is magically spun into gold.

OLD EBBITT GRILL
675 15th St. NW, Washington, DC
(202) 347-4800

AMERICAN   🦽

Breakfast: M-Th 7:30-11, Sat 8-11:30 **Entrees:** $4.50-$7
Lunch: M-Th 11-5, Sat 11:30-4 **Entrees:** $6.25-$14
Dinner: Daily 5-midnight **Entrees:** $10-$19
Late Night: Daily midnight-1 am **Entrees:** $6.75-$18
Brunch: Sun 9:30-4 **Entrees:** $6-$14
Credit Cards: All major, DIS, DC
Reservations: Recommended **Dress:** Casual
Parking: Complimentary valet, dinner, brunch **Metro:** Metro Center

Once upon a time Clyde's was the hottest news in town. Now Clyde's has become a conglomerate of restaurants, ranging from the family-oriented Tomato Palace in Columbia to the OLD EBBITT GRILL downtown, to the colonial dowager 1789 in Georgetown.

What's amazing is that this high-intensity restaurant chain, with its predictable pub fare (fried calamari, Buffalo wings, chili, Caesar salad, the usual pastas, barbecue, crab cakes), comes up with some wonderful seasonable surprises. The few days of halibut season in Alaska mean fresh halibut on the menus at Clyde's and the OLD EBBITT. In the summer, the OLD EBBITT GRILL is probably the only downtown pub serving fresh corn on the cob, local green beans and new potatoes, as well as pies and cobblers made with berries from nearby farms.

Even so, we'd all like to retire on a dollar for every burger the OLD EBBITT sells. What once was Clyde's claim to fame is now the OLD EBBITT'S: a thick, handsome patty of juicy, coarsely ground

> **"We'd all like to retire on a dollar for every hamburger the Old Ebbitt sells."**

and loosely packed beef, as crusty outside and as pink inside as you want, on a seeded bun with lettuce, tomato (ripe in season), pickle and utterly indifferent french fries. Ask for the green beans instead.

OLD GLORY (ALL-AMERICAN BARBEQUE)
3130 M St. NW, Washington, DC
(202) 337-3406

AMERICAN/SOUTHERN/BARBECUE

Open: M-Th 11:30am-11:30pm, F-Sat 11:30am-12:30pm, Sun 11am-11:30 pm **Entrees:** $6.50-$16 **Late Night:** Sun-Th 11:30-1 am, F-Sat 12:30-2 am **Late Night Entrees:** $5.25-$6.75
Brunch: Sun 11-3, $12 buffet
Credit Cards: All major **Reservations:** No **Dress:** Casual
Parking: Street **Entertainment:** Blues Tu, Th, F-Sat at 10:30

If a restaurant is this noisy, throbbing with rock music and flickering with big-screen TV, and it still manages to attract diners beyond their twenties, it must be serving awfully good food. And so OLD GLORY does, for the most part. It's a two-story, tightly packed barbecue joint, with lean, tender and juicy ribs and brisket that envelop your table in wood smoke, as well as some terrific side dishes.

At most barbecues, the chicken is overcooked, dry and far too smoky to taste like bird. And so it is here. But the Buffalo wings are a succulent appetizer. So is barbecued shrimp in the shell. For entrees, the ribs and brisket can't be beat, and the burgers are substantial.

An array of sauces representing eight barbecue regions provides mix-and-match games. And the basket of corn muffins and biscuits tastes of Southern pride. Getting more Southern, mellow collard greens, creamy succotash and barely greasy hush puppies are among the side dishes. The potato salad is worthy of a church picnic, and the mashed potatoes are the real thing. Too bad that the coleslaw and the french fries taste like leftovers.

Few real barbecues have desserts that warrant saving room, but here, too, OLD GLORY exceeds expectations. Apple crisp and cherry-coconut cobbler taste homey and look it, in their Pyrex measuring cups. And cookie-topped chocolate pudding, served in a flowerpot with candy gummy worms peering through, is far more delicious than most practical jokes.

OODLES NOODLES
1120 19th St. NW, Washington, DC
(202) 293-3138

ASIAN   ♿

Lunch: M-F 11:30-3   **Dinner:** M-Th 5-10, F-Sat 5-10:30
Entrees: $7-$9   **Closed:** Sun   **Credit Cards:** All major, DC
Reservations: Recommended for dinner   **Dress:** Casual
Parking: Street   **Metro:** Dupont Circle, Farragut North

Whereas a decade or two ago we might have gone to a coffee shop and had a sandwich when we sought an uncomplicated, unpricey lunch, now we go to an Asian noodle parlor. OODLES NOODLES answers the need reliably, which is why its downtown branch has a line out the door at lunch and its Bethesda branch is packed with families at dinner.

Its menu is like those long lists of sandwich variations delis used to offer, only instead of corned beef or hoagies, the modern diet dictates that the choice be light and lean noodles with chicken or shrimp or—for the daring eater—beef or pork. The menu is a little Thai, somewhat Japanese, with touches of Chinese, Indonesian and Vietnamese.

Few dishes are really spicy, and much of the food is approximately what you'd put together for a Sunday supper if your refrigerator was particularly well stocked with Asian leftovers:

> **"For such an on-the-run, jam-packed eatery, the waiters maintain remarkably good cheer."**

A Thai fried rice with spurts of chilis, peanut-sauced or sesame-sauced noodles with chicken, or all kinds of soups packed with noodles, vegetables and meats (my perennial favorite is grilled-chicken noodle soup with cilantro, fried onions and flat noodles).

Some of the doughy appetizers—fried beef pancakes, pan-fried meaty Japanese dumplings or scallion cakes—are more authentically ethnic and often delicious. And for such an on-the-run, jam-packed eatery, the waiters maintain remarkable good cheer.

Oodles Noodles' Maryland branch is at 4907 Cordell Ave., Bethesda, (301) 986-8833.

OVAL ROOM
800 Connecticut Ave. NW, Washington, DC
(202) 463-8700

AMERICAN   👌

Lunch: M-F 11:30-3 **Entrees:** $10.50-$18.50
Light Fare: Daily 3-5:30 **Entrees:** $6-$9
Dinner: M-Th 5:30-10:30, F-Sat 5:30-11 **Entrees:** $14.50-$22
Pre-Theater: M-Sat 5:30-6:30, $24.50 **Closed:** Sun
Credit Cards: All major, DC **Reservations:** Recommended
Dress: Casual **Parking:** Complimentary valet after 6 pm
Metro: Farragut West **Entertainment:** Pianist Tu-Sat 6:30-9:30

This OVAL ROOM is not very far from its White House namesake, so you can expect to see the faces in the news as well as those who report it. Thus it serves as a comfortable, quiet haven of traditional furniture and modern curved walls painted with a whimsical mural of Washington political life.

The OVAL ROOM has always served with expertise: It's a safe, reliable and luxurious place for a business lunch if your business involves the movers and shakers of the capital. And if your budget allows for a measure of opulence.

Its food is hardly traditional. It's always been modern and adventurous. Now, under a new chef—RJ Cooper—the OVAL ROOM seems to be simplifying—a bit. So far, Cooper seems particularly attentive to fish, serving it crusty-skinned and velvet-fleshed. He dresses halibut with a fragrant mushroom risotto and a reduction of red wine; it's lively and not the least bizarre. Rockfish is even closer to the mainstream, with its bed of pleasantly bitter broccoli rabe and a haze of garlic. Cooper presents pork elegantly with a timbale of pasta that encloses red cabbage, and he pays attention to vegetarians' needs. He's ambitious—smoking his own duck breast, playing *foie gras* against scallops and flavoring ice cream with black pepper and a sauce of balsamic vinegar (it's sensational!). He's still too new to this kitchen to judge for the long haul. But he's made a promising start in a restaurant that brings along lots of environmental and geographical advantages.

> **" . . . a safe, reliable, luxurious place for a business lunch if your business involves the movers and shakers of the capital."**

PAN ASIAN NOODLES AND GRILL
2020 P St. NW, Washington, DC
(202) 872-8889

ASIAN/THAI

Lunch: M-F 11:30-2:30, Sat noon-2:30 **Entrees:** $5.25-$7
Dinner: Sun-Th 5-10, F-Sat 5-11 **Entrees:** $7.25-$12
Credit Cards: All major **Reservations:** Recommended
Dress: Casual **Parking:** Street **Metro:** Dupont Circle

When a gust of cold weather reminds you that winter has settled in, PAN ASIAN NOODLES AND GRILL is at its best. For a pittance you can order a giant bowl of noodles, meat and broth, with mix-and-match choices of rice or egg noodles, chicken or spicy beef broth, sliced beef, pork or wontons with pork. Pay a couple bucks more and you get seafood.

In any case, these are filling meals of warming, aromatic broth heady with fresh coriander and Oriental spices. They're served in spiffy-looking black bowls with red rims, in tune with the neon and lacquered colors of this cheerful, clever little restaurant. Even

"When a gust of cold weather reminds you that winter has settled in, Pan Asian Noodles and Grill is at its best."

if the day is not cold enough to shout soup, PAN ASIAN is popular for its plates of noodles topped with every Asian flavor, from Thailand's *pad thai* (which unfortunately is too sweet) to Canton's *chow fun*.

The most addictive, though, is drunken noodles, the wide noodles topped with ground chicken and basil in an aromatic, faintly sweet and fairly spicy sauce. Again, the price is well under $10. And the relative splurges of the menu, the appetizers, include lovely little grilled skewered bits, crisply fried nuggets and the spring rolls of several nations.

PANJSHIR
224 W. Maple Ave., Vienna, VA
(703) 281-4183

AFGHAN   ♿

Lunch: M-Sat 11-2 **Entrees:** $6-$7.25
Dinner: Tu-Sat 5-10, Sun-M 5-9 **Entrees:** $10-$13.25
Credit Cards: All major, DC **Reservations:** Recommended
Dress: Casual **Parking:** Free lot **Metro:** Vienna

A fter years of near-addiction to *aushak*, the leek-stuffed Afghan noodles buried in yogurt, tomato sauce and mint, I discovered PANJSHIR'S *muntoo*, a meat-stuffed version of *aushak*. It became a new love. What all this adds up to is that the same dish can be made many different ways and be wonderful in all its variations, despite the stubborn loyalty we have for our taste memories.

Beyond boiled dumplings, the area's Afghan menus are similar right through dessert. Virtually all offer deep-fried turnovers, usually as appetizers. Entrees are kebabs with seasoned rice, stewed lamb with rice, and (the glory of Afghan cooking) vegetables seasoned with such aromatics as ginger or coriander, moistened with yogurt and tomato sauce, sometimes sweetened with brown sugar or prunes. If you don't order an entree that comes with vegetables, you should include a side dish. And even if you consider pumpkin fit only for pies and jack-o-lanterns, try *kadu*—sautéed pumpkin with tomato and yogurt—lest you miss one of the greatest vegetable dishes ever contrived.

PANJSHIR'S outstanding kebab is lamb chops—called Chopped Kebab on the menu. Marinated for a spicy and vinegary tang, the chops are trimmed well, cut thin and cooked until their edges are crisp. Lamb outshines beef here. If you like a sweet main dish, try *quabili palow*— tomatoey lamb stew with rice, topped with glazed carrot shreds, almonds and raisins—or one of the vegetable combinations: apples with prunes and walnuts, brown-sugared turnips, carrots with prunes and walnuts or the wonderful, soft and aromatic pumpkin. On the less sweet side is eggplant with tomato sauce, and there's spinach with onion and garlic if you prefer no sweetness at all. All are preceded by a nice crisp green salad and accompanied by typical Afghan bread.

Panjshir also has a branch at 924 W. Broad St., Falls Church, VA, (703) 536-4566.

PAOLO'S
1303 Wisconsin Ave. NW, Washington, DC
(202) 333-7353

ITALIAN	&#9855;

Open: Sun-Th 11:30am-11:30pm, F-Sat 11:30am-12:30pm
Entrees: $9-$19 **Brunch:** Sat-Sun 11:30-3 **Entrees:** $7-$13
Credit Cards: All major, DIS, DC **Dress:** Casual **Parking:** Street
Reservations: Lunch and brunch only **Entertainment:** Jazz Sun brunch

No matter what else might have gone to pot in recent decades, chain restaurants have improved. In an earlier era, nothing could be more predictable—or boring—than an Italian-American restaurant with branches in the major suburbs. No longer. PAOLO'S is a restaurant of considerable comfort (except for the noise level) and the visual enticements of an open kitchen and a wood-burning oven. Its servers are well trained, and it offers food that is imaginative and made from fresh ingredients. Most important, it has added personality to formula cooking.

I like PAOLO'S at off hours, when the place burbles rather than shouts. And I'm impressed by the attractive listings among the pizzas, pastas and grilled dishes. What's more, PAOLO'S has added a little extra zest to the same old salads that everyone else serves. It's got a Caesar (but with *pecorino* Romano and garlic croutons) and the usual mixed greens (in this case with olives, pine nuts and Gorgonzola). Its grilled seafood salads include calamari with hearts of palm, pine nuts and tomato in orange-basil vinaigrette, and grilled salmon and shrimp with olives and dried tomatoes in sherry-herb vinaigrette. While you might think you've seen everything a chicken salad could offer, the grilled-chicken-and-greens toss at PAOLO'S includes eggplant, olives, capers and feta as well.

"The main reason for going to Paolo's is for what comes free."

The main reason for going to PAOLO'S, though, is what comes free: warm, soft, seeded bread sticks and the sensational chickpea-eggplant-olive spread that accompanies them.

For the two other Paolo's branches, in Virginia and Maryland: 11898 Market St., Reston, VA, (703) 318-8920, and 1 W. Pennsylvania Ave., Towson, MD, (410) 321-7000.

PATISSERIE POUPON
1645 Wisconsin Ave. NW, Washington, DC
(202) 342-3248

FRENCH

Open: Tu-Sat 8-6:30, Sun 9-5 **Entrees:** $5.25-$9
Closed: M **Credit Cards:** All major
Dress: Casual **Parking:** Street

All of Georgetown—the real Georgetown—seems to stop at this friendly little cafe for lunch. Stylish young men, serious-looking couples and women "of a certain age" wait for one of the tiny tables, chat and fortify themselves with soups, spare salads or lean sandwiches in this handsome old brick-walled townhouse.

"All of Georgetown —the real Georgetown— seems to stop at this friendly little cafe for lunch."

Then they finish up with a chocolate bombe or a *mirabelle* tart. And we thought such fashionable people didn't indulge in fat and sugar. Here they do. And who could resist? The rows and rows of pastries are perfect little rounds or pyramids, lustrous and colorful, far too sumptuous to resist. Of course they outshine the simple baguette sandwiches of ham, turkey or prosciutto. And certainly they upstage the smoked salmon plate, the charcuterie, the pâtés and the crudites. The small quiches and olive-topped pizzas can't compete with this sugar glory. The savories are hardly more than a shill: Who would dare go to lunch just for pastry?

There is another location at 820 E. Baltimore St., Baltimore, MD, (410) 332-0390.

PEKING GOURMET INN
6029 Leesburg Pike, Falls Church, VA
(703) 671-8088

CHINESE   ♿

Lunch: Daily 11-3   **Entrees:** $8-$10
Dinner: Sun-Th 3-10:30, F-Sat 3-11   **Entrees:** $10-$15
Credit Cards: All major   **Dress:** Casual
Reservations: Preferred on weekends   **Parking:** Free lot

Did success spoil the PEKING GOURMET INN? This was once one of the best Chinese restaurants in Virginia, and in the Bush administration it was in the spotlight as a favorite presidential retreat. Now it seems like a standard pack-em-in-and-feed-em-quick Chinese restaurant, even if it does still grow its own Chinese leeks and feature them in several dishes.

Two dishes still show what this restaurant used to be. Salt-baked shrimp are large and juicy, crisped in a hot pan with lots of garlic. String beans with pork and chili are lightly cooked and strongly seasoned, just as they should be. Crispy beef with sesame seeds is still crunchy, but it is all sweet and no heat. The saddest change is that PEKING GOURMET chicken, which once was glorious, is now soggy and gluey. The skin on the Peking duck is crisp and fat-free, but the meat is dry and overcooked. Even the dumplings are thick and gummy, and it's hard to find a dumpling that isn't lovable.

"Did success spoil the Peking Gourmet Inn?"

Yet the PEKING GOURMET INN has weathered decades, expansion, fame and loss of fame. I wouldn't be surprised if it got itself back in shape again.

PERSIMMON
7003 Wisconsin Ave., Bethesda, MD
(301) 654-9860

AMERICAN   🕭

Lunch: W-F 11:30-2 **Entrees:** $7-$12 **Dinner:** M-Sat 5:30-10
Entrees: $17-$22   **Closed:** Sun **Credit Cards:** All major, DC
Reservations: Recommended **Dress:** Casual **Parking:** Lot in rear
(free after 7 pm and weekends) **Metro:** Bethesda

PERSIMMON is off to a nice start for a young, fresh restaurant. The place hints of a tight budget, with chairs that are only barely comfortable and tablecloths that always seem to need ironing. Still, the dining room and the menu present a lot of style for the price.

Dinner begins on a generous note with a basket of bread and a small crock of liver pâté. Don't fill up on it, though; portions are generous, so you'll need to pace yourself.

Hidden among the salads is a trio of tartares, an offering that turns out to be a lush disk of chopped raw salmon topped by a layer of raw tuna, both lightly dressed, with bits of mild seviche shrimp. A couple of the first courses are pasta variations — mushroom-filled ravioli with a salty, glossy brown sauce and Chinese pot stickers that are really fried won tons filled with a jarring barbecued chicken. Far more disconcerting, though, is the carrot ginger soup, which has such a wallop of ginger that it brings tears to your eyes.

Given that all the fish is fresh and flawlessly cooked, you might decide to choose yours by its accompaniments. The smoked-trout spring roll with the grilled mahi-mahi is crisp and interesting. Sautéed halibut rests on a delicious mushroom risotto cake. And sautéed salmon comes with ratatouille and wonderful spinach as well as crispy potato. Among the meats, roast chicken stands out. It's a mite overcooked, but its crisp skin is irresistible.

Something creamy for dessert will end dinner impressively. PERSIMMON serves *crème brûlée* that reminds you how elegantly smooth and rich it can be. And you can hope to hit a night when the house-made ice cream is lemon. The wine list here is modest in size and price, just like the menu. It's one more factor that invites you to give PERSIMMON a chance.

PESCE
2016 P St. NW, Washington, DC
(202) 466-3474

AMERICAN/SEAFOOD	&#9855;

Lunch: M-F 11:30-2:30, Sat noon-2:30 **Entrees:** $12.50-$17
Dinner: M-W 5:30-10, Th-Sat 5:30-10:30, Sun 5-9:30
Dinner Entrees: $13.75-$18.50 **Credit Cards:** All major, DIS, DC
Reservations: Accepted for lunch, 6-plus at dinner **Dress:** Casual
Parking: Valet (fee) at dinner Th-Sat **Metro:** Dupont Circle

C ooking seafood seems simple, but with the new abundance of sea-food restaurants in town, we've learned that sparklingly fresh fish is rare. Properly prepared fish is more so, and moderately priced excellent fish is beyond that. Yet PESCE offers all this and more. This small, clat-tery, crowded and whimsically decorated seafood cafe uses the same sea-food sources as the city's top restaurants. The lengthy list of dishes is mar-ket driven, changed daily and chalked on a board brought to each table. It reflects a wider range of seafood than you're likely to find at any other casual seafood restaurants, and if you can't make a choice, you can look over the specimens in the glass-fronted case to see which glistens most.

You'll probably have to wait in line, and this is not a place you expect to linger. The tables are close, the chairs are firm and the waiting throngs suggest otherwise. Nor are you likely to rush through, not with such a nicely chosen wine list and such breezy, agreeable service.

In 1998, though, a new chef was installed in PESCE'S kitchen, and he's yet to regain the excitement that was lost in the transition. I would no longer seek out the creative and possibly risky dishes here. For the time being, at least, I'd place my money on the plain, straightforward and uncomplicated: Let the fish itself shine.

PESCE sometimes offers gigantic grilled, fresh, head-on shrimp with extraordianary flavor. Each costs as much as a normal appetizer, but the portion of two is very filling. The daily list occasionally offers opa, which tastes like a hybrid of tuna and swordfish and is one of Hawaii's best kept secrets. The menu includes a long list of appetizers and salads—which often sound more intriguing than the entrees. A few pastas are always available, some of them vegetarian. But the emphasis in entrees is fish fillets with garnishes and sauces from Europe, Asia, Latin America. One thing you can count on at PESCE: The seafood itself is nothing but the best.

PHO 75
1711 Wilson Blvd., Arlington, VA
(703) 525-7355

VIETNAMESE   🦽

Open: Daily 9 am-8 pm **Entrees:** $4.25-$6
Credit Cards: None; cash only **Reservations:** No
Dress: Casual **Parking:** Free lot **Metro:** Roslyn, Courthouse

When the first PHO 75 opened in Arlington decades ago, nobody had heard of the Internet. Now, every person at its long communal tables might have an e-mail address, but this Vietnamese soup restaurant hasn't changed a whit. It still looks like an institutional dining hall and serves only one dish—long-simmered, fragrant beef noodle soup with a long list of garnishes (brisket, fatty brisket, eye of round, bible tripe, tendon, meatballs and so on). The regular bowl is still a full meal and the large bowl an ordeal, and the highest price is $6.

"Rarely does such a modest expenditure in time and money yield such satisfying eating."

The soup is terrific, but the scene makes it even better. Those long tables fill with Vietnamese expatriates. If you're a novice, watch and you will learn how to personalize your soup with vinegar, soy, fresh chilies, bean sprouts and basil leaves, and how to squirt hot sauce and *hoisin* into your porcelain spoon, then dip your noodles and meat lightly into it. You will eventually develop your own preferences among the condiments available on the table.

And you'll discover such beverages as lemonade made from salted preserved lemons, coconut milk with scrapings of gelatinous baby coconut, sweet or salty plum juice, and coffee or tea brewed to dark intensity, then muted by ice and condensed milk. Rarely does such a modest expenditure in time and money yield such satisfying eating.

Pho 75 has three other locations in the Washington area: 3103 Graham Rd., Unit B, Falls Church, VA, (703) 204-1490; 771 Hungerford Dr., Rockville, MD, (301) 309-8873; and 1510 University Blvd. East, Langley Park, MD, (301) 434-7844.

PO SIAM
3807 Mt. Vernon Ave., Alexandria, VA
(703) 548-3925

THAI ♿

Lunch: M-Sat 11:30-4, Sun noon-4 **Entrees:** $5-$8
Dinner: M-Sat 4-10, Sun 4-9:30 **Entrees:** $7-$12
Credit Cards: All major **Dress:** Casual
Reservations: Recommended **Parking:** Street

A recent search for Thai dishes that go beyond the ordinary started with PO-SIAM, which long had been touted to me as a terrific neighborhood Thai restaurant. I probably came too late, after it opened a noodle parlor across the street that siphoned off some of its energy.

In the fashion of countless ethnic, storefront eating places, it's a mingling of Old World artifacts with plastic: plastic tablecloths, plastic ceiling fans, plastic greenery. Yet there are also sophisticated modern metal sculptures on the walls. Service is efficient as well as lively and friendly. It's a neighborly place.

I could skip the entrees here and never miss them; none has been impressive, and my Thai grilled chicken tasted like something that had been forgotten in the refrigerator. Yet the Chef's Special appetizers include an unusually spicy version of the standard open-top steamed dumplings. There's a clay pot of small and very tasty mussels in a broth of coconut milk and lime leaves with the fragrance of anise and basil— and a too-hot dipping sauce that cauterizes their flavor away.

Seafood with crispy-fish maw salad isn't nearly as scary as it sounds. It's instant tears, but worth the pain. Curls of tender squid and shrimp are littered with faintly fishy fluffs of crisp-fried maw, and tossed with onion, cilantro, lemon galore and well-browned cashews. There's also a catfish variation, of puffy crisp fish threads with cashews and slivered apples.

PIZZERIA PARADISO
2029 P St. NW, Washington, DC
(202) 223-1245

ITALIAN

Open: M-Th 11 am-11 pm, F-Sat noon-midnight, Sun 11 am-10
Entrees: $5-$10 **Credit Cards:** V, MC, DC **Reservations:** No
Dress: Casual **Parking:** Street **Metro:** Dupont Circle

This small, cheerful and jam-packed restaurant shows how starved we are for good pizza—the lines form early and long. There's no secret to its success, just attention to the details that turn flour, water, yeast, tomatoes and cheese into greatness.

It's fun to watch the pizzas baking in the wood-burning oven. The dough is flavorful from slow rising, and it is good enough to be eaten without any adornment. The toppings are uncomplicated and fresh: tomatoes as tasty as the season allows, dewy fresh mozzarella, green herbs and a modest list of extras, from vegetables to Italian cold cuts to fragrant cheeses. My favorite is the rich and pungent four-cheese, though I like the tomato toppings as well.

You can also get a well chosen and modestly priced wine or fresh lemonade. And a salad at PARADISO, either a simple mixture of greens or a *panzanella* salad of diced raw vegetables, is marvelous, piled on bread that soaks up the juices. That brings us to the superb offshoot of PARADISO'S dough making: great crackly loaves of bread, which become the makings of memorable sandwiches. Go for the lamb, and stay for a dish of house-made *gelato*.

Turning "flour, water, yeast, tomatoes and cheese into greatness."

THE PRIME RIB
2020 K St. NW, Washington, DC
(202) 466-8811

AMERICAN/STEAKHOUSE

Lunch: M-F 11:30-3 **Entrees:** $11-$19
Dinner: M-Th 5-11, F-Sat 5-11:30 **Entrees:** $18-$30
Closed: Sun **Credit Cards:** All major, DC
Reservations: Recommended **Dress:** Jacket & tie required
Metro: Farragut West, Foggy Bottom
Parking: Complimentary valet at dinner
Entertainment: Pianist and bassist at dinner, pianist at lunch

Washington has plenty of restaurants that serve first-class steaks. But it has only two places to get top-notch, inches-thick, juicy and—most important—flavorful roast beef, and those are the PRIME RIB and Morton's (which only serves it as a sideline and runs out early).

When you taste this meat for which the PRIME RIB restaurant is named, you realize that most competitors don't even come close. It's great meat, and it is cooked so that even the rare cuts benefit from a crusty brown edge. It's accompanied by fresh shredded horseradish, a vegetable that could be the best buttery broccoli you'll find this season, and baked, fried or real mashed potatoes.

Don't stray. Rather, don't stray beyond the crab imperial or crab cakes, which are similarly sumptuous and

> **"The Prime Rib does a few things memorably and makes you want to forget the rest."**

flawless. The PRIME RIB does a few things memorably and makes you want to forget the rest: the soggy and slapdish Caesar salad (though with an admirable dose of anchovy), the weird tomatoey clams casino, the unfathomly bitter blackened fish, the waiters who are chilly and supercilious unless you're one of its crowd. Prices are high, but at lunch the roast beef is a bargain. The wine list is legendary. And the urbane black walls with gold trim are almost as romantic at noon as at dinner.

The PRIME RIB is one of those restaurants that can outrage you; but if you play to its strengths, it is right up there among the best.

There is another location at 1011 N. Calvert St., Baltimore, MD, (410) 539-1804.

QUEEN BEE
3181 Wilson Blvd., Arlington, VA
(703) 527-3444

VIETNAMESE   🏂

Lunch: M-F 11-3   **Dinner:** M-F 3-10, Sat-Sun 11-10
Entrees: $6.50-$10   **Lunch Special:** M-F 11-3, $3.50
Credit Cards: All major, DC, CB   **Dress:** Casual
Reservations: Accepted for 6 or more   **Parking:** Street
Metro: Clarendon

Every neighborhood has a favorite Vietnamese restaurant by now, and a few neighborhoods such as Clarendon have a half dozen favorites. Still, you can't beat QUEEN BEE, which is among the oldest and still holding its own. Its menu is extensive, its service is efficient, its prices are low and its cooking is reliable (if you ignore some oversalting here and there). It's a cavernous restaurant that frequently has a line waiting for tables.

Nobody makes better *cha gio*, the crisp, rice-paper wrappers with a savory stuffing of ground pork, vegetables and thin vermicelli. Appetizers also include meaty or vegetarian summer rolls, skewered beef or shrimp and wonderful, plump, roasted quail. Entrees cover everything from noodle soups to stir-fried and sauced meats or seafood.

But my favorites are the grilled dishes. Vietnamese cooking at its best, so far as I'm concerned, is bits of pork, marinated with soy sauce, scallions and sometimes honey, cooked over charcoal until the edges are crisp and served with thin, white noodles or, even better, rice-flour cakes. The cakes are made of a slippery and slightly chewy wad of steamed rice-flour dough, here studded with bits of scallion. The contrast of crisp, sweet-salty meat and bland dough is irresistible, particularly when you wrap it in lettuce with marinated carrots and cilantro and dip it in the faintly fishy clear sauce.

Wash it down with sparkling fresh lemonade, Vietnamese beer or creamy-rich and intense iced coffee, and you'll have found one of Asia's best meals for under $10.

RT's
3804 Mount Vernon Ave., Alexandria, VA
(703) 684-6010

AMERICAN/CREOLE/SEAFOOD   ⑤

Lunch: M-Sat 11-2:30 **Entrees:** $6.50-$15
Light Fare: M-Sat 2:30-5 **Entrees:** $6.50-$10
Dinner: M-Th 5-10:30, F-Sat 5-11, Sun 4-9 **Entrees:** $13-$22
Credit Cards: All major **Reservations:** Recommended
Dress: Casual **Parking:** Street

Okay, so the expansion of RT's to a second location (or a third, if you count the Warehouse in Old Town Alexandria) hasn't done it any good. The Acadian peppered shrimp, last time I tried it, was all pepper and no salt, and the shrimp didn't taste fresh enough. Our party left two, whereas we usually fight over the last nibble.

The she-crab soup was crabby, creamy and nicely spirited, even if it wasn't as luscious as we'd last found it. The shrimp cakes were crumbly, and the shrimp in the "Jack Daniel's" shrimp with lump crabmeat had a bleary, watery taste (though its rich, pale-pink sauce was worth dunking and swabbing to the last smidgen).

Maybe RT's was having a bad-shrimp day. After all, the smothered catfish was luscious under its spicy *etouffe* sauce. And always, when the fish of the day is coated with pecans and livened with creole mustard sauce, you really don't need to know about anything else.

While RT's—at both locations—shows signs of slipping, its Louisiana specialties remain seasoned as they should be. So the talent is still there. Both restaurants have a homey style, but since the Alexandria outpost is older and smaller, it is all the more neighborly.

The second RT's location, which has somewhat different hours and prices, is at 2300 Clarendon Blvd., Arlington, VA, (703) 841-0100.

RAKU
1900 Q St. NW, Washington, DC
(202) 265-7258

ASIAN   ♿

Open: Sun-Th 11:30-10, F-Sat 11:30-midnight **Entrees:** $8-$13
Credit Cards: All major **Reservations:** No **Dress:** Casual
Happy Hour: M-F 4-7, $2.95-$4.95 (dim sum) **Parking:** Street
Metro: Dupont Circle

R AKU'S New Wave Asian diner is designed to be replicated, from downtown to Bethesda, then around the country. It signals a shift from the pasta to the noodle era, from casual abundance to studied austerity, from the group to the individual. Most of the seating at RAKU is not at companionable tables but at loners' counters. Single diners perch on backless stools, peering through green lacquered bamboo poles to the street scene, sipping cold sake or designer tea, eating a bowl of noodles or three tiny skewers of *yakitori*—nothing that invites sharing. Forget the menu; I love the stone floors and the mossy, sponged-looking wall panels, the *shoji* screens and the Japanese videos.

The cooking is assembly-line fast food. Morsels of chicken are skewered and grilled as yakitori or arranged on a bowl of broth with Japanese *udon* noodles and a handful of vegetables. Rich, yellow, coconut curry broth is ladled over thin rice noodles with a few shrimp and vegetables (Bangkok noodles) or over thicker, wiry egg noodles with chicken and pretty much the same vegetables (Chiang Mai noodles). Those same egg noodles form the base of Kowloon noodles. Or if the meat is changed to sliced beef and *kim chee* is stirred in to fire up the chicken broth, it becomes Korean chili beef.

The chicken broth tastes real, and the vegetables are crunchy-fresh. The ingredients cooperate rather than clash. Still, there's no escaping the fact that this is mass cooking. *Dim sum* taste as if they've been cooked in a crockpot. And the shrimp paste is starchy. What work best are skewers, of Nonya pork, diced shark meat rubbed with Thai green curry paste, the little chicken morsels or flat slabs of squid. And the most popular dish— deservedly so—is Hunan chicken salad. As for dessert, the sorbets are the class acts on the list.

Raku has a second branch at 7240 Woodmont Ave., Bethesda, MD, (301) 718-8680, where the menu is smaller, the hours are shorter and there are sushi and saki bars.

RAVI KABOB HOUSE
305 N. Glebe Rd., Arlington, VA
(703) 522-6666

PAKISTANI

Open: Daily 11-3 am **Entrees:** $5.25-$6.30
Lunch Special: Daily 11 am-1 pm, $5
Credit Cards: None; cash or check only
Dress: Casual **Parking:** Free lot

A bright, clean little storefront, RAVI KABOB HOUSE is a bit of a community center, with three cooks in back schmoozing with friends in the front, who are eating their curries in true Pakistani fashion, with their hands. It's a friendly scene.

Like many other kabob houses, it displays refrigerator cases of raw meats on skewers, marinated to a bright orange and ready to grill. The steam table offers a half dozen vegetable side dishes from which to choose.

Here a meal is priced like a sandwich, so even if the gigantic portion of lamb is gnarly and sinewy, it's still quite a buy. Chicken kabobs are also huge, rubbed with yogurt and yellow spices and grilled to a juicy and slightly crusty finish. With your choice of lentils or chickpeas or whatever else is on the day's steam table, and a little salad, it would be meal enough. But add the big, puffy bread cooked to order in a tandoor oven while you watch, and it's a feast. Quick and cheap, too.

RED HOT & BLUE
1600 Wilson Blvd., Arlington, VA
(703) 276-7427

AMERICAN/BARBECUE   🦽

Open: Sun-Th 11 am-10 pm, F-Sat 11 am-11 pm
Entrees: $7-$13   **Credit Cards:** All major, DIS, DC
Reservations: Accepted for 15 or more   **Dress:** Casual
Parking: Street   **Metro:** Rosslyn
Happy Hour: M-F 4-6, $1 off drafts, half-price appetizers

While it's spinning off branches as fast as a pig produces piglets, RED HOT & BLUE'S original Arlington location always seems to attract a crowd. So expect to wait and not to linger at the table. What's worth waiting for are not just the ribs but also the side dishes. The ribs come wet or dry, and while I usually like the dry—heavily sprinkled with spices rather than sodden with sauce—I don't like the grittyness that comes from pouring on the spices at the end; they should be cooked on the ribs.

So I opt for wet ribs, basted with a thick, sweet-hot sauce that has enough tang to balance the sugar. If you hit it right, the ribs will be crusty and chewy, lightly perfumed with smoke, but sometimes they are overcooked so they are falling off the bone and soft rather than crusty. The accompanying coleslaw is fine, the meaty barbecued beans are nicely spiced, and the beer is icy. Go whole hog and add a loaf of onion rings, thin and crunchy and freshly made.

RED HOT & BLUE also serves pulled chicken, barbecued beef brisket and pulled pig, which is a refined version of North Carolina chopped barbecue with big, soft, lean chunks of smoked pork butt brushed with barbecue sauce. Again, I miss the crustiness, but the pulled pig is a generous sandwich served with potato salad. RED HOT & BLUE has hit the right chord in a city that's been whining for good barbecue, and now that it's going national, maybe Washington will become known as a barbecue capital.

Red Hot & Blue's other locations: 4150 Chain Bridge Rd., Arlington, VA, (703) 218-6989; 208 Elden St., Herndon, VA, (703) 318-7427; 16809 Crabbs Branch Way, Gaithersburg, MD, (301) 948-7333; 677 Main St., Laurel, MD, (301) 953-1943, and 200 Old Mill Bottom Rd. (Rte. 50 & Exit 28), Annapolis, MD, (410) 626-7427. There is also a takeout-only location at 3014 Wilson Blvd., Arlington, VA (703) 243-1510.

RED SAGE
605 14th St. NW, Washington, DC
(202) 638-4444

AMERICAN/SOUTHWESTERN ♿

Grill Lunch: M-F 11:30-2 **Entrees:** $12-$20
Grill Dinner: M-Th 5:30-10, F-Sat till 10:30, Sun 5-10 **Entrees:** $17-$28
Border Cafe: M-Sat 11:30-11:30 pm, Sun 4:30-11 pm **Entrees:** $7-$11
Credit Cards: All major, DIS, DC, CB
Reservations: Recommended for Grill only
Dress: Casual (Grill: business attire suggested)
Parking: Validated at dinner **Metro:** Metro Center

The trick to enjoying RED SAGE, so far as I'm concerned, is not to treat it like a Big Deal. As a serious restaurant, worthy of a big-bucks grilled swordfish or rack of lamb, it has too many flaws. Although the dining rooms are dramatic and colorful, with luxurious little Western details that somehow added up to millions spent on the construction, the place is noisy and clattery, too large to be personal. And the *haute* South-western food, brilliant though its colors and concepts may be, shows more flair than finesse.

Yet while a $70 dinner may be disappointing, a $20 lunch or a $15 cafe meal can be great fun. I like RED SAGE when I can eat with a minimum of ceremony—a bowl of chili or a glamorized burrito at an upstairs bar table at off hours, a quick lunch at the counter of the downstairs bar. RED SAGE, despite its (inflated) reputation and its dinner prices, is not a Temple of Gastronomy. It is a sprawl of a restaurant that cooks to dazzle the eye and wake up jaded taste buds. It is a smashingly vivid site that tourists flock to see, and it adds spice and color to the downtown local's lunch scene.

"While a $70 dinner may be disappointing, a $20 lunch or a $15 cafe meal can be great fun."

RED TOMATO
2030 M St. NW, Washington, DC
(202) 463-9030

AMERICAN   ♿

Lunch: M-F 11:30-3, Sat noon-3   **Entrees:** $5-$10
Dinner: M-F 5-10, Sat 5-11, Sun 5-9:30   **Entrees:** $8.50-$17
Credit Cards: All major, DIS   **Dress:** Casual
Reservations: Recommended   **Parking:** Street

Food is not the raison d'être at RED TOMATO; it's just part of the young singles meet-greet-eat, salad-lunch and martini-evening downtown scene. The most appetizing element is the color scheme.

RED TOMATO'S management describes it as a fun place. It employs cheerful servers, but nobody fusses with such details as waiting until you've finished your appetizer before bringing your entree. Still, I've rarely found waiters more eager to make diners feel welcome.

Entree salads are big and vinegar-sharpened. Some feature interesting combinations while others fall flat, especially the signature Red Tomato Salad, which is served in a silly balloon of pizza dough. The dough needs work. Despite the "brick oven" bragging on the menu, it is more like tandoori bread left out to grow stale. If you must, have the white pizza.

At lunch I'd turn to the pastas for something more substantial than the somewhat pedestrian sandwiches. Saffron *bucatini* is a surprising but addictive combination of elements. Despite timid bits of *langostino*, the wiry red tomato linguine with sugar snap peas and mushrooms is almost as good. At dinner, the treat is rustic green tortellini topped with a thick tomato sauce and a mound of broccoli. Dinner also features a few up-market entrees including a huge veal chop that oozes mozzarella, prosciutto, even tomato and basil from a hidden pocket. Desserts are all show, with a predominant taste of sugar; even a lemon pine-nut torte is achingly sweet.

Red Tomato has a certain electric quality, a bustling energy. As for the food, it's about what I'd expect from a restaurant where the manager is far less interested in talking about the food than the fun.

There is another Red Tomato at 4910 St. Elmo Ave., Bethesda, MD, (301) 652-4499.

RESTAURANT NORA
2132 Florida Ave. NW, Washington, DC
(202) 462-5143

AMERICAN

Dinner: M-Th 6-10, F-Sat 6-10:30 **Entrees:** $20-$29
Closed: Sun **Credit Cards:** MC, V
Reservations: Recommended **Dress:** Casual
Parking: Valet (fee) **Metro:** Dupont Circle

Nora Pouillon took organic vegetables out of the tofu casserole and into the world of haute cuisine decades ago when she opened her environmentally savvy restaurant. Then she reached for the stars, upgrading the dining room, hanging it with museum-quality quilts and tacking on a skylit back room and private dining spaces. She laid in a supply of wines for connoisseurs and restyled her menu for elegance rather than homeyness. She also raised her prices to vie with the highest.

Now she's taken on a new *chef de cuisine*, and he's yet to move beyond cleverness to excellence. The ingredients are invariably the best—from Mennonite organic cream and butter to certified organic and free-range eggs and chickens to meats of impeccable breeding. The fault is in fussiness, overreaching and a technique that needs honing. It's a treat to find kidneys among the appetizers, particularly teamed with potato *galette* and spinach. But half the kidneys are overcooked and chewy, and the galette is limp. Rockfish tastes weary, its lobster mashed potatoes gluey and heavily salted. Delicate supple pork is lost in a bewilderment of cumin, *pasilla* chiles and *tomatillos*. One can only hope that Nora Pouillon's palate will soon exert its influence.

Desserts, though, remain fine, still showing a homestyle charm. Fruit pies that are exactly tart enough, in a crust that shatters at a touch, with housemade ice cream that melts into unsullied cream: That's NORA at its best.

RICHLAND
865-B Rockville Pike, Rockville, MD
(301) 340-8778

CHINESE   🕭

Lunch: Daily 11-3 **Entrees:** $5-$7
Dinner: Sun-Th 3-10, F-Sat 3-11 **Entrees:** $7-$12.50
Credit Cards: All major **Reservations:** Recommended
Dress: Casual **Parking:** Free lot **Metro:** Rockville

G iven RICHLAND'S shopping-strip location, its big, boxy dining room decorated with gilded fans, and the plates of *moo goo gai pan* and shrimp fried rice on the tables, you'd think this was just another updated Chinese restaurant left over from the '50s. But its reach is much wider, from bargain combination plates to the esoteric. The dinner menu goes on for pages—with eight duck dishes, for example. Entrees you can count on are shredded pork with bean curd strips, lamb with green onions or garlic sauce, and steamed fish that's cooked only until it's barely gelatinous. Even better are sautéed baby shrimp on a bed of spinach, and eggplant with garlic sauce.

But what makes RICHLAND a standout is its appetizer list, at least 30 items, among them a Chinese pizza that is similar to the white pizza Italian restaurants sell for four or five times the price. The greatest treat is the *dim sum*, available at dinner as well as at lunch: *shao my*; spicy, tangy dumplings; and my favorite, deep-fried radish cake, with bits of ham and scallion, wrapped in crisp, flaky dough reminiscent of Italian *sfogliatelle*. The pan-fried radish cake is far less interesting. Hot appetizers also include other fried items—egg rolls, spring rolls, shrimp toast, chicken wings —as well as more steamed dumplings, spareribs and kebabs. Cold appetizers provide contrasts in crunch, tang and lightness. Spicy pickled cabbage is outstanding, and there are bean curd sheets rolled around black mushrooms and cut into handsome slices that look like mushroom strudel. Finally, there's stewed duck in spicy salt water, its flavor reminiscent of France's *confit*.

RICHLAND serves large portions at low prices in a comfortable dining room, which is enough to make it a solidly successful suburban Chinese restaurant. But it is more. Its service is solicitous and its cooking is highly competent. And it provides excellent dim sum at any time of day.

RIO GRANDE CAFE
4919 Fairmont Ave., Bethesda, MD
(301) 656-2981

AMERICAN/SOUTHWESTERN

Lunch: M-F 11:30-3 **Entrees:** $7-$10.75
Dinner: Sun-Th 3-10, F 3-11:30, Sat 11:30am-11:30pm
Entrees: $7.50-$21 **Brunch:** Sun 11:30-3 **Entrees:** $6.25-$8
Credit Cards: All major, DIS, DC **Reservations:** No
Dress: Casual **Parking:** Street **Metro:** Bethesda
Happy Hour: M-F 4:30-6:30, 75 cents off margaritas/beer

E ven our children have more worldly palates nowadays, if you can judge from the early-evening lines of strollers and baby carriers in front of RIO GRANDE CAFES. Who would have thought that suburban toddlers would clamor for enchiladas and soft tacos? Of course, one big draw at these family-friendly Tex-Mex restaurants is the tortilla machine, a Rube Goldberg sort of contraption that forms and bakes truly delicious flour tortillas before your eyes.

That leads to the second draw: really good food, better than we expect at noisy, jam-packed restaurants where many prices are under two digits. The chips are thin and crisp, though the salsa is a quirky, near-liquid concoction. The sauces have potent flavor as well as bite,

> **You'll find "really good food, better than we expect at noisy, jam-packed restaurants . . ."**

the fajitas' meats are smoky, the guacamole and seviche taste perfectly fresh, the beans are subtly excellent, and my quarrels with the tamales are minor in light of all that seems so painstakingly consistent.

The menu moves into glamorous territory with quail and frogs' legs, and even for vegetarians the possibilities are exciting. Portions are large enough to share—right down to the ice cream. And the servers, who are as cheerful and efficient as if they'd been trained by Mary Poppins, warn you when you're over-ordering. Which isn't hard to do.

Other Rio Grande Cafe branches: 4301 North Fairfax Dr., Arlington, VA, (703) 528-3131; 1827 Library St., Reston, VA, (703) 904-0703.

RISTORANTE TERRAZZA
2 Wisconsin Circle, Chevy Chase, MD
(301) 951-9292

ITALIAN   🛆

Lunch: M-F 11:30-2:30 **Entrees:** $6-$13
Dinner: M-Sat 5:30-10 **Entrees:** $6-$23
Closed: Sun **Pre-Theater:** 20% discount M-F 5:30-7
Credit Cards: All major, DIS, DC **Dress:** Casual
Reservations: Required F-Sat (dinner) **Parking:** Free lot
Metro: Friendship Heights **Happy Hour:** M-F 5:30-7, $1 off drinks

The old Duca di Milano has come down to earth as TERRAZZA, with new owners, a redecoration and a far more modest menu. There's nothing you haven't heard of, nothing constructed into a tower, no ingredient you might not find in a well-stocked home kitchen. As this restaurant site has matured, so have its patrons. While the bar may still attract a young crowd, the tables have been filled with couples more Neiman Marcus than Gap—those who don't want the noise of Clyde's up the street. TERRAZZA seems to be addressing diners who care about service.

Osso buco is the highlight of this menu. The thick, meaty veal shank is braised until it nearly melts off the bone, and the dish achieves one of those mystical transformations of ordinary diced root vegetables, tomato, sage, rosemary, wine and meat juices into a radiant sauce. The waiter said this osso buco takes two days to make. It's worth every minute.

The rest of the cooking: nice. Some is awfully nice, some just nice enough. The house-made fettuccine comes with *mascarpone* and spinach, an appealing balance of creaminess and green freshness. I'm impressed with the silky *pappardelle*; but its duck *ragu* tastes harsh—perhaps an excess of juniper berries. The menu also offers pastas with shrimp, scallops and leeks, white clam sauce, tomato with pesto, ricotta with spinach and the simple, pepper-spiked, tomato-based *arrabbiata*.

If osso buco sounds too heavy an entree after pasta, there is a beautifully cooked rockfish, pristine and moistened with Italy's *tocai* wine, sprinkled with asparagus slices and accompanied by braised red onion. The desserts are classics. Of course there's tiramisu. The *crema catalana* is less the Italian classic, though, than a clumsy French *crème brûlée*.

TERRAZZA is a perfectly nice restaurant. In many a neighborhood it would thrive. But it's tackled one of those difficult locations where everyone wonders what's going to show up next. At least it's trying with a new formula: not grandeur, but modest satisfactions.

ROCKLANDS
2418 Wisconsin Ave. NW, Washington, DC
(202) 333-2558

AMERICAN/BARBECUE   🚻

Open: M-F 11:30-10, Sat 11-10, Sun 11-9
Entrees: $3-$17 **Credit Card:** AE **Reservations:** No
Dress: Casual **Parking:** Free lot

It's no longer necessary to drive to Georgia for a barbecue menu that offers a long list of fresh vegetables as side dishes. Glover Park or Arlington will do.

That's where you'll find ROCKLANDS, the small, in-town one with just a few seats and mostly carryout, or the barnlike spinoff in an ex-gas station near Ballston. I like the smaller place, with its bowls of peanuts in the shell to entertain you while you wait and its walls of hot sauces. But each has its funky charm, and both have top-notch ribs, smoked over real wood and just chewy enough, seasoned rather than just peppered.

"Few places anywhere make available such satisfying, down-home, from-scratch American cooking at fast-food prices."

The chopped pork sandwich is outstanding meat, with juicy and crunchy bits of meat piled high on a bun—though I prefer my sauce less tomatoey. The grilled leg of lamb is elegant, the grilled fish fillet—usually salmon— even more so. Only the chicken could use more attention to keeping it juicy. Among the side dishes, the macaroni and cheese is so zingy that it should star as a main course. There are fine corn pudding and mashed potatoes, baked beans and cooked greens, a mild and fresh corn salad and tart, thick, fresh apple compote. The potato salad has an unfortunate tendency to be undercooked, and some of the salads yearn for salt. In all, though, few places anywhere make available such satisfying, down-home, from-scratch American cooking at fast-food prices.

There is another Rocklands at 4000 Fairfax Dr., Arlington, VA, (703) 528-9663.

RUPPERTS

1017 7th St. NW, Washington, DC
(202) 783-0699

AMERICAN   [&]

Lunch: Th only 11:30-2:30 **Entrees:** $25
Dinner: Tu-Th 6-10, F-Sat 6-11 **Entrees:** $25
Closed: Sun-M **Credit Cards:** All major, DC
Reservations: Recommended **Dress:** Casual
Parking: Street **Metro:** Mount Vernon, Gallery Place/Chinatown

Freshness and purity are almost a religion at RUPPERTS, which is the good news and the bad news. With a small dining room as spare as a temple, and waiters wearing khakis yet serving with reverence, this restaurant is focused squarely on the food. I appreciate that seriousness of purpose, but I need to suppress a giggle when I encounter a single green bean as a centerpiece or I am presented with a gift from the chef that consists of a lone leaflet of greenery—lightly dressed—in the bowl of a spoon. What would happen if I asked for seconds?

Yet the wine list is a marvel, none of it predictable. Its exuberance is in contrast to the menu, which offers a mere five choices at a standard price for each course (an expensive $9 for soup, a bargain $9 for *foie gras*; every entree $25), and identifies dishes but doesn't describe them ("Veal loin and sweetbread with mashed potato": Is that grilled? Sautéed? Sauced? As a shepherd's pie?). What impresses me is the clarity, the intensity with which each food tastes of itself. Soft-shell crabs are grilled and unsullied by flour or batter. Even the rhubarb that accompanies the foie gras seems to have no sugar, yet is neither puckery nor bitter. A vegetarian melange here—say, wild mushrooms with arugula and asparagus—retains the distinction of each vegetable (except when the vegetables come out too raw). Duck is rare and pink, yet expresses the developed flavor of cooked meat.

Some might find the food unexciting in its plainness, and not worth a price that suggests a more elaborate preparation or setting. There's a penchant for underseasoning, and this is not the kind of restaurant that offers salt on the table (or butter as an alternative to herbed fresh cheese with the hearty, rough, hot-from-the-oven country breads). Desserts tend to be so undersweetened that you might mistake them for savories (indeed, the assorted cheeses are my favorite ending, since their condition is magnificent). The coda here is a plate of cookies, luscious little morsels, though some are as small as a punctuation mark and too little to truly taste. Much about RUPPERTS is sublime. A few of the details are ridiculous.

SAIGON CRYSTAL
536 S. 23rd St., Arlington, VA
(703) 920-3663

VIETNAMESE   &

Lunch: M-F 11-5 **Entrees:** $5-$7
Dinner: Sun-Th 5-10, F-Sat 5-11 **Entrees:** $9-$17
Dress: Casual **Reservations:** Recommended (esp. weekends)
Parking: Free lot **Metro:** Crystal City

Just down the street from the stark, high-rise slabs of Crystal City architecture is one of the most varied restaurant strips in the metropolitan area. Among the dozen or so ethnic groups represented is SAIGON CRYSTAL, a Vietnamese restaurant that twinkles and glows with neon and strings of tiny lights. It's probably the funkiest restaurant of them all. Indoors, it's a sea of green and sparkle. Outdoors, there's a narrow wooden deck that allows a view of the neighborhood dining scene.

The menu goes on for pages, and if you look around, you'll see that the place serves countless inexpensive meals of noodle soups and grilled meats on rice. The house specialties, though, are seafood combinations— hotpots, grills and casseroles of shellfish in creamy curry sauces or Asian herb broths.

Regulars know to ask whether soft-shell crabs are available, or to inquire about the whole fish of the day. This is a kitchen that understands the intricacies of frying. Those soft-shells are veiled in light batter and fried at a temperature sufficient to seal in the juices. They're great. And whole fish can be ordered with ginger or black bean sauce—or even steamed rather than fried. Other shellfish is not so impressive, though the sauces are fragrant and worthy of being spooned over rice.

The Washington area has a multitude of good Vietnamese restaurants, and this is a modest example. Its rustic deck and its fried seafood lift it a notch above the crowd.

SALA THAI
2016 P St. NW, Washington, DC
(202) 872-1144

THAI

Lunch: M-F 11:30-3 **Entrees:** $6.25-$9
Dinner: M 5-10:30, Tu 5-11, W-F 5-11:30, Sat 12-11:30, Sun 12-10:30
Entrees: $7.25-$13 **Credit Cards:** All major, DC
Reservations: Accepted for 5 or more **Dress:** Casual
Parking: Street **Metro:** Dupont Circle

Downtown Thai restaurants are a treasure, many of them serving elegant food in casual surroundings at easygoing prices. And SALA THAI was the first to venture to Dupont Circle. This downstairs cafe is brightly furnished with laminated tables and spiffy folding chairs. Its menu is extensive, and the waiters warn you if you are ordering dishes that are similar.

There is no stinting on the chilies in this kitchen. If the waiter tells you a dish is hot, watch out. But under the heat is a frenzy of intriguing flavors—this is invigorating food. The hot-and-sour chicken-coconut soup tingles with peppery and cool flavors. Among the most familiar entrees is a faintly sweet and homey *pad thai* that is as good as any you'll find. The curry of the day is intricate and aromatic, though its sauce has sometimes been too thin to cling well to the meat or seafood.

If you are inclined to splurge a bit, the shrimp fried in eggroll wrappers—Pinky in the Blanket—is enough to

"If the waiter tells you a dish is hot, watch out."

share as an appetizer or even to serve one as an entree. Above all, however, check out the list of daily specials outside the door (the seafood dishes are meant to compete with Pesce next door). That's where you'll find the newest, the freshest, and often the best buys.

SAM & HARRY'S
1200 19th St. NW, Washington, DC
(202) 296-4333

AMERICAN/STEAKHOUSE   ♿

Lunch: M-F 11:30-2:30 (2:30-5:30 at the bar) **Entrees:** $9-$26
Dinner: M-Sat 5:30-10:30 **Entrees:** $18-$32
Closed: Sun **Credit Cards:** All major, DIS, DC, CB
Reservations: Recommended **Dress:** Business attire suggested
Parking: Complimentary valet at 5:30 pm **Metro:** Dupont Circle

Washington has plenty of luxurious steakhouses that are branches of national chains. SAM & HARRY'S is homegrown, though, and has a keen idea of what Washingtonians like. In addition to top-of-the-line steaks, it features fish, shellfish and hearty lunchtime salads. And it used to serve some of the closest-to-ideal crab cakes. But as it's spread to the suburbs, SAM & HARRY'S seems to have spread itself too thin.

Meat's the ticket here. The kitchen still understands what rare means, and its beef is still serious meat. Lamb chops, too, are fine, and the house salad of romaine, corn, peppers, onions and blue cheese dressing is a good balance. But anything more complicated is beyond this kitchen nowadays. Lobster bisque tastes like creamy, salty clam juice; crab cakes are bready and tasteless, and salmon tartare begs for seasoning.

"Sam & Harry's remains a solid steakhouse, but beyond red meat it stumbles."

Little detracts, though, from the clubby and handsome dining room that's cleverly divided into manageable and intimate sections. Nothing but overly pushy service, that is. Thus SAM & HARRY'S remains a solid steakhouse, but beyond red meat it stumbles.

There is another Sam & Harry's at 8240 Leesburg Pike, Vienna, VA, (703) 448-0088. It has additional hours on Sundays, from 5:30 to 10:30, and a fireplace.

SAVORY
7071 Carroll Ave., Takoma Park, MD
(301) 270-2233

AMERICAN   🦽

Open: M-Th 7 am-9 pm, F 7 am-10, Sat 8 am-10, Sun 9-4 pm
Entrees: $6-$11 (dinner), $3.50-$6 (lunch), $3.50-$8 (brunch)
Credit Cards: V, MC **Reservations:** No **Dress:** Casual
Parking: Free lot (limited) **Metro:** Takoma Park

It's not that I truly love SAVORY, rather that I appreciate it. I think how much I would adore it if I lived in the neighborhood and had small children.

SAVORY is a sort of Mary Poppins restaurant, with toys and little tables available for children, healthy and fresh foods geared for them and their parents, prices that allow eating out to fit into an everyday budget and a pleasantly artistic environment for even adults without kiddies in tow.

It's really an upscale carryout with tables (a few outdoors). So you pick your meal from a display case of salads, pastas, quiches and such and wait for them to be microwaved and served. Wait patiently, that is, for the easygoing staff to wade through the orders. The food is all made on the premises, much of it aimed at vegetarians, and the bright colors speak of careful marketing. The asparagus salad is green and crisp, the wild rice or bowtie pasta or mixed green salad is as vivid as a garden in summer. And such hot dishes as seafood creole are made with respectable basics, though nothing is seasoned as much as its description would lead you to expect.

"Savory is a sort of Mary Poppins restaurant, with toys and little tables available for children . . ."

Think dough. Crust. Pastry. The talent at SAVORY is concentrated in the baker. The quiches are fragile and flaky-crusted, and the fruit tarts are marvelous: mostly fruit, bursting through rustic yet delicate dough. The dessert case is as abundant as the choice of savories, with big cookies such as "snickerdoodles" and shortbread, doubly chocolatey brownies and a bread pudding that makes you want to clean your plate so you'll qualify for such a treat. For the kids: 25-cent ice cream cones.

SEA CATCH RESTAURANT
1054 31st St. NW, Washington, DC
(202) 337-8855

SEAFOOD   ♿

Lunch: M-Sat noon-3 **Entrees:** $11-$23
Dinner: M-F 5:30-10:30 **Entrees:** $15-$25
Closed: Sun **Credit Cards:** All major, DIS, DC, CB
Dress: Casual **Reservations:** Required for dinner, large parties
Parking: Complimentary valet

The SEA CATCH is a handsome, brick-walled place, but its great attraction is its view of the C&O Canal. Tables on the balcony practically hang over the towpath.

For two sitting in the sunshine one day at lunch, the setting was perfect. We started with house-smoked salmon that was light and refined but pricey. Tuna sashimi also suited a spring day. Soft-shell crabs were an entree special, sprinkled with diced tomato and pecan halves. Splendid idea, even if the pecans weren't crisp and the crabs were a little flabby. Ling cod, another special, was the ideal of simplicity.

Usually a restaurant puts its best kitchen crew on in the evenings. At the SEA CATCH, though, a subsequent dinner might as well have been prepared by the third string. Manhattan clam chowder tasted as if it had been stretched to feed a multitude. A crab cake was more respectable. The most appealing dish of the evening was an appetizer of steamed mussels in a straightforward briny broth.

We should have skipped entrees altogether. The rockfish turned out to be dry and bland. Scallops, too, tasted blank. And the scampi was not enhanced by a dull tomato sauce that cascaded over freshly made linguine. In the company of these entrees, the swordfish was a relief, even if it was cooked a mite too long. All in all, though, the highlight of this course was an à la carte order of sautéed spinach.

The SEA CATCH has a proficient pastry chef, but perhaps not an enthusiastic enough clientele. The tarts are full of lovely flavors but have tasted soggy, as if we'd caught them a day past their peak. Cheesecake left us with no complaints.

So I haven't found the seafood restaurant of my dreams. I've just rediscovered an eternally pleasant dining room with a balcony that's idyllic on a sunny day, and with a kitchen that might, just might, live up to its surroundings.

SEASONS

Four Seasons Hotel
2800 Pennsylvania Ave. NW, Washington, DC
(202) 342-0810

AMERICAN/FRENCH   ♿

Breakfast: M-F 7-11, Sat-Sun 8-noon   **Entrees:** $4.75-$17 (prix fixe)
Lunch: M-F noon-2:30   **Entrees:** $13.75-$23
Dinner: Daily 6-10:30   **Entrees:** $21-$34   **Tea:** Daily 3-5, $14.75
Credit Cards: All major   **Reservations:** Preferred
Dress: Jacket, tie suggested   **Parking:** Complimentary valet, lunch, dinner

Hotel restaurants often are at a disadvantage. It can be hard to rev up a bureaucratic staff to go beyond minimally doing its job. Yet, at SEASONS, the staff seems—pardon the pun—well seasoned, yet not jaded. An advantage hotel restaurants have is the space and budget for luxurious decoration, and SEASONS is a cross between a staid country club and an urban park. An indoor garden is backed by a window wall overlooking Rock Creek Park, as if both garden and park were one. A few curved banquettes create coves of privacy that feel almost like picnic areas, separated not by trees and hills but by carpet and potted plants.

Overall, I often like the food at SEASONS better than at most luxury hotels. It may sometimes fall short of expectations, but it isn't silly or overcomplicated. At its best it seems designed to satisfy more than to impress. Still, it too often seems like food cooked by a committee. Soft-shell crabs are ethereal in a tempura batter, but crab cake is dry and oddly bitter. Roast chicken is elevated by a *duxelles* stuffing under its skin, but that duxelles is watery even if the bird itself is as juicy and crisp as one could hope. The risotto doesn't seem even vaguely Italian but more a pilaf. Thus, one enticing dish is followed with another that's missed its potential. Given the high prices, the food is risky. Dessert tends to smooth away disappointments, though. The pastries—particularly chocolate—are pristine and elegant.

"This hotel's banquets are even better than the restaurant meals."

That's why the meals that most draw me to this soothing luxuriance are afternoon tea —the pastries are designed to make you salivate with your eyes—and Sunday brunch, which revels in grand simplicity. And in case your romantic dinner at SEASONS develops into planning for a wedding, this hotel's banquets are even better than the restaurant meals—in fact, they may be the best in town.

701
701 Pennsylvania Ave. NW, Washington, DC
(202) 393-0701

AMERICAN/INTERNATIONAL   🚻

Lunch: M-F 11:30-3 **Entrees:** $12.50-$17.50
Light Fare: M-F 3-5:30 **Entrees:** $9-$12
Dinner: M-Tu 5:30-10:30, W-Th 5:30-11, F-Sat 5:30-11:30, Sun 5-9:30
Entrees: $15-$22 **Pre-Theater:** Daily 5:30-7, $22.50
Credit Cards: All major, DC **Reservations:** Recommended **Dress:**
Casual **Parking:** Complimentary valet at dinner (except Sun)
Metro: Archives/Navy Memorial **Entertainment:** Jazz/blues daily 6-close

Shakespeare and caviar—that's what I call a spectacular evening. Instead of preceding the theater with a dinner heavy enough to make me doze through the second act, I'd rather splurge on an invigorating and luxurious snack at 701, which is a comfortable walk from the downtown stages. Cocktail dining tempts me here.

The dining room is spacious, quiet and comfortable. A pianist makes it even more festive. The service borders on royal. And the menu goes beyond caviar to a long list of contemporary dishes.

I settle into one of the downy, soft armchairs at a table in the lounge. I examine the page-long list of vodkas. As for the caviar, you can go all-out with *osetra* (my preference) or *beluga*, or pull your punches deliciously with salmon

"The service borders on royal."

caviar. Each is served with tiny *blini* and *brioche* toast. And since you can hardly fill up on caviar, order something else from the appetizer list—tuna tartare built into an architectural marvel or maybe smoked salmon combined with seviche, or an updated Caesar salad.

If a more conventional meal tempts you, the entrees range from seafood through steaks, with a particularly inventive vegetarian platter. The cooking doesn't necessarily soar, but it is always attractive and fresh. Look for light sauces made with seasonal ingredients, as well as accents from the Southwest, New Orleans or the Mediterranean. Above all, keep in mind that the pastry chef does wonders with chocolate.

If it's not a caviar evening, consider 701 for a business lunch. The space and luxury—at moderate price—make it an always safe choice.

1789
1226 36th St. NW, Washington, DC
(202) 965-1789

AMERICAN

Dinner: Sun-Th 5-10, F-Sat 5-11 Entrees: $18-$32
Pre-Theater: Daily until 6:45 pm, $25
Credit Cards: All major, DIS, DC Reservations: Recommended
Dress: Jacket required Parking: Complimentary valet

While discovering a wonderful new restaurant is exciting, even more so is discovering that a promising restaurant has become wonderful. That's what's happened with 1789.

It has always had a great architectural advantage, this handsome antique on a Georgetown side street. Its dining rooms are small and vary from an 18th-century tavern look to a Colonial showpiece with a fireplace, to illuminate its old Washington etchings and mahogany furnishings. The service is dignified, and some of the waiters have been here for decades.

Now it has magnificent cooking, too. Chef Ris Lacoste, having worked with Bob Kinkead in his three successive restaurants, has developed her own style and assurance since leaving Kinkead's. Her emphasis is on seafood, and her oyster stew—its thick cream sparkling with the crunch of minced celery, walnuts and prosciutto—is one of the best dishes I've tasted in a year. She calls her monkfish steak an "osso buco," and serves it on a wonderfully chewy and creamy champagne-leek risotto with lobster and wild mushrooms. Her salmon steak has a jolt of Persian spices.

"A promising restaurant has become wonderful."

On the meaty side is an oversize veal chop from Virginia's Summerfield Farm, which also supplies the venison. Of utmost importance, though, are the vegetables, cooked with precision and combined with reason. The mashed potatoes with fennel, portobellos and roasted peppers with lemon herb sauce and prosciutto under the succulent pine nut chicken could star on their own. And then there's dessert, with much to consider, unless you already know that it would be foolhardy to miss the chocolate terrine.

SHAMSHIRY
8607 Westwood Center Dr., Vienna, VA
(703) 448-8883

PERSIAN

Open: Daily 11:30 am-10:30 pm **Entrees:** $6-$10
Credit Cards: All major **Reservations:** Accepted for 10 or more
Dress: Casual **Parking:** Free lot

The first thing you see in this Persian kebab restaurant is a window overlooking the grill. Metal skewers of meats and fish rotate over flames: chunks of salmon (among the best kebabs), long, nubby, sausage shapes of *kubideh* (ground beef), filet mignon threaded as flat strips or rolled around onions and herbs, plain marinated chicken in addition to fiery-herbed tandoori, and the star of the lineup, Cornish game hen "marinated in Grand Fathers original recipe."

These skewers and rice are most of what you need to know about SHAMSHIRY. It offers no entrees besides kebabs. It serves no alcoholic beverages; nearly everybody drinks tea or *doogh*, an astringent combination of yogurt, club soda and dry herbs. Appetizer choices consist simply of raw or pickled vegetables, but a sufficient beginning to the meal is the basket of flat bread, with a dish of green herb paste peppery enough to clear any winter stuffiness. Try this fiery condiment, but only after you've buffered the bread with a thin veneer of butter.

White rice, served with beef dishes, achieves greatness when you order a raw egg yolk on the side, to stir in so that the egg coats all the grains as the heat cooks it. Also stir in as much butter as you dare, and sprinkle on the dark, brown, powdered sumac that's in a shaker on the table. The other rice variations are recommended with chicken dishes. Sweet rice is perfumed with sugared orange peel and crunchy with pistachios and almonds. Cherry rice is topped with syrupy preserved cherries, and barberry rice is studded with tart dried red currants. Finally, the unpromisingly named "veggie rice," which comes with the salmon and can be ordered with other kebabs, is tinted an intriguing greenish beige and seductively flavored by dill and soft, delicious fava beans.

Though decorations are simple, the dining room feels like a Persian dinner party; on some Saturday nights when there's taped Persian music and tables are filled, you might feel like the guest at a Persian wedding.

192

SHOLL'S COLONIAL CAFETERIA
1990 K St. NW, Washington, DC
(202) 296-3065

AMERICAN   ♿

Breakfast: M-Sat 7-10:30, Sun 8-3 **Lunch:** M-Sat 11-2:30, Sun 1-3
Dinner: M-Sat 4-8 **Brunch:** Sun 8-3 **Entrees:** $1.85-$5.55
Credit Cards: Cash only **Dress:** Casual **Reservations:** No
Parking: Street **Metro:** Farragut West, Farragut North

Your mother doesn't make rice pudding anymore? She buys her biscuits from the refrigerator case and her pies from the freezer? You need SHOLL'S, the venerable cafeteria that starts the morning with fresh doughnuts and brightens the evening with seasonal vegetables and house-made rolls, biscuits, cakes and pies. It's hardly more expensive than cooking for yourself, and while the food is as plain as plain can be, it is all made from scratch.

"Pennywise lawyers dine a table away from homeless people on a splurge."

Maybe you've forgotten old-fashioned chopped steak, flavorful and juicy even though it is worlds away from rare. It's my favorite entree here, with mashed potatoes and the thin brown pan gravy. Chicken is apt to be dry, and fish can go either way; look carefully before you choose. But anything that's braised, stewed or immersed in gravy has a homey goodness. Crab cakes are as creamy as croquettes, and though they may be more filler than crab, they have a powerful charm.

SHOLL'S is a crossroads. It serves both old-timers who probably eat all their meals there and busloads of schoolkids on field trips. Pennywise lawyers dine a table away from homeless people on a splurge. It's friendly, wholesome and as reliable as 70 successful years can promise.

SKEWERS
1633 P St. NW, Washington, DC
(202) 387-7400

MEDITERRANEAN

Open: Sun-Th 11:30-11, F-Sat 11:30-1 am
Entrees: $10-$13 **Credit Cards:** All major, DIS, CB
Reservations: Recommended **Dress:** Casual
Parking: Street **Metro:** Dupont Circle

A few steps above street level, this is one of Dupont Circle's long-running bargain restaurants. The list of appetizers has expanded beyond the original *tabouleh*, hummus and *baba ghanouj* to nearly two dozen *mezze*, including carrot puree with *harissa* spice, *kibbeh* of meat or vegetables and two additional versions of hummus and of eggplant salads. Yet the entree list remains simple—kebabs on rice, kebabs on fettucine, kebabs on salad or kebabs with romaine and crisped pita topped by yogurt and pine nuts, plus a few pastas.

The primary draws at SKEWERS are its homey environment and its modest prices. The dining room has a cheerful, palm-tree theme, and the service is personable, even if it is not very efficient.

Given the basically simple menu, though, SKEWERS has surprisingly erratic cooking. At one meal the filet mignon kebab might be spicy and juicy while the chicken and shrimp are bland and limp. Baba ghanouj and tabouleh might taste fresh and lively, while stuffed grape leaves and hummus have no taste at all. The trick is to order a mezze—an appetizer combination for two or four people—which offers an assortment of little dishes and a basket of warm pita. It's enough for a light meal, and it allows you to hedge your bets.

"This is one of Dupont Circle's long-running bargain restaurants."

SOPER'S ON M
1813 M St. NW, Washington, DC
(202) 463-4590

AMERICAN

Lunch: M-F 11:30-4 **Entrees:** $7-$12
Light Fare: M-Sat 4-5 **Entrees:** $5-$9
Dinner: M-Sat 5-10 **Entrees:** $13-$19
Closed: Sun **Credit Cards:** All major, DC **Dress:** Nice casual
Reservations: Recommended **Parking:** Valet (fee) at dinner only
Metro: Farragut North, Farragut West

Don't try to squeeze salmon tartare out of a meatloaf-and-mashed-potatoes kind of chef. Over the years Mike Soper has become a legend for his inspired menus, but the things he's always done best are foods that look a mess yet are as soothing as an old quilt. The problem with Chef Soper is that his food is incomprehensibly inconsistent. Just plain moody.

Dinner at his new white-tablecloth restaurant starts with a basket of assorted breads that shows how hard he's trying. But then Soper gets fashionable. His Land & Sea Carpaccio is a light and refreshing start, but a salmon tartare was more like overcured seviche. Conch puppies— chewy little fritters with rubbery bits of conch—are pretty good if you think of them as slightly fishy hush puppies. The most distinctive appetizer is callaloo-stuffed shrimp—available as a "small plate," or light entree, at lunch. It's SOPER'S kind of reinvented soul food, the shrimp and greens nestled on a big, moist, corn griddlecake.

Those corn griddlecakes are the key. They show up in the Pinebark Stack, the best of the dinner entrees. It's seared swordfish layered with cheddar mashed potatoes and drenched in oyster cream gravy. At lunch, it appears as the Eastern Shore Stack, with chicken breast instead of swordfish.

What goes the extra mile on the lunch list is the Cuban pork po' boy, because its toasted roll is piled with soft and spicy hunks of irresistible roast pork. Dinner hasn't half the gutsy stuff as lunch.

Desserts recapture Soper's talent for homeyness. The fruit cobblers arrive hot and oozing not-too-sweetened berries under a bit of crunch. Lime meringue pie is also as tart as you'd wish. At SOPER'S, the cooking is hit or miss; the thing to remember is that the best dishes are ugly and mushy. But when SOPER'S works, it's downright therapeutic— emotionally, if not nutritionally.

SOSTANZA
1606 20th St. NW, Washington, DC
(202) 667-0047

ITALIAN

Lunch: M-F noon-2 **Entrees:** $6.75-$9.75
Dinner: M-Sat 6-10 **Entrees:** $13.75-$19.75
Closed: Sun **Credit Cards:** All major, DC, CB
Dress: Casual **Reservations:** Recommended
Parking: Street **Metro:** Dupont Circle

Two decades ago, when Vince MacDonald opened Vincenzo, it served practically nothing but fish. Now it's called SOSTANZA, after the legendary Florentine trattoria where the specialty is a big, thick porterhouse steak seared over a wood fire and accompanied by a torrent of fried potatoes.

So, naturally, the specialty here is steak. But this SOSTANZA doesn't cook over a wood fire, and that's a critical difference. The smoky flavor is missing. Even more important, these lean, part-Chianina beef steaks are tricky to time; SOSTANZA turns out steaks that are at best rare near the bone and a juiceless gray here and there. The menu includes a couple of fish dishes, and soft-shell crabs in season. What's surprising, given this restaurant's origins, is that these simple dishes aren't nearly as delicious as they used to be.

If SOSTANZA doesn't quite have a great steak, and if the accompanying potatoes turn out to be soggy, it still does some things uncommonly well. As always, this restaurant excels at understatement. The fried zucchini side dish is impeccable, and the grainy, chewy Italian bread is perfectly correct. Appetizers are straightforward and of the highest quality.

Vincenzo taught us a lesson all those years ago when it first opened. It served only dry pastas, from a box, and they were irresistibly delicious. Now there are half a dozen pastas on the menu, and the best ones are still those that began in a box.

Desserts are modest and homey, even beyond the berries and house-made ices. And you can still depend on Vince MacDonald for a classic espresso. The dining rooms are as serene as ever, and the waiters have that quiet expertise that makes Italy's restaurants gently agreeable.

I expect that SOSTANZA will be just a blip in Vincenzo's history. First all-fish, then mostly meat: Can vegetarian be far behind?

SOUTHSIDE 815
815 S. Washington St., Alexandria, VA
(703) 836-6222

AMERICAN/SOUTHERN   ♿

Lunch: M-Sat 11:30-4 **Entrees:** $6-$11
Dinner: Sun-Th 4-10:30 **Entrees:** $6-$14
Brunch: Sun 11:30-4, $6-$11 **Credit Cards:** All major, DIS, DC, CB
Reservations: Accepted for 6 or more **Dress:** Casual
Parking: Free lot **Metro:** King St. **Happy Hour:** M-F 4-7, various
drink specials; 25-cent Buffalo wings, half-price burgers

Bring a big appetite to SOUTHSIDE 815, because the best of its dishes are the heavy, rich, homey Southern classics. The Low Country Shortcake says it all: It's layers of corn bread, mashed potatoes, oysters and chicken drenched in succotash gravy.

Okay, so you want something lighter? There's a thick, grilled tuna steak, flavored with lemon and pepper. But be warned: As good as the tuna is, it pales beside its vegetable accompaniments of peppered and vinegared Southern greens, wildly rich cream grits and those drive-you-crazy mashed potatoes. Another of the potential stars on this menu is Charleston Chicken, the breast topped with shrimp, corn and sausage in sherry butter. The sandwich choices are equally interesting, from the catfish po' boy to the pulled pork to the burger with fried oysters.

With all this, you surely don't need an appetizer. But there are oysters three ways, which means with heady seasoned spinach (Rockefeller), creamy crab (Virginia) and bacon (Maryland). It's enough for two to share, as are the crab and corn drop fritters and the sweet potato biscuits smothered with crab, Virginia ham and cream gravy. Likewise, you ought to share a side dish of fried green tomatoes.

The only trouble is the kitchen is no longer as reliable as it was in SOUTHSIDE 815's early days. You can hope to catch it on a good day.

STARDUST
608 Montgomery St., Alexandria, VA
(703) 548-9864

AMERICAN/THAI/SEAFOOD

Lunch: M-F 11:30-5 **Entrees:** $7-$9
Dinner: M-Th 5-10:30, F-Sat 5-11 **Entrees:** $11-$19
Credit Cards: All major, DC, DIS **Dress:** Casual
Reservations: Recommended **Parking:** Street **Metro:** Braddock Rd.
Happy Hour: (twilight time) M-F 5-7, discounted drinks, half-price
appetizers

You'd never know that STARDUST began life as Kristos' Charcoal House. Its dining rooms resemble a frozen confection: walls the color of mint green ice cream in one room, blackberry ice cream in another. In both you dine under a painted sky, its stars seemingly reflected in the carpet.

The apricot-painted bar is probably going to be best known for its half-price happy-hour appetizers. Even at full price, they're very appealing. Oysters on the half shell sparkle with salty flavor, and tiny steamed clams keep you spooning up the garlicky broth. A creamy seafood stew is downright sumptuous. Not all the appetizers exceed expectations. As in many restaurants, the more complicated the dish, the more chances it has to fail.

STARDUST'S chef, Pat Phatiphong, is Thai, and while he brings an Asian flavor to some dishes, his menu covers the globe. Yet the sea is clearly his favorite hunting ground. The major temptations among the entrees are seafood: whole fish grilled or—as a special—fried in a light tempura batter. Salmon crab rolls are pretty and greaseless, but the crabmeat is compacted shreds. For a safe choice, go with the trout with lemon dill sauce.

For dessert, choose among the European offerings, and remember that extravagance succeeds far better than simplicity. Head right for the sumptuous bittersweet chocolate macadamia torte or the strawberry chocolate-cream shortcake.

STARDUST is a restaurant with considerable polish as well as thoughtful service (though the kitchen can bog down on a busy evening). The mood is hospitable. And while appetizers and desserts are stars, even the lesser dishes are exuberant. When STARDUST'S kitchen makes mistakes, they stem from trying too hard rather than not trying enough.

STARLAND CAFE
5125 McArthur Blvd. NW, Washington, DC
(202) 244-9396

AMERICAN

Lunch: M-F 11:30-3 **Entrees:** $6-$13
Dinner: Sun-Th 5:30-9:30, F-Sat 5:30-10:30 **Entrees:** $11-$16
Brunch: Sun 11-3 **Entrees:** $4-$13
Credit Cards: All major **Dress:** Casual **Reservations:** Accepted
Parking: Street **Entertainment:** Acoustic groups at Sun brunch

S TARLAND CAFE is named after the Starland Vocal Band (band member Bill Danoff is a co-owner), and it has the lilting presence of "Afternoon Delight," the group's hit song from the 1970s. It's fresh and airy, part open-air roofed terrace, part glassed-in front room, part romantic back room.

So far, STARLAND CAFE has seemed solid, reliable. Not wonderful, not a temple of gastronomy, but a very agreeable place to spend an evening without spending a lot of money. The menu is of modest length with neighborly prices. Even at dinner it offers such casual options as sandwiches and steak salad. Recently it's hired a new chef, and he's added his own elaborately constructed modern dishes.

Start with a salad. You might find arugula with portobello and cheese or spinach with Smithfield ham, pecans and blue cheese, even pulled duck with watercress and gorgonzola.

When it comes to entrees, the new chef is attempting a few high-wire acts with complicated mixes of ingredients: The salmon is seared with almonds and caraway, sauced with bitter orange. Barbecued lobster and shrimp are served over biscuits with creamed brussels sprouts and bourbon corn mash. On the other hand, steamed fish is seasoned with cilantro, ginger, soy, shiitakes and sesame oil—which sounds a good bit more sensible. And chicken—always a strong suit here—is left alone with just its own *jus*. Vegetarians are paid some attention, as are steak-and-potatoes tastes—the potatoes mashed with garlic and the steak topped with house-made worcestershire.

For dessert, STARLAND CAFE stays close to home, offering such cozy sweets as bread pudding with whiskey pecan butter, pot au chocolate and seasonal fruit cobblers.

STRAITS OF MALAYA
1836 18th St. NW, Washington, DC
(202) 483-1483

| MALAYSIAN | ♿ |

Lunch: M-F noon-2 **Entrees:** $7-$12
Dinner: Sun-Th 5:30-10, F-Sat 5:30-11 **Entrees:** $10-$15
Credit Cards: All major **Dress:** Casual
Reservations: Recommended weekends **Parking:** Street
Metro: Dupont Circle

S ome say Singapore has the world's best food, and STRAITS OF MALAYA encourages me to believe that. Its cooking hints of China and India, with the tropical fragrances of coconut and ginger, *galanga* and lemon grass, chilies and tamarind, plus strong overtones of cilantro. Dine on these highly perfumed, family-style dishes on the roof terrace, and you'll feel closer to Singapore than to Washington.

STRAITS OF MALAYA'S menu can be daunting, even though the entrees are almost all based on chicken or shrimp. You can order many dishes in vegetarian versions, with or without tofu and seasoned highly or gently. And the staff will guide you to the best dishes.

Among entrees, don't miss *poh pia*. It's served with pancakes a la mu shu pork, but the similarities pretty much end there. Its vegetables— including jicama—are crunchier, and the spicing—incorporating dried shrimp—is more exotic, while the dark sauce for smearing on the pancakes is far more pungent than hoisin. The noodle dishes—*cha kway teow, bee hoon* and Singapore rice noodles—are a pleasant balance to the hotter, creamy, coconut-based curries, such as the pink-sauced shrimp or the more familiar yellow chicken curry. A consistent favorite is small Chinese eggplants curried with chunks of carrots and chicken. And the *nasi goreng*—Indonesian fried rice—is one of those dishes you can't resist nibbling to the last morsel.

As for appetizers, be sure to try the crisp, fried, beef-stuffed curry puffs and the *rojak*, an unusual salad made with jicama, cucumbers, carrots and pineapple coated with a savory shrimp paste marinade. Then there are the flat scallion-and-cilantro shrimp pancakes with a bright red peanutty hot sauce, the fried tofu with a similar sauce, five-spice roll (an exotic cousin of meat loaf) and the meal-in-itself soup called *laksa*.

SUMAH'S
1727 7th St. NW
(202) 462-7309

WEST AFRICAN

Open: M-Sat 11-10 **Entrees:** $6-$8
Closed: Sun **Credit Cards:** Cash only **Dress:** Casual
Reservations: Accepted **Parking:** Street **Metro:** Shaw-Howard

Y ou get a lot of politics to spice your food at this small West African carryout, despite the hand-lettered sign: "Warning—No loud political debates in this restaurant." But the guys have got to do something while they wait at the counter for their *jollof* rice. The service is laid-back, which often translates as mighty slow. The half dozen tables seem more for waiting than for eating.

"You get a lot of politics to spice your food at this small West African carryout."

Still, this city hasn't got so many places to buy house-made ginger beer—strong and syrupy—or rice *akras*, small fritters, faintly sweet. The pepper soup—undoubtedly a forerunner of pepperpot—is a thin, fiery, red broth with slices of tripe, bracing if you're a tripe fan. Peanut butter soup is thick enough to eat with a fork, ladled over a huge portion of rice and topped with chewy but flavorful chicken. The menu goes on to okra, couscous, rice *pap* and agreeably grassy and peppery cassava leaf stewed and ladled over rice.

There are entrees even less familiar: potato leaf, *crain crain*, *tola*, *fufu*, *eba*. And for the less adventurous, fried fish and plantain. This is basic, down-home cooking at prices to match.

SUPORN'S
2302 Price Ave., Wheaton, MD
(301) 946-7613

THAI   ♿

Lunch: Tu-F 11:30-3 **Dinner:** Tu-F 5-10, Sat-Sun 11:30-10
Closed: M **Entrees:** $5.50-$10 **Credit Cards:** All major, DC, DIS
Reservations: Recommended for large parties **Dress:** Casual
Parking: Free lot after 6 pm **Metro:** Wheaton

Sunday afternoon. The quiet time between customers. The staffers at
SUPORN'S—few enough to fit at a single table—have apparently
finished their lunch and are keeping busy stripping the leaves from stems
of basil. When we arrive, three of them jump up and head for the kitchen.
I haven't been to SUPORN'S for years, and I'm immediately glad that
fate has brought me back.

The restaurant looks soft and sweet, with white lace curtains, pink vinyl
tablecloths and baby-blue banquettes. Tiny colored lights twinkle across
the walls; it's as if we were inside a Christmas tree. A small box on the
counter holding tissues to dry chili-teared eyes is slipcovered as a minia-
ture couch. You'll need those tissues if you've ordered right. Even mild
dishes sometimes come with a little bowl of chili sauce to dab or dip.
And each sauce is likely to be different: tart with lime, salty with soy, or
thick and vivid with red chili paste. The sauces make dishes with bright
red and green bell peppers, carrots and asparagus taste even brighter, as
if colors were reverberating in your mouth.

Appetizers and salads could keep you happy meal after meal. *Sakooh sai
gai*, tapioca dumplings not much bigger than teardrops, have a fascinating
glutenous chew to them, and they are filled with a sweet-hot dab of chicken
and peanuts. Among the cold appetizers, *yum pla krob* is a salad of salty
slivers of tilefish, as thin and crisp as turkey skin, and startlingly tart.

Not so the "*suki yaki*," which owner Suporn Ringo herself insisted we
order. Sounds like pseudo-Japanese food, doesn't it? It's better than that.
The thin noodles are tossed with egg, scallion, napa cabbage and the
meat of your choice, then brought out with a red chili sauce that makes
them quiver with flavor.

Few small storefront restaurants serve quality seafood. Thus it amazes
me that SUPORN'S shrimp are fresh, with their heads on. They're worth
a messy peeling job to taste them, either stir-fried or spicily steamed.

SUSHI-KO
2309 Wisconsin Ave. NW, Washington, DC
(202) 333-4187

JAPANESE	♿

Lunch: Tu-F noon-2:30 **Entrees:** $7.50-$17
Dinner: M-Th 6-10:30, F-Sat 6-11, Sun 5:30-10 **Entrees:** $9-$18.50
Credit Cards: All major **Reservations:** Recommended
Dress: Casual **Parking:** Valet (fee) at dinner

W ho would have predicted that Americans, too squeamish to eat the innards that the rest of the world covets, would fall in love with raw fish? These days we even pick up plastic trays of sushi from the supermarket for a last-minute weekday supper.

As the city's first sushi bar, SUSHI-KO started the raw-fish trend in Washington years ago. Now it has hired back sushi chef Tetsuro Takanashi and redecorated its two-story dining rooms in an excess of understatement. It's also expanded its all-important list of daily specials to teach us a thing or two we haven't yet learned about sushi.

The standing menu has the tempuras, teriyakis and sushi rolls you'll find at any Japanese restaurant. What sets SUSHI-KO apart is the daily sheet of small dishes that reflects the seasons and the creativity of Takanashi and his American *chef de cuisine*, Duncan Boyd. That's where you'll find a napoleon of chopped raw sea trout with peanuts and cilantro on crisp fried wonton, or pan-roasted monkfish with tiny bits of green beans, corn kernels and green soybeans.

In addition to modernizations of Japanese tradition, this menu offers rarities: monkfish pâté that is like *foie gras* of the sea, baby conch grilled and stuffed back into their cornucopia shells, extraordinary *onna nakase* sake served cold in a small iron kettle, cherry tomato salad with *shiso* or mozzarella marinated in miso. Extravagant versions of sushi show up here, and for $2 you can splurge on fresh *wasabi* rather than the usual reconstituted powder.

The new SUSHI-KO can still produce excellent raw tuna, sea urchin, yellowtail and the other familiar sushi favorites. It can also introduce a sushi-wise clientele to the pleasures of grilled baby octopus with mango and *daikon* salad.

SWAGAT
2063 University Blvd. E., Adelphi, MD
(301) 434-2247

INDIAN   🔳

Open: Tu-Sun 11:30-9:30 **Entrees:** $5-$14 **Closed:** M
Credit Cards: All major, DIS **Dress:** Casual
Reservations: Recommended **Parking:** Free lot

You'd never anticipate it from the bare facade on a raucous stretch on University Boulevard, but SWAGAT has a serene and exotic dining room. White lace is painted on the walls to frame evocative photos of India, and waiters serve with quiet solicitude.

The menu is South Indian—all vegetarian—and ranges from snack foods such as the yard-long rolled rice pancakes called *dosas* to multi-course dinners of three curries. If you want a sample, you can start with an assorted appetizer platter. Or just order *khasta kachori*, a pair of fragile, grainy puffed breads stuffed with a sharp and tangy mix of raw onions, yogurt and chutney. Beyond that, the highlights include a particularly vibrant version of spinach with house-made cheese or the same cheese with various gravies, the soft vegetable-nut patties called vegetable *korma*, spinach with the sweet touch of corn kernels, curries of potatoes and cauliflower or eggplant.

Unfortunately, a sameness has crept into many of the curries, the South Indian pancakes, crepes, fritters and breads are sometimes heavy-handed, and the mango *lassi* is cloying. One can hope this is just a temporary lassitude, for here is a restaurant with such promise that *dals* include not just the usual yellow lentils, but more flavorful black lentils and kidney beans, or a combination of five lentils.

Swagat has another location near the Woodley Park-Zoo Metro station: 2604 Connecticut Ave. NW, Washington, DC 20008, (202) 462-4786.

TABARD INN
1739 N St. NW, Washington, DC
(202) 331-8528

AMERICAN

Breakfast: M-F 7-10, Sat 8-10, Sun 8-9:30 **Entrees:** $2.50-$7.50
Lunch: M-F 11:30-2:30 **Entrees:** $9.50-$14.50
Dinner: Sun-Th 6-10, F-Sat 6-10:30 **Entrees:** $19-$28
Brunch: Sat 11-2:30, Sun 10:30-2:30 **Entrees:** $9-$15
Credit Cards: All major, DC **Reservations:** Recommended
Dress: Casual **Parking:** Street **Metro:** Dupont Circle
Entertainment: Jazz Sun 7:30-10:30

There's nothing fancy about this tile-floored dining room in the English basement of a small Victorian hotel. But there's plenty that's tasteful. The greatest of its charms lie outside the dining room proper: There's a lounge full of aging sofas and a fireplace on one side, and a lyrically pretty, walled garden for lunching on the other. The dining room is laconically artistic, with contemporary art on the walls and white cloths on the small tables.

The cooking, too, is contemporary and artistic, with many of its ingredients coming from TABARD INN'S own farm. It's an immensely satisfying little tucked-away restaurant, except that it has mainstreet prices. And pitted against such similarly priced American restaurants as Kinkead's and Vidalia, it seems priced above its scale.

The current chef, David Craig, came from Pesce, and brings with him a repertoire of fish dishes that sounds exciting. Their execution tends to need some work; while the fish itself is impeccable, the sauces seem like works in progress. A sparkling fresh and delicious whole yellowtail snapper loses the battle for dominance with its plate of marinated fennel with wine, anchovies and tomatoes. A crusty whole bluefish is drowned in butter. Wonderful, crisp-skinned red trout is upstaged by sweet beet puree. Meat dishes stand up better to their surroundings. A veal chop is handsome in every way, and rigatoni has a bolognese sauce so savory you might wish for a bowlful and a spoon. Most impressive are Craig's vegetables, particularly one day's spinach-green risotto with tiny tomatoes and butter beans that was risotto nirvana.

The menu changes daily and is full of dishes that sound wonderful, but Craig seems to have started by feeling his way and experimenting on his clientele rather than presenting finished dishes. Still, they're in the good company of a fine wine list, some seductive breads and satisfyingly seasonal desserts such as fruit cobblers and house-made ice creams.

TABERNA DEL ALABARDERO
1776 I St. NW, Washington, DC
(Entrance on 18th Street)
(202) 429-2200

SPANISH ♿

Lunch: M-F 11:30-2:30 **Entrees:** $17.25-$20.75
Dinner: M-Th 6-10, F-Sat 6-11 **Entrees:** $19-$29.50
Pre-Theater: M-Sat 6-8 pm, $30 **Closed:** Sun
Tapas: Served throughout the day, $5-$8.75
Credit Cards: All major, DIS, DC **Reservations:** Recommended
Dress: Jacket required **Parking:** Complimentary valet at dinner
Metro: Farragut West **Happy Hour:** M-F 4-6, half-price drinks

Don't go to TABERNA DEL ALABARDERO for something that sounds French. You can probably find a better value elsewhere. Search the menu for something distinctively Spanish: Anything with almonds or Spanish cheese. Duck and game and lamb. Fresh sardines and cuttlefish. This handsome and formal restaurant shows a style you won't find elsewhere in town.

The tapas menu is shorter than Jaleo's or Coco Loco's and concentrates on the classics. They're usually fine, though the cold ones are more reliable than the hot: A tapas portion of paella has tasted like leftovers (and unfortunately, the entree paella is for only two people).

I particularly like TABERNA DEL ALABARDERO for lunch, for it's then that I've found a gratin of cauliflower and scallops glazed with sharp cheese, all melting together in a cream sauce, and game patties that are a succulent amalgam of squab, rabbit, duck, whatever the kitchen has trimmings of. Even grilled lamb steak has a remarkable woodsy and juicy flavor. The dishes at lunch are more homey, less formal than at dinner, and all the better for it.

At any meal, though, the dessert list is worth examining. Flan is, after all, a Spanish specialty. And velvety sweet custard cream made with cheese, buried under a honeydew melon granita, is the opposite of *crème brûlée*, an unexpected match that's reason alone to seek out TABERNA.

TAHOGA
2815 M St. NW, Washington, DC
(202) 338-5380

AMERICAN/SEAFOOD   ♿

Lunch: M-F 11:30-2 **Entrees:** $7.50-$11
Dinner: Sun-Th 5:30-10, F-Sat 5:30-11 **Entrees:** $17.50-$24
Credit Cards: All major, DC **Dress:** Nice casual
Reservations: Recommended **Parking:** Valet (fee) at dinner
Metro: Foggy Bottom

Pick a mild evening and reserve a table in the brick-walled garden, and you'll see TAHOGA at its best. Yet even indoors it has a style that befits Georgetown: cool, chic minimalism, with light used as art in this contemporary dining room.

The menu is also up-to-date, with only pork and herb-roasted chicken to distract you from seafood. Salmon, monkfish, scallops, shrimp, trout and clams dominate the menu. The dishes are complicated and eclectic, drawing from the South's grits cake, Italy's balsamic vinegar, the Middle East's bulgur, Mexico's tequila. And sometimes they confuse the palate. But when the ingredients are in harmony—as in an appetizer of steamed clams with cilantro, lime and chorizo—you're reminded what pleasure America's freewheeling approach to food can provide.

Your seafood will almost always be beautifully cooked, and you can count on finding something of interest among such accompaniments as corn risotto and fennel *confit*. Still, the menu is small and less adventurous than it once was. Desserts return to yesteryear with an authentic apple-apricot strudel. And the wine list shows a generosity of spirit: It's a top-notch array—particularly from California—and priced modestly.

TAIPEI TOKYO
11510-A Rockville Pike, Rockville, MD
(301) 881-8388

CHINESE / JAPANESE   ♿

Open: M-Th 11:30-9:30, F-Sat 11:30-10, Sun 11:30-9
Entrees: $5-$15   **Credit Cards:** V, MC   **Dress:** Casual
Reservations: Not accepted   **Parking:** Free lot

I t has all the earmarks of a great ethnic find. This storefront Asian restaurant is around the side of a shopping strip, so you have to know about it already. It's busy and clattery, a madhouse at the height of lunch or dinner.

Its distinction is that it's two restaurants in one, Japanese on the left, serving sushi and tempura, and Chinese on the right, with stir-fries, noodle soups and hot pots. It's fun. It's cheap. But is it good?

The sushi is uncharacteristically a little sloppy, its rolls unraveling and its fish not quite tasty enough. The Chinese food, though, makes the sushi look good. Dumplings are soggy, salt-and-garlic fried chicken tastes only of the salt, and crisp fried noodles with beef are no such thing (they are gluey instead).

TAIPEI TOKYO isn't much more than a place to fill up in a hurry for little money. But the lines attest that it fulfills its purpose.

Another nearby branch: 1596-A Rockville Pike, Rockville, MD, (301) 881-8533.

TARA THAI
4828 Bethesda Ave., Bethesda, MD
(301) 657-0488

THAI   占

Lunch: M-F 11:30-3, Sat-Sun noon-3:30 **Entrees:** $5-$8
Dinner: Sun-Th 5-10, F-Sat 5-11 **Entrees:** $7-$13
Credit Cards: All major, DIS, DC **Reservations:** Recommended
Dress: Casual **Parking:** Street **Metro:** Bethesda

Bethesda teems with new restaurants, and while many of them capsize, TARA THAI—there and at its other three branches—keeps floating along. No wonder: They provide some of the most scintillating Thai food around, in a colorful, mock-underwater environment, at prices no higher than at more drearily decorated Thai restaurants.

Their menus are—as the decor would suggest—strong on seafood. And while the service can be forgetful and even rude, the place is fun. Just keep a hand on your plate lest a waiter grab it while you're still eating, and you'll do fine.

The standard dishes are good here, but the seafood is more of an accomplishment. A large bowl of juicy little mussels steamed in lemon grass and basil, served with a sweet-hot chili and basil dip, is a mere $4.95. As an entree, sautéed with chili paste and basil, mussels are just $7.95. Whole fish is a specialty, the rockfish grilled in banana leaves or steamed with plum sauce or the flounder fried crisp with chili and garlic sauce or black beans, mushrooms and ginger. Soft-shell crabs are fried, but out of season they're served frozen, so it's worth asking and waiting for the fresh ones. Far better than the usual American surf and turf is a mating of big grilled tiger shrimp with crabmeat and sweet-hot ground chicken sauce. And if you're tired of the ubiquitous *pad thai*, switch to wide rice noodles, here topped with shrimp and chicken in a spicy basil sauce. TARA THAI encourages vegetarians to specify if they don't want their dishes seasoned with fish sauce. It also promises extra-spicy food for chiliheads, and for everyone else it keeps the pepper level pronounced but not outrageous.

For other Tara Thai locations: 226 Maple Ave., Vienna, VA, (703) 255-2467; 7501 E. Leesburg Pike, Falls Church, VA, (703) 506-9788; 4001 N. Fairfax Dr., Arlington, VA, (703) 908-4999. A fifth Tara Thai was scheduled to open at 12071 Rockville Pike, Rockville, Md., in January 1999.

TEAISM
2009 R St. NW, Washington, DC
(202) 667-3827

ASIAN

Breakfast: M-F 8 am-11:30 am, Sat-Sun 9 am-2:30 pm **Entrees:**
$2.50-$6.25 **Dinner:** Sun-Th 11 am-10 pm, F-Sat 11 am-11 pm
Entrees: $4.75-$7.75 **Credit Cards:** All major **Reservations:** No
Dress: Casual **Parking:** Street **Metro:** Dupont Circle

An interlude at TEAISM makes me feel serene. It's a tiny place, with counters downstairs and silky little wood tables and benches upstairs, every lovely bit of it looking handcrafted. It makes an art of tea, an education of every cup, with sweet-spiced milky *chai*, poetic spring blossom pekoe, mysterious three-cups fragrance, bracing *sencha* or disconcerting *pu-erh* camel breath.

> **"It makes an art of tea, an education of every cup."**

The accompanying foods are simple and delicate, an Asian sampling from Thai noodle salad to Japanese *bento* boxes. India contributes a couple of curries, chutneys and flat breads, and America has inspired the chiffon cake and the homestyle cookies. There's an ecumenical ostrich burger with Asian barbecue sauce, sesame mustard and an inventive *wasabi* potato salad.

For breakfast you can find familiar granola, French toast and waffles or exotic scrambled eggs with cilantro or with deliciously suave tea-cured salmon—which is also worth seeking among the bento boxes at lunch or dinner. For any time of the day, the most restorative dish is *ochazuke*, a bowl of sticky rice topped with shreds of salmon and seaweed or with *bok choy* and pickled plum, over which you pour sencha green tea to turn it into a soup that tastes as healthy as a morning hike.

THAI FLAVOR
2531 Ennalls Ave., Wheaton, MD
(301) 946-6602

THAI   🦽

Lunch: Daily 11:30-3 **Entrees:** $5-$7, $7 (buffet)
Dinner: Daily 3-10 **Entrees:** $8-$11
Credit Cards: All major, DIS, DC, CB **Dress:** Casual
Reservations: Recommended **Parking:** Free lot
Metro: Wheaton **Entertainment:** Thai music F-Sat 10-2am

It's awfully small and has a makeshift air, but THAI FLAVOR flashes some charm in its carved-wood room dividers and glimpses of a small red shrine in the kitchen. What's more, its prices are about as low as fresh-cooked food is ever likely to get, and its service is hospitable. But the pacing makes you wonder whether there is more than one person in the kitchen. Apparently not.

Everything looks handmade, from the pan-fried dumplings folded into rough triangles to the baton-shaped spring rolls and the salad *khaek*, which has an air of being inspired by a trip to the market. It's a platter of peanut-sauced lettuce arranged with rows of fried tofu, tomato, onions, hard-cooked egg and a flurry of house-made potato chips scooped over all.

The sauces here, pooled on the plate rather than served in little side dishes, are concocted with a painter's eye. *Yum talay*, the usual seafood salad, is a skimpy array (what would you expect at $5.95?), and the dressing is a bit watery, but it's all tinted a bonfire red. *Keow saa*, those triangular shrimp dumplings, are adrift on a gold-brown ginger-sesame-soy sauce. And the familiar open-top pork and crab dumplings are on a glossy brown sweetened soy, with a pouf of julienned raw vegetables in the center.

It all tastes mild, as if the chef were afraid to offend American palates: The pad thai is far more sweet than savory; a dramatic whole fried flounder comes with a chili glaze that isn't as fiery as it looks, and the beige sauce on the chicken and shrimp with asparagus is restrained in everything but sugar. All the sauces are light and pretty, but few have much impact —except the one with the "wild chicken," which has little branches of green peppercorns to enliven it.

Dessert is the most interesting part of the meal. What Americans would order wedges of acorn squash with spongy gray filling to end a meal? Smart ones. The airy custard filling is perfumed with coconut milk, and the sugared squash tastes like fruit. What's more, the plate is splashed with strawberry and chocolate sauces, and finished with lovely coconut ice cream and whipped cream. Nobody will believe me, but it's scrumptious.

THAI SQUARE
3217 Columbia Pike, Arlington, VA
(703) 685-7040

THAI   ♿

Open: M-Th 11:30-10:30, F 11:30-11, Sat noon-11, Sun noon-10:30
Entrees: $6-$9 **Lunch Special:** M-F 11:30-3 **Entrees:** $5.50-$7.25
Credit Cards: All major **Dress:** Casual
Reservations: Required for 5 or more **Parking:** Free lot in back

You can keep your insider's stock tip. The secret that moves me to action is a new, little-known restaurant with authentic food from somewhere-or-other. Thus, when a guy told me he knew of a place that served the only authentic Thai food he'd tasted in the United States, I pulled out my note pad. That scared him off; he didn't want to "ruin" the restaurant. I nagged until he relented.

THAI SQUARE immediately lived up to my imaginings. It was small and tidy, with just a couple of waitresses and an effusively hospitable host. Most telling, every other table was taken by a group of Thais. The menu, however, was long and ordinary. My attention wandered to the next table. What fascinating-looking dishes were being served there! Turns out they were on the Thai menu, which the owner hadn't translated yet.

After having the Thai carryout translated, I discovered that long-stewed pig is akin to Chinese pork stewed with rock sugar. And the spicy catfish entree is crisp and chewy at the same time. The host eventually understood our tastes and steered us deftly, recommending pork *larb* rather than the more familiar chicken version of this salad. All the appetizer salads are refreshingly tart and stunningly hot; we loved them. The single best dish was the first our host recommended, the special of mussels.

Some of the best entrees are Thai versions of Chinese classics. There are the wide rice noodles—the *chow foon* of Chinatown—as well as a form of egg *foo yung* that's quietly delicious. Noodle soups are intense, while curries range from watery to sinus clearing.

On every visit, I ordered one dish on a whim; each one made me want to return the next day. Now I can't wait to go back. Will I ever work up to spice beef tripe soup in hot pot? Will the guy who steered me to THAI SQUARE ever forgive me?

THAT'S AMORE
5225 Wisconsin Ave. NW, Washington, DC
(202) 237-7800

ITALIAN   ♿

Dinner: Sun-Th 4-10:30, F-Sat 4-midnight **Entrees:** $8-$17 (family style $15-$29) **Credit Cards:** All major, DIS, DC, CB
Dress: Casual **Reservations:** Recommended (for 6 or more F-Sat only)
Parking: Validated **Metro:** Friendship Heights
Entertainment: Jazz W-Th 7-10, F-Sat 8-11
Happy Hour: M-F 5-7, reduced-price drinks and appetizers

There's no point going to dinner at THAT'S AMORE as just a couple. This home-style Italian restaurant specializes in abundance, big groups of noisy families passing around multiple platters of fragrant pastas, fish, meats and side dishes.

The bread basket is filled with standard focaccia and Italian loaves, but their fortunes are much improved when the waiter pours a pool of olive oil onto a plate and sprinkles it with Parmesan and freshly grated pepper. You could dip a tablecloth in this oily paste and it would taste delicious.

Sensible diners will steer away from the crumb-laden shrimp, clams or mussels in favor of the lighter, char-grilled appetizers. Almost reaching greatness is the calamari with its crisp edges; grilled chicken strips are also excellent. The immense mixed green salad is a sleeper, and the mozzarella in *carrozza* is sheer excess.

The problem is, all that won't leave you enough appetite for the grilled chicken breast adorned only with lemon and butter, the choicest of the entrees. A close second is the whole roast chicken seasoned with a profligate amount of well-browned garlic, enough to fend off a lifetime of vampires. The steak is also terrific. As for pastas, the waiter was right to suggest the rigatoni with sausage. The only truly dreary dish I've found is the mixed seafood pasta: This kitchen's strength is gutsiness, not delicacy.

Desserts are weak. But would anybody notice? At THAT'S AMORE the food is primarily a backdrop for the service—thoughtful, energetic, fun-loving. It's as if the restaurant hired babysitters not just for children but for their moms and dads, too.

Other branches: 15201 Shady Grove Rd., Rockville, MD, (301) 670-9666; 10400 Little Patuxent Pkwy., Columbia, MD, (410) 772-5900; 720 Kenilworth Dr., Towson, MD, (410) 825-5255; 150 Branch Rd. SE, Vienna, VA, (703) 281-7777, and 46300 Potomac Run Plaza, Sterling, VA, (703) 406-4900. Branches are open for lunch 11:30-4 (entrees $5-$12).

3RD & EATS
500 3rd St. NW, Washington, DC
(202) 347-8790

AMERICAN/SOUTHERN

Breakfast: M-F 7-10 **Lunch:** M-F 10-3 **Entrees:** $2.50-$5
Closed: Sat-Sun **Credit Cards:** None; cash only **Reservations:** No
Dress: Casual **Parking:** Street **Metro:** Judiciary Square

You can put your money where your mouth is at 3RD & EATS, doing good while eating well. This small, self-service restaurant, open weekdays for breakfast and lunch, is a training ground for the unemployed and a source of funds to aid the poor and homeless. It's also an awfully nice place to eat.

In fact, few luncheonettes around town serve food that is fresher or more likely to be made from scratch. And certainly none offers lower prices. Breakfast begins the day with house-made biscuits that are crunchy and flaky enough for the most persnickety Southerner, layered with scrambled eggs, American cheese and bacon or a sausage patty. The blueberry muffins are soft and moist, thick with berries. The raisin bread is also made in-house, but it tends to be a little dry; it's better toasted. There are bagels, English muffins, cereals and just-cut fresh fruit, plus juices and coffees to serve yourself. Regulars have learned to check the lunchtime special when they stop in for breakfast. Some days it's short ribs, other days ham hocks with red beans and rice or ham with macaroni and cheese. It could be stuffed flank steak or stuffed peppers, tuna noodle casserole or spaghetti with meat sauce. There is also a house-made soup each day.

Every day the display case is filled with salads, including a wonderful home-style chicken salad with raisins, walnuts and celery plus a carefully restrained dose of mayonnaise. Sandwiches are the usual deli choices —roast beef, corned beef, turkey, ham, tuna, chicken or egg salad. They are nothing special—the meat is prepackaged and the bread is squishy. There is always a red-cabbage slaw, and sometimes the kitchen has time to make potato salad.

" . . . a training ground for the unemployed and a source of funds to aid the poor and homeless. It's also an awfully nice place to eat."

TIFFIN RESTAURANT
1341 University Blvd. East, Langley Park, MD
(301) 434-9200

INDIAN   ゙

Lunch: Daily 11:30-3 **Dinner:** Daily 5-10 **Entrees:** $6.50-$17
Buffet: Daily 11:30-3; $6 (M-F), $8 (Sat-Sun) **Dress:** Casual
Reservations: Recommended **Parking:** Free lot

They start arriving before noon, and within an hour the trickle becomes a torrent. A line forms along the buffet table, lunchers of myriad sizes, heights, weights and ages, all of Indian descent.

TIFFIN is an upscale spinoff of Udupi Palace, the bargain-priced vegetarian restaurant down the street. The lunch buffet, which stretches along three tables, starts with soup and ends with dessert. In between it offers three meat dishes, plus vegetables as well as the chutneys, salads and other condiments that make an Indian meal such an intricate feast. Yet the display doesn't even include the highlight: hot breads. Lunchtime keeps the bread maker in perpetual motion over the deep tandoor oven, stretching the balls of dough much like a pizza chef and slapping it onto the inside wall of the tandoor, where it blisters and browns.

At lunch, just about everyone opts for the buffet, even though the à la carte menu is far more extensive. The trick is to figure out the kitchen's strengths. Appetizers aren't among them. There's one exception, an unusual and savory Delhi fried fish. Nor are meats and poultry the talent of this kitchen. Goat curry has an agreeable sauce shot through with slivers of ginger, and the inevitable lamb *rogan josh* is fine. But they're not really memorable, and chicken dishes feature juiceless, bland meat. The vegetable dishes—especially the eggplant, spinach and cheese, okra—are the dazzlers. As are the breads. A *dosa* is as voluminous as a tablecloth loosely rolled to a half-foot in diameter. TIFFIN'S *naan* is outstanding, and onion-stuffed *kulcha* is its match. But nothing competes with the *puri*, a bubble of whole-wheat dough that's served puffed as large as a sofa pillow.

TIFFIN is large enough to seat nearly a hundred, yet it's pretty, and it aspires to elegance. Most endearing, its service is as attentive and personal as a private home. All this and great bread, too.

TONY CHENG'S SEAFOOD RESTAURANT
& MONGOLIAN BARBECUE
619-621 H St. NW, Washington, DC
(202) 371-8669 (Seafood)
(202) 842-8669 (BBQ)

CHINESE

Lunch: M-Sat 11-3 **Entrees:** $8-$10 (**BBQ:** $9 buffet)
Dinner: M-Th 3-11, F-Sat 3-midnight, Sun 11am-11pm
Dinner Entrees: $9-$18 (**BBQ:** $15 buffet)
Dim Sum: Daily 11-3 **Entrees:** $2.35-$8
Credit Cards: All major **Reservations:** Recommended
Dress: Casual **Parking:** Street **Metro:** Gallery Place-Chinatown

Washington hasn't much more than a hint of a Chinatown, but through the years Tony Cheng has populated it with several restaurants. These days, he's concentrating on two restaurants in one building: TONY CHENG'S SEAFOOD RESTAURANT (second floor) and his MONGOLIAN BARBECUE (first floor).

The seafood restaurant is enormous, anchored with a tank of live lobsters and Dungeness crabs. The menu, too, is extensive, going well beyond seafood. At lunch dim sum is served; on Sundays it's wheeled around on carts. But if you tried only dim sum, you'd think this was a pretty pedestrian place. In fact, much of the menu would leave that impression. The most worthwhile dishes are seafood, especially fresh shrimp, wrapped in lotus leaves and steamed in spicy soybean paste, and Dungeness crab strewn with scallions, ginger and onions. It's the ingredients that stand out here: whole fish, shrimp with their heads, snails, clams, oysters. And the choices are many. Two pages of dim sum, dozens of noodle dishes, and a wide selection of vegetables keep company with the Chinese restaurant standards.

At the MONGOLIAN BARBECUE, self-service combines with showmanship to produce a favorite meal of the $10 lunch crowd. The salad bar is raised to new heights as customers circle the buffet, piling bowls with sliced raw meats and vegetables that the chefs season and cook on a big grill. The browned ingredients are flipped into a clean bowl, and that's lunch. Back at the table, the mixture is stuffed into sesame-studded rolls or piled on rice. With a free nibble of roasted peanuts and spicy pickled cabbage and a fortune cookie for dessert, the MONGOLIAN BARBECUE can offer a hefty lunch tailored to your taste.

216

VIDALIA
1990 M St. NW, Washington, DC
(202) 659-1990

AMERICAN/SOUTHERN   ♿

Lunch: M-F 11:30-2:30   **Entrees:** $6.75-$18.75
Dinner: M-Th 5:30-10, F-Sat 5:30-10:30, Sun 5-9:30
Entrees: $19.50-$27   **Credit Cards:** All major, DIS, DC
Reservations: Preferred   **Dress:** Nice casual
Parking: Complimentary valet at dinner   **Metro:** Dupont Circle

Restaurants, unlike books and movies, are far from static. Dig out that old review from your files and you're likely to find the opinions outdated. If you have rare luck, the changes will prove to have been for the better. That's what you'd find with VIDALIA: This always-good restaurant has become superb.

The underground dining room is still so fresh and airy that you don't miss windows, and the service has that smooth flow that comes from a team's long experience together. The wine list has matured as only a passionate cellarmaster can make it do.

Most important, chef Jeff Buben's talent in the kitchen has matured. Be forewarned that this food is rich. His somewhat Southern cooking uses country ham and grits in sophisticated guises—don't miss the appetizer of fried grits cake with portobellos, arugula and goat cheese—and offers

"This always-good restaurant has become superb."

the creamiest and most wonderful corn bread along with biscuits and onion focaccia. The Shenandoah trout is sumptuously stuffed with crabmeat, hominy, bacon and baby limas. Crab cakes are updated with roasted peppers, cilantro and mustard, all to their advantage, though in another chef's hands the combination might be a mess. Only shrimp and grits has been disappointing, though the grits themselves were grand.

For dessert, restraint is not an option. Even the sorbets have lemon-grass syrup or coconut tuiles. Give in to the lemon chess or pecan pie.

VILLA FRANCO
601 Pennsylvania Ave. NW, Washington, DC
(Entrance on Indiana Ave.)
(202) 638-2423

ITALIAN   🦽

Lunch: M-F 11-3 **Entrees:** $11-$22
Dinner: M-F 5:30-10:30, Sat 5:30-11, Sun 5-10:30 **Entrees:** $13-$30
Pre-Theater: Daily 5:30-7, $20 **Credit Cards:** All major, DC
Dress: Nice casual **Reservations:** Recommended
Parking: Complimentary valet at dinner **Metro:** Archives/Navy Memorial
Entertainment: Piano Sat 7:30-9:30

I f you don't fall prey to sticker shock, VILLA FRANCO is a vital and exciting place. It's run by Franco Nuschese, the first maitre d' at Bice who went on to start up Cafe Milano. Now he's serving the food of his home ground, the Amalfi coast. With its tropical blue dining room, stone columns and attentive service, VILLA FRANCO is given to classical flourishes. It plays at being a setting for emperors. Mostly, it gets senators and other politicos.

At one table, every one of the men was served a double veal chop, spectacular, juicy slab of meat. It's the most expensive—and the best—entree in the house, best shared between two people. The other big seller is a showy whole fish, most often grilled. It's more exciting on the platter than on your palate, though. There's one entree for which it's worth straying from the veal, but it's not for the squeamish: baby octopus stew.

Like Cafe Milano, VILLA FRANCO composes colorful and impeccable salads. As for appetizers, there's a wonderful fried mixed seafood and an eggplant parmigiana that's lighter than most. And while the pastas sound far from ordinary, their execution isn't nearly as appealing as their descriptions.

A whole fish doesn't leave room for much more dessert than a little sorbet, but what sorbets! Rough and icy, in improbable flavors.

Franco Nuschese understands the value of style and service. He's dressed up and given a make-over to an old favorite: red-sauce southern Italian cooking. If you're looking for an evening made to seem important, it's here.

VILLAGE BISTRO
1723 Wilson Blvd., Arlington, VA
(703) 522-0284

AMERICAN/INTERNATIONAL   ♿

Lunch: M-F 11:30-2:30 **Entrees:** $6-$13
Dinner: M-Th 5-10:30, F-Sat 5-11, Sun 5-10 **Entrees:** $8-$19
Pre-Theater: Sun-Th 5-7, $15 **Credit Cards:** All major, DIS, DC
Dress: Casual **Reservations:** Preferred **Parking:** Free lot
Metro: Rosslyn, Court House

Nothing inspires more trust in a kitchen than a long list of seasonal daily specials. At the VILLAGE BISTRO the specials run half as long as the regular menu, and they include rarities the season evokes: shad in the spring (the fish, not just the roe), soft-shells in summer, roast goose in winter.

From the street, the VILLAGE BISTRO would seem to be just another neighborhood restaurant in a shopping strip that is fraying at the edges. Inside, though, it's dressed with bouquets of flowers and so friendly that after your first few visits the waiter is likely to know your preferences without being reminded. While such personal service may be noteworthy in this chain-restaurant era, the VILLAGE BISTRO'S quality/price ratio is even more remarkable. At chicken-carryout prices the VILLAGE BISTRO offers a long list of fresh fish and seafood, luxurious choices among the meats, nicely dressed pastas. Except for the uninteresting pizzas, the cooking is a sure-handed and creative mingling of French, Italian, Indian, Middle Eastern and American.

"You can wear jeans or jewels and eat Broadway cooking at movie-house prices."

Even so, appetizers are the winners, from steamed clams fragrant with orange and lemon to calamari sautéed with an herbed *beurre blanc*. Those buttery yet light sauces for seafood and Mediterranean garnishes of olives, arugula and balsamic vinegar or pernod and garlic are the kitchen's signatures, so when in doubt, choose fish. And if you find a disappointment—dry crab cakes, for instance—remind yourself that those generous and elaborately garnished cakes cost little more than a sandwich elsewhere. Here is a place where you can wear jeans or jewels and eat Broadway cooking at movie-house prices.

VINTAGE WINE BISTRO
2809 M St. NW, Washington, DC
(202) 625-0077

FRENCH   ♿

Lunch: M-F 11:30-3   **Entrees:** $10-$18
Dinner: M-Sat 5:30-11   **Entrees:** $14.50-$21   **Closed:** Sun
Dress: Casual   **Reservations:** Recommended   **Parking:** Street

R eal, old-fashioned French onion soup. What an astonishment! The stock is made from scratch and the crouton floating in the bowl is of hearty country bread. And it's a bargain. You might also be captivated by the simple, homey French salads. In fact, you might think you had stumbled upon a corner of provincial France in Georgetown.

This is the bistro of Gerard Pangaud, who brought his two Michelin stars to Washington, then opened Gerard's Place. VINTAGE got a shaky start under various *chefs de cuisine*; now Pangaud himself has promised to take charge of the kitchen at dinner in hopes of polishing its performance.

If the day doesn't warrant hot soup, there's one promising cold appetizer: Roquefort terrine with *frisee* salad; it's a tiny, wonderful balanced meal. The duck terrine, though, has been too compact and bland. Snails in puff pastry are elaborate; they are more of a showcase for garlic and butter than snails.

Except for an evocative veal casserole, the long-cooked entrees have seemed more slapdash than lovingly tended; surely Pangaud can correct that. Cassoulet has been merely a pot of salty beans, with a few chewy chunks of meat. *Choucroute* has tasted flat. Dishes more quickly cooked —fish, mussels, steak, roast lamb and chicken—depend on the luck of the moment. I've had flawlessly sautéed cod and a roast chicken that was sadly overcooked, nicely sautéed skinless duck with figs and pleasant salmon, deliciously sharpened by sorrel.

Whatever style this restaurant has is concentrated on wine, and the prices are nearly saintly. Where else will you find a serious French champagne for $9.50 a glass?

Desserts are neither dazzlers nor afterthoughts, with such classic choices as *oeufs à la neige* and poached pears. VINTAGE in its first year was merely a moderately priced, simple French restaurant, a place you might stop for a glass of wine and a little lunch or dinner when you happen to be in the neighborhood. It could yet become a moderately priced showcase for Gerard Pangaud.

VOX ARTIS
839 17ᵗʰ St. NW, Washington, DC
(202) 974-4260

FRENCH   [♿]

Breakfast: M-F 7-9:45 **Entrees:** $5.75-$13.75; prix fixe: $8, $13.50
Dinner: M-F 11:30-9:30, Sat 5:30-9:30 **Entrees:** $15-$25
Pre-Theater: M-F 5-6:30, Sat 5:30-6:30, $19 **Closed:** Sun
Credit Cards: All major, DC **Dress:** Casual
Reservations: Required for lunch, accepted for dinner
Parking: Street **Metro:** Farragut West

V OX ARTIS, charming and evocative yet fresh and new, has a lot going for it—but not the food. To find a meal as pleasurable as the setting, you have to tread carefully.

Start out as the French bistro-goer does, with a little salad. The melange of celery root *remoulade* and shredded carrot, set on a bed of Boston lettuce and surrounded with sliced tomatoes and haricots verts, is the classic *hors d'oeuvre varie*. For an appetizer slightly more substantial, there's a Nicoise salad that features strips of grilled fresh tuna. So what if the tuna is overcooked; it's an accent here, not the focal point. Even heartier, and welcome if that breeze from the street turns chilly, is the Mediterranean fish soup, a distinctly French treat. Of course, if you must have sausage in brioche; it's not bad here, just a little stolid.

Entrees are a trickier choice. The duck *confit* looks and tastes like boiled meat, and the glamorous-sounding pastas are pallid and heavy. Tuna is more palatable—cut thin but cooked accurately and enlivened by a lemony dark sauce. Pork loin, cut even thinner, still stays remarkably juicy. The most flavorful of the entrees is leg of lamb, sliced across the bone and smoky from the grill. If only its flageolets hadn't been undercooked, this would be prime bistro fare.

The strangest dish I've encountered is herb-grilled shrimp with seared fruit: Its large, chewy shrimp rest in a sauce that tastes like warm milk, dotted with cooked strawberries, pineapple and kiwi. If it weren't for the white rice, I'd have wondered whether the shrimp had blundered into a dessert gratin of fruit. Desserts tend to be prettily undistinguished, from a medium-brown chocolate mousse served in a martini glass, to a frozen version with walnuts on a sunny mango *coulis*, to a decent *crème brûlée*. The standout is a wild berry cake that's tart and sparkling on the tongue. It hardly needs its pool of *crème anglaise*. Even unsauced, this berry pastry is the highest artistry at VOX ARTIS.

WEISSBLATT'S
7913 Tuckerman Lane, Potomac, MD
(301) 299-1740

JEWISH DELI   [♿]

Open: Daily 7-9   **Entrees:** $8-$12
Breakfast: (all day) $4-$9   **Credit Cards:** All major, DIS, DC **Dress:**
Casual   **Reservations:** No   **Parking:** Free lot

Okay, so it isn't the deli of our dreams. But WEISSBLATT'S has many of the qualities that we expect to surround a corned beef sandwich.

The plates are piled high with enough food for the entire day—even if they are only appetizers. The breakfast specials specialize in overkill: lox, onions and eggs over potato pancakes, for example. In all, the menu is like an historical record of Eastern European immigrants: *kishke*, *kasha*, stuffed cabbage, knishes (though the waiter reveals that they are not homemade, as the menu promises, but frozen). It also lists modern alternatives "on the healthy side," the likes of turkey pastrami, turkey burger and grilled tuna sandwich.

As for whether WEISSBLATT'S traditions taste authentic, they're halfway there. The corned beef, to its great credit, tastes of more than salt, but the rye bread—baked off in this kitchen—is pale and flabby. The matzo ball soup could use a flavor boost, the chopped liver has a fetching rough texture but also a bitter aftertaste. Smoked fish looks plump and fresh, and whitefish salad is just fine.

In all, WEISSBLATT'S serves all that you'd hope to find, but it doesn't set any new standards for a Washington-area deli.

"It doesn't set any new standards for a Washington-area deli."

WEST END CAFE
Washington Circle Hotel
1 Washington Circle NW, Washington, DC
(202) 293-5390

AMERICAN/MEDITERRANEAN   ♿

Breakfast: M-F 7-10:30, Sat-Sun 8-10 **Entrees:** $1.75-$5.25, $9 (buffet)
Lunch: M-F 11:30-2:30 **Entrees:** $7.50-$13, $10 (buffet)
Dinner: Tu-Th 5:30-11:30, F-Sat 5:30-midnight, Sun-M 5:30-10
Dinner Entrees: $11-$21 **Pre-Theater:** $18 (during dinner hours)
Brunch: Sun 11:30-3, $16 buffet **Credit Cards:** All major, DC
Dress: Casual **Reservations:** Recommended
Parking: Complimentary valet **Metro:** Foggy Bottom
Entertainment: Pianist Tu-Th 7:30-11, F-Sat 8-12

WEST END CAFE, with its glass walls curving overhead like a greenhouse, lets you feel the sun, see the sky and eat your smoked salmon in cool comfort. Given Washington summers, it's even better than an outdoor cafe.

This creative American restaurant has two dining rooms with a hallway between. The Garden Room has lush greenery and floral upholstery, art deco fashion prints and taped classical music amid sunshine or starlight. The Piano Room, a bar and lounge, is a darker nook, decorated more with sound—a pianist in the evenings—than with light. I've been eating Caesar salad on this site since back when the West End theater showed plays rather than films. And the Caesar is still good, though the WEST END CAFE has modernized it with baked Parmesan crisps.

Over the years, many of Washington's best young chefs have come through this kitchen on their way up the ladder. This is the place where much of the city's New American cooking got its start. Smoked salmon, fried oysters, grilled fish, seasonal soups—they take on new character with each chef. And there's always an array of informal dishes, even at dinner: burgers, pizzas, antipasto samplers, omelets and sandwiches. Vegetarians have plenty to choose from. So dinner can be elaborate or simple, leisurely or quick.

At midday, though, there is an à la carte menu. The highlight is a Mediterranean antipasto buffet: an array of salads—asparagus, baby artichokes, couscous with dried fruit. A quiche—a little bland and soggy, though still better than most—adds heft, as do salamis. With serve-yourself soup to start and slices of melon for dessert, the buffet is a three-course meal for hardly more than the price of a sandwich.

WILLARD ROOM

Willard Hotel
1401 Pennsylvania Ave. NW
Washington, DC
(202) 637-7440

AMERICAN/FRENCH   ♿

Breakfast: M-F 7:30-10 **Entrees:** $7.50-$12.75; prix fixe: $12, $17.50
Lunch: M-F 11:30-2 **Entrees:** $16-$24; prix fixe: $26
Dinner: M-Sat 6-10 **Entrees:** $24-$32
Pre-Theater: M-Sat (fall-spring) 6-7, $35 **Closed:** Sun
Credit Cards: All major, DIS, DC, CB **Reservations:** Preferred
Dress: Jacket & tie preferred **Metro:** Metro Center
Parking: Complimentary valet (dinner)
Entertainment: Pianist F-Sat 6:30-10:30

On the off chance that you aren't invited to dine at Versailles this year, you can always make do with the WILLARD ROOM. Few grander spaces are open for public dining.

All that's been needed here is cooking to match the beauty. So Gerard Madani, a new *chef de cuisine* with impressive credentials, has been hired. He spent his last four years in Florida, which translates to one piece of advice: Order seafood. The spring menu features warm oysters, mussel soup, *langoustines* with risotto, and crab roll as appetizers, and half the entrees are seafood—the better half.

On both the winter and spring menus, every dish that's soared has been something simple. The more complex the dish, the more disillusioning. The entree that has dazzled me is Dover sole, steamed, then swathed in a vermouth cream sauce flavored with sorrel leaves. The sour herb weaves in an acidity that is like sparklers in a dark sky. The modern touch: The fish is cunningly braided before it is steamed. Madani understands rockfish, too, and treats it gently. Squab and duck star in the cooler seasons. You might also find kidneys with mustard sauce, tenderloin with bordelaise, duck breast or rack of lamb.

Desserts are dramatic. The best are *tarte Tatin* and a still-crisp *millefeuille* of puff pastry with lemon cream and a scoop of wonderful lemon sorbet. The grapefruit terrine, however, is like expense account Jell-O, pretty and refreshing until you consider that it costs $8.

XAVIER & BRUNO PATISSERIE CAFE
(Formerly Patisserie Cafe Didier)
3206 Grace St. NW, Washington, DC
(202) 342-9083

FRENCH   🦽

Open: Tu-Sat 7:30 am-7:30 pm, Sun 8 am-6 **Entrees:** $6-$10
Tea: Tu-Sat 4-7 **Entrees:** $1.50-$5.50 **Closed:** M
Credit Cards: V, MC, DIS, DC, CB **Dress:** Casual
Reservations: 5 or more only **Parking:** Street

A tiny pastry shop on Georgetown's most hidden street, XAVIER & BRUNO PATISSERIE CAFE has a new owner, pastry chef Bruno Felheisen from New York's Four Seasons Hotel. What he's taken over has until now been a kind of gastronomic antique shop; he plans to maintain that Old World character while he expands its offerings and its hours.

That means continuing the lunches of savory soufflés or tall, quivery quiches, the authentic kind that the French would eat. Onion soup starts in-house with onions, left to sweat on the stove until they sweeten and nearly melt from the heat. XAVIER & BRUNO serves the kind of French tearoom food that suggests the old genteel Georgetown rather than the noisy, modern-day M Street with its Boston Market and French-from-Texas chain, La Madeleine.

XAVIER & BRUNO is decorated with a gleaming array of fruit tarts and creamy cakes, flowered tablecloths and vases with a single flower or a small bouquet. For breakfast it serves croissants, muffins, scones and the only honestly buttery, delicate and flaky Danish I can find in this town. The fruit juices are freshly squeezed. And for lunch there's a small selection of salads, cold cuts on French bread, a hot entree such as a grilled chicken breast or that evocative quiche.

It's no bargain, and the portions are, let's say, restrained. But some might consider that an asset, considering the richness of the food. And an afternoon break of thick, creamy, Old World, bittersweet hot chocolate and a few airy ladyfingers to dip into it, with classical music in the background, is an indulgence beyond price.

ZUKI MOON NOODLES
824 New Hampshire Ave. NW, Washington, DC
(202) 333-3312

JAPANESE

Lunch: M-F 11:30-2:30 **Dinner:** M-Sat 5-11, Sun 5-10
Entrees: $9-$17 **Credit Cards:** All major, DC **Dress:** Casual
Reservations: Recommended **Parking:** Valet (fee)
Metro: Foggy Bottom

I'd given up on finding good food, much less reasonable prices, within walking distance of the Kennedy Center. But then chef Mary Richter opened ZUKI MOON NOODLES. It's a small, high-style Asian noodle parlor with handmade pottery and chairs (which look like overgrown kindergarten furniture) as well as hand-tended noodles and broths. If the night is balmy, you can dine outdoors, in a spot that's private if not beautiful.

And if the weather is warm, try the cold noodles, which are light, pristine and refreshing. An appetizer of green tea noodles is one of the best uses

"Just the right prelude to the National Symphony."

of smoked salmon I've encountered, the chilled, slippery, thin green noodles tangled with julienned cucumber and carrots in a lilting sesame-ginger dressing. For a more traditional Japanese starter, there are fragile and tangy *gyoza*, meat-filled, pan-fried dumplings. Other appetizers range through spring rolls and seaweed combinations, tempura and sushi—though made with noodles rather than rice—and even oysters on the half shell.

Entrees include a few grilled meats and fish with accents of soy sauce, sesame seeds and ginger; rare tuna with ginger and *wasabi* is terrific. There are tempuras and a stir-fry or two. Most of the entree menu is devoted to noodles, of wheat or buckwheat, thick or thin, in cold or hot broths, with a variety of meats and fish. When in doubt, look for dishes named after the restaurant. *Zuki udon*, for example, is a bowl full of treasures: a crisp and flavorful tempura shrimp, moist grilled chicken, scallops, bright vegetables, thick white noodles and, buried in the middle, a whole poached egg to puncture and stir into the broth.

All in all, ZUKI MOON NOODLES is just the right prelude to the National Symphony.

GUIDE
LISTINGS

Finding
what you want ...
the food, the features,
the atmosphere, and
all the right places

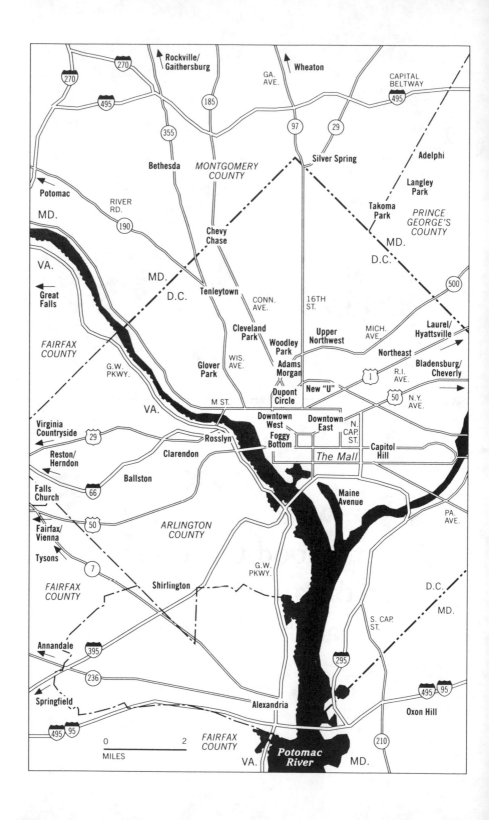

District of Columbia

ADAMS MORGAN
Addis Ababa
Cashion's
Cities
Fasika's
Felix
Grill from Ipanema
I Matti
La Fourchette
Lauriol Plaza
Meskerem

CAPITOL HILL
Anatolia
B. Smith's
Banana Cafe
Barolo
Bis
Cafe Berlin
Capitol City Brewing Company
Capitol View Club
Dubliner
La Colline
Market Lunch

CHEVY CHASE
Chadwick's
Cheesecake Factory
Clyde's
Maggiano's Little Italy
That's Amore

CHINATOWN
Burma
Eat First
Full Kee
Golden Palace
Mr. Yung's

CLEVELAND PARK
Ardeo
Coppi's Vigorelli
Greenwood
Lavandou
Nam Viet

DOWNTOWN – 16TH STREET AND EAST
A.V. Ristorante
Austin Grill
BET on Jazz
Cafe Atlantico
California Grill
Capitol City Brewing Company
Capital Grille
DC Coast
District Chophouse
El Catalan
Georgia Brown's
Gerard's Place
Haad Thai
Isabella
Jaleo
Les Halles
Lespinasse
Luigino
The Mark
Marrakesh
Mike Baker's
Morrison-Clark Inn
Old Ebbit Grill
Pan Asian Noodles & Grill
Red Sage
Rupperts
701
3rd & Eats
Tony Cheng's
Villa Franco
Willard Room

DOWNTOWN – 16TH STREET AND WEST

Bombay Club
Bread Line
Daily Grill
Galileo
Goldoni
Jefferson Restaurant
Kinkead's
Legal Sea Foods
Max's
McCormick & Schmick
Morton's
Mykonos
Oodles Noodles
Oval Room
Prime Rib
Sam & Harry's
Sholl's
Soper's on M
Taberna del Alabardero
Vidalia
Vox Artis

DUPONT CIRCLE

Al Tiramisu
Bacchus
BeDuCi
Blue Plate
Brickskeller
C.F. Folks
Caravan Grill
City Lights of China
Eleventh Hour
Gabriel
Georgetown Seafood Grill
I Ricchi
Il Radicchio
Jockey Club
La Tomate
Luna Grill & Diner
Obelisk
Pan Asian Noodles & Grill
Pesce
Pizzeria Paradiso

Raku
Red Tomato
Retaurant Nora
Sala Thai
Skewers
Sostanza
Straits of Malaya
Tabard Inn
Teaism

FOGGY BOTTOM/ WEST END

Aquarelle
Asia Nora
Galileo
Melrose
West End Cafe
Zuki Moon Noodles

GEORGETOWN

Bistrot Lepic
Bistro Francais
Cafe Milano
Ching Ching Cha
Clyde's
Enriqueta's
Hibiscus Cafe
Houston's
Il Radicchio
La Chaumiere
Martin's Tavern
Mendocino
Michel Richard's Citronelle
Music City Roadhouse
Nathan's
Old Glory
Paolo's
Patisserie Poupon
Sea Catch
Seasons
1789
Tahoga
Vintage Wine Bistro
Xavier & Bruno Patisserie Cafe

GLOVER PARK
Austin Grill
Busara
Rocklands
Sushi-Ko

NEW U
Coppi's

NORTHEAST
Ella's
Ellis Island

MAINE AVENUE WATERFRONT
Le Rivage
Maine Avenue Wharf

PALISADES
Makoto
Starland Cafe

SHAW
Sumah's

TENLEYTOWN/ CATHEDRAL
Amazonia Grill
Cafe Deluxe
Cafe Ole

UPPER NORTHWEST – EAST OF ROCK CREEK
Fio's

WOODLEY PARK
Lebanese Taverna
New Heights

Maryland

ANNAPOLIS
Red Hot & Blue

BETHESDA
Austin Grill
Bacchus
Cafe Bethesda
Capitol City Brewing Company
Cesco Trattoria
Cottonwood Cafe
Faryab
Houston's
Matuba
Oodles Noodles
Persimmon
Raku
Red Tomato
Rio Grande Cafe
Tara Thai

BLADENSBURG
Cielito Lindo

CHEVERLY
Fratelli

CHEVY CHASE
La Ferme
Ristorante Terrazza

COLLEGE PARK
Food Factory

COLUMBIA/TOWSON
Clyde's
Paolo's
That's Amore

EASTERN MD.
The Narrows

LANGLEY PARK/ ADELPHI/HYATTSVILLE
Ledo
Pho 75

Swagat
Tiffin

LAUREL
Red Hot & Blue

POTOMAC
Old Angler's Inn
Weissblatt's

**ROCKVILLE/
N. BETHESDA/
GAITHERSBURG**
A & J
Bombay Bistro
Cheesecake Factory
Crisp & Juicy
Houston's
Mykonos
Pho 75
Red Hot & Blue
Richland
Taipei Tokyo
Tara Thai (opening in Rockville
   soon)
That's Amore

**SILVER SPRING/
WHEATON/TAKOMA
PARK**
Crisp & Juicy
Hollywood East
Malaysian Satay House
Savory
Suporn's
Thai Flavor

Virginia

ALEXANDRIA
Afghan
Austin Grill
Bilbo Baggins
Bombay Curry Company
Clyde's
Evening Star Cafe
Generous George
Haad Thai
La Bergerie
Le Gaulois
Po Siam
RT's
Southside 815
Stardust

**ANNANDALE/
SPRINGFIELD**
Austin Grill
Generous George

**ARLINGTON/
CLARENDON/
SHIRLINGTON**
Atilla's
Cafe Dalat
Carlyle Grand Cafe
Costa Verde
Crisp & Juicy
Food Factory
La Cote D'Or
Layalina
Legal Sea Foods (National
   Airport)
Luna Grill & Diner
Matuba
Pho 75
Queen Bee
Ravi Kabob House
Red Hot & Blue
Rio Grande Cafe
Rocklands
Tara Thai
Thai Square
Village Bistro

CRYSTAL CITY
Demera
Saigon Crystal

FAIRFAX/VIENNA
Asian Flavor
Bombay Bistro
Clyde's
Dolce Vita
Il Radicchio
Nizam's
Panjshir
Sam & Harry's
Shamshiry
Tara Thai

FALLS CHURCH
Duangrat's
Huong Que
Panjshir
Peking Gourmet Inn
Pho 75
Rabieng
Tara Thai

GREAT FALLS
L'Auberge Chez Francois

McLEAN
Afghan
Busara
Daily Grill
Legal Sea Foods
Maggiano's Little Italy

RESTON/HERNDON
Clyde's
McCormick & Schmick
Paolo's
Red Hot & Blue
Rio Grande Cafe

ROSSLYN
Il Radicchio
Mezza 9

SHIRLINGTON
Capitol City Brewing Company

STERLING
That's Amore

VIRGINIA COUNTRYSIDE
Ashby Inn
Inn at Little Washington

WHERE TO GET BREAKFAST

Aquarelle	Luna Grill & Diner	Seasons
Bis	Maine Avenue Wharf	Sholl's
Bread Line	Market Lunch	Tabard Inn
California Grill	Martin's Tavern	Teaism
Dubliner	Melrose	3rd & Eats
Gabriel	Mezza 9	Vox Artis
Jefferson Restaurant	Michel Richard's	Weissblatt's
Jockey Club	Citronelle	West End Cafe
La Colline	Old Ebbitt Grill	Willard Room
Ledo	Patisserie Poupon	Xavier & Bruno
Lespinasse	Savory	Patisserie Cafe

Rupperts
Sam & Harry's
Savory
Seasons
701
1789
Sholl's
Soper's on M
Southside 815
Stardust
Starland Cafe
Tabard Inn
Tahoga
3rd & Eats
Vidalia
Village Bistro
West End Cafe
Willard Room

AMERICAN/BARBECUE
Ella's
Market Lunch
Old Glory
Red Hot & Blue
Rocklands

AMERICAN/CREOLE
RT's

AMERICAN/SEAFOOD
DC Coast
Georgetown Seafood
  Grill
Kinkead's
Legal Sea Foods
Maine Ave. Wharf
Market Lunch
McCormick &
  Schmick
Narrows
Pesce
RT's
Sea Catch
Stardust
Tahoga

AMERICAN/SOUTHERN
Georgia Brown's
Morrison-Clark Inn
Music City
  Roadhouse
Old Glory
Southside 815
3rd & Eats
Vidalia

AMERICAN/ SOUTHWESTERN
Austin Grill
Cottonwood Cafe
Houston's
Red Sage
Rio Grande Cafe

ASIAN
Asia Nora
Oodles Noodles
Pan Asian Noodles &
  Grill
Raku
Teaism

BRAZILIAN
Amazonia Grill
Grill from Ipanema

BURMESE
Burma

CARIBBEAN
Banana Cafe
BET on Jazz
Cafe Atlantico
Hibiscus Cafe

CHINESE
A & J
Ching Ching Cha
City Lights of China
Eat First
Full Kee
Golden Palace

Hollywood East
Mr. Yung's
Peking Gourmet Inn
Richland
Taipei Tokyo
Tony Cheng's

ETHIOPIAN

Addis Ababa
Demera
Fasika's
Meskerem

FRENCH

Bis
Bistro Francais
Bistrot Lepic
Gerard's Place
Jockey Club
L'Auberge Chez
  Francois
La Bergerie
La Chaumiere
La Colline
La Cote D'Or
La Ferme
La Fourchette
Lavandou
Le Gaulois
Le Rivage
Les Halles
Lespinasse
Michel Richard's
  Citronelle
Patisserie Poupon
Seasons
Vintage Wine Bistro
Vox Artis
Willard Room
Xavier & Bruno
  Patisserie Cafe

GERMAN

Cafe Berlin

GREEK

Mykonos

INDIAN

Bombay Bistro
Bombay Club
Bombay Curry
  Company
Swagat
Tiffin

IRISH

Dubliner
Ellis Island

ITALIAN

Al Tiramisu
A.V. Ristorante
Barolo
Cafe Milano
Cesco Trattoria
Coppi's
Dolce Vita
Fio's
Fratelli
Galileo
Generous George
Goldoni
I Matti
I Ricchi
Il Radicchio
La Tomate
Ledo
Luigino
Maggiano's Little
  Italy
Obelisk
Paolo's
Pizzeria Paradiso
Ristorante Terrazza
Sostanza
That's Amore
Villa Franco

JAPANESE

Asian Flavor
Hee Been
Makoto

Matuba
Sushi-Ko
Taipei Tokyo
Zuki Moon Noodles

JEWISH DELI
Weissblatt's

KOREAN
Hee Been

LATIN AMERICAN
Cafe Atlantico
Crisp & Juicy
Gabriel

LEBANESE
Bacchus
Lebanese Taverna

MALAYSIAN
Malaysian Satay
  House
Straits of Malaya

MEDITERRANEAN
BeDuCi
Cafe Olé
Gabriel
Isabella
Mezza 9
Nizam's
Skewers
West End Cafe

MEXICAN
Cielito Lindo
Enriqueta's
Lauriol Plaza

MORROCAN
Marrakesh

PAKISTANI
Food Factory
Ravi Kabob House

PERSIAN
Caravan Grill
Shamshiry

PERUVIAN
Costa Verde

ROTISSERIE CHICKEN
Crisp & Juicy

SPANISH
El Catalan
Gabriel
Jaleo
Lauriol Plaza
Taberna del
  Alabardero

STEAKHOUSE
Capital Grille
Les Halles
Max's of Washington
Morton's
The Prime Rib
Sam & Harry's

SYRIAN
Layalina

TEX/MEX
Banana Cafe

THAI
Asian Flavor
Busara
Duangrat's
Haad Thai
Pan Asian Noodles &
  Grill
Po Siam
Rabieng
Sala Thai
Stardust
Suporn's
Tara Thai
Thai Flavor
Thai Square

TURKISH
Anatolia
Atilla's
Nizam's

VIETNAMESE
Cafe Dalat
Huong Que
Nam Viet
Pho 75
Queen Bee
Saigon Crystal

WEST AFRICAN
Sumah's

CHEAP EATS – DINNER ENTREES STARTING UNDER $10

Addis Ababa
A & J
A.V. Ristorante
Afghan
Asian Flavor
Austin Grill
Banana Cafe
Blue Plate
Bombay Bistro
Bombay Club
Bombay Curry Company
Brickskeller
Burma
Cafe Dalat
Cafe Deluxe
Cafe Olé
Capitol City Brewing Company
Caravan Grill
Carlyle Grand Cafe
Chadwick's
Cheesecake Factory
Ching Ching Cha
Cielito Lindo
City Lights of China
Clyde's of Chevy Chase
Clyde's of Georgetown
Coppi's

Costa Verde
Crisp & Juicy
Daily Grill
Demera
Dolce Vita
Dubliner
Eat First
El Catalan
Ella's Barbecue
Enriquetta's
Evening Star
Faryab
Fasika's
Fio's
Food Factory
Fratelli
Full Kee
Generous George
Golden Palace
Grill from Ipanema
Haad Thai
Hee Been
Hibiscus Cafe
Hollywood East
Huong Que
Il Radicchio
Isabella
La Fourchette
Lauriol Plaza
Ledo
Le Gaulois
Luna Grill & Diner
Maine Avenue Wharf
Makoto
Malaysian Satay House
Matuba
Mike Baker's
Meskerem
Mr. Yung's
Monroe's
Music City Roadhouse
Nam Viet

Old Glory
Oodles Noodles
Pan Asian Noodles & Grill
Paolo's
Pho 75
Pizzeria Paradiso
Po Siam
Queen Bee
RT's
Rabieng
Raku
Ravi Kabob House
Red Hot & Blue
Red Tomato
Richland
Rio Grand Cafe
Ristorante Terrazza
Rocklands
Saigon Crystal
Sala Thai
Savory
Shamshiry
Sholl's
Southside 815
Sumah's
Suporn's
Sushi-Ko
Swagat
Taipei Tokyo
Tara Thai
Teaism
Thai Flavor
Thai Square
That's Amore
3rd & Eats
Tiffin
Tony Cheng's
Village Bistro
Weissblatt's
Zuki Moon Noodles

WHERE LATE-NIGHTERS GO

The following hours apply mainly to weekends, though more than a few restaurants also keep late hours during the week.

4 AM
Bistro Francais

3 AM
Brickskeller
Full Kee
Mike Baker's
Ravi Kabob House

2 AM
Hollywood East
Les Halles
Old Glory

1 AM
Addis Ababa
Cafe Milano
Chadwick's
Clyde's of Georgetown
Dubliner
Fasika's
Martin's Tavern
Meskerem
Music City Roadhouse
Old Ebbitt Grill
Skewers

12:30 AM
Cheesecake Factory
Clyde's of Chevy Chase
Paolo's

MIDNIGHT
A.V. Ristorante
Austin Grill
B. Smith's
BET on Jazz

Busara
Cafe Atlantico
Cafe Olé
Capitol City Brewing Company
Caravan Grill
Cities
Coppi's
Daily Grill
Demera
Generous George (summer)
Georgia Brown's
Golden Palace
Grill from Ipanema
Hee Been
Hibiscus
Houston's
Jaleo
Lauriol Plaza
Ledo
Luna Grill & Diner
Malaysian Satay House
McCormick & Schmick
Pizzeria Paradiso
Raku
That's Amore
Tony Cheng's
West End Cafe

11:30 PM
Amazonia Grill
Ardeo
Luigino
Prime Rib
Red Sage
Rio Grand Cafc
Sala Thai
701

ROOMS WITH A (SPECIAL) VIEW
Aquarelle
Capitol View Club
Le Rivage
Old Angler's Inn

FOR LIVE ENTERTAINMENT OR DANCING
(D) indicates dancing

Addis Ababa
Amazonia Grill
Atilla's
B. Smith's
Banana Cafe
BET on Jazz
Bombay Club
Cafe Olé
Capitol View Club
Cities (D)
Clyde's of Chevy Chase
Costa Verde
Demera
Dolce Vita
Duangrat's
Dubliner
Eleventh Hour (D)
Felix (D)
Generous George
Georgia Brown's
I Matti (D)
Jaleo
Kinkead's
La Ferme
La Tomate
Lespinasse
Marrakesh
Melrose (D)
Meskerem
Music City Roadhouse
Nathan's (D)
Old Glory
Oval Room
Paolo's
The Prime Rib
701
Starland Cafe
Tabard Inn
Thai Flavor

That's Amore
Villa Franco
West End Cafe
Willard Room

RESTAURANTS WITH PRIVATE DINING ROOMS

A.V. Ristorante
Afghan
Aquarelle
Ardeo
Ashby Inn
Asia Nora
Bacchus
Banana Cafe
Barolo
BeDuCi
Bis
Bistro Francais
Brickskeller
Burma
Busara
Cafe Berlin
Cafe Milano
Capitol City Brewing Company
Capital Grille
Capitol View Club
Cielito Lindo
Cities
City Lights of China
Clyde's of Georgetown
Cottonwood Cafe
Daily Grill
DC Coast
District Chophouse
El Catalan
Eleventh Hour
Enriqueta's
Fasika's
Felix
Fio's

Fratelli
Gabriel
Galileo
Generous George
Golden Palace
Goldoni
Hee Been
Hibiscus Cafe
Hollywood East
I Matti
I Ricchi
Jefferson Restaurant
Jockey Club
Kinkead's
La Bergerie
La Chaumiere
La Colline
La Cote D'Or
La Ferme
La Tomate
Lauriol Plaza
Layalina Restaurant
Le Gaulois
Lebanese Taverna
Legal Seafoods
Les Halles
Lespinasse
Luigino
Maggiano's Little Italy
The Mark
Martin's Tavern
McCormick & Schmick
Melrose
Meskerem
Mezza 9
Michel Richard's Citronelle
Mike Baker's
Morrison-Clark Inn
Morton's of Chicago
Music City Roadhouse
Mykonos
Nizam's
Old Angler's Inn

Old Ebbitt Grill
Oval Room
Pan Asian Noodles
Peking Gourmet Inn
The Prime Rib
RT's
Red Hot & Blue
Red Sage
Restaurant Nora
Ristorante Terrazza
Sam & Harry's
Sea Catch
Seasons
701
1789
Soper's on M
Sostanza
Stardust
Straits of Malaya
Swagat (MD only)
Tabard Inn
Taberna del Alabardero
Tahoga
That's Amore
Tiffin Restaurant
Vidalia
Villa Franco
Vintage Wine Bistro
Vox Artis
West End Cafe
Willard Room

FAMILY-FRIENDLY RESTAURANTS

Addis Ababa
A & J
A.V. Ristorante
Afghan
Asian Flavor
Atilla's
Austin Grill
Anatolia

Blue Plate
Bombay Curry Company
Bread Line
Cafe Dalat
Cafe Deluxe
California Grill
Caravan Grill
Chadwick's
Cheesecake Factory
Cielito Lindo
Clyde's of Chevy Chase
Coppi's
Crisp & Juicy
Demera
Fasika's
Fio's
Food Factory
Fratelli
Full Kee
Generous George
Golden Palace
Hee Been
Hollywood East
Houston's
Huong Que
Il Radicchio
Lebanese Taverna
Ledo
Ella's Barbecue
Layalina
Luna Grill & Diner
Maggiano's Little Italy
Maine Avenue Wharf
Market Lunch
Music City Roadhouse
Old Glory
Oodles Noodles
Paolo's
Patisserie Poupon
Peking Gourmet Inn
Po Siam
Ravi Kabob House
Red Hot & Blue
Red Tomato

Richland
Rio Grand Cafe
Rocklands
Saigon Crystal
Shamshiry
Southside 815
Savory
Sholl's
Swagat
Taipei Tokyo
Tara Thai
That's Amore
3rd & Eats
Tony Cheng's
Weissblatt's
Xavier & Bruno Patisserie
    Cafe

THE SUNDAY BRUNCH BUNCH

Aquarelle
Ardeo
Ashby Inn
Austin Grill
B. Smith's
Banana Cafe
BET on Jazz
Bistro Francais
Blue Plate
Bombay Club
Cafe Deluxe
Carlyle Grand Cafe
Cashion's Eat Place
Chadwick's
Cheesecake Factory
Cities
Clyde's of Chevy Chase
Clyde's of Georgetown
Daily Grill
Dubliner
Ellis Island
Evening Star Cafe

Felix
Fratelli
Gabriel
Georgia Brown's
Grill from Ipanema
Jaleo
Jefferson Restaurant
Kinkead's
La Cote D'Or
Lauriol Plaza
Luna Grill & Diner
The Mark
Martin's Tavern
Melrose
Morrison-Clark Inn
Music City Roadhouse
Narrows
Nathan's
New Heights
Old Angler's Inn
Old Ebbitt Grill
Old Glory
Paolo's
Rio Grande Cafe
Seasons
Sholl's
Southside 815
Starland Cafe
Tabard Inn
West End Cafe

AFTERNOON TEA

Ching Ching Cha
Jefferson Restaurant
Lespinasse
Melrose
Seasons
Teaism
Xavier & Bruno Patisserie
Cafe

BUFFETS

These buffets are mostly for lunch or brunch.

Afghan
Amazonia Grill
Bombay Bistro
Bombay Club
Bombay Curry Company
Cafe Dalat
Capitol View Club
Caravan Grill
Costa Verde
Gabriel
Hee Been
Generous George (Annandale
   & Springfield)
Michel Richard's Citronelle
Old Glory
Thai Flavor
Tiffin
Tony Cheng's
West End Cafe

PRE-THEATER BARGAINS

Aquarelle
BeDuCi
Bistro Francais
Bombay Club
Cafe Atlantico
Carlyle Grand Cafe
Clyde's of Georgetown
Felix
Generous George
Isabella
La Cote D'Or
Lavandou
Le Rivage

Ledo
Luigino
Luna Grill & Diner
The Mark
Melrose
Oval Room
Ristorante Terrazza
701
1789
Taberna del Alabardero
Villa Franco
Village Bistro
Vox Artis
West End Cafe
Willard Room

OUTDOOR DINING

A.V. Ristorante
Amazonia Grill
Ashby Inn
Austin Grill (Bethesda)
Bacchus (Bethesda)
Banana Cafe
BeDuCi
BET on Jazz
Bis
Bombay Bistro
Bombay Club
Bread Line
Busara
C.F. Folks
Cafe Atlantico
Cafe Berlin
Cafe Bethesda
Cafe Ole
Cafe Dalat
Cafe Deluxe
Cafe Milano
California Grill
Capitol City Brewing Company
Caravan Grill
Carlyle Grand Cafe

Cashion's Eat Place
Cesco Trattoria
Chadwick's
Cottonwood Cafe
DC Coast
Dubliner
Eleventh Hour
Ellis Island
Evening Star Cafe
Fasika's
Gabriel
Galileo
Georgetown Seafood Grill
Gerard's Place
Goldoni
Grill from Ipanema
Hibiscus Cafe
I Ricchi
Isabella
Kinkead's
La Cote D'Or
La Ferme
La Fourchette
La Tomate
L'Auberge Chez Francois
Lauriol Plaza
Layalina Restaurant
Le Gaulois
Le Rivage
Lebanese Taverna
Les Halles
Luigino
Luna Grill & Diner
Martin's Tavern
McCormick and Schmick
Melrose
Monroe's
Morrison-Clark Inn
Morton's of Chicago
Music City Roadhouse
New Heights
Old Angler's Inn
Oval Room
Paolo's
Patisserie Poupon
Po Siam

Raku
Ristorante Terrazza
Saigon Crystal
Savory
Sea Catch
701
Skewers
Southside 815
Starland Cafe
Straits of Malaya
Tabard Inn
Taberna del Alabardero
Tahoga
That's Amore
Villa Franco
Village Bistro
Vox Artis
Zuki Moon Noodles

TAKING NO CREDIT

Almost a dozen restaurants in this book do not accept credit cards, only cash or, in some cases, checks as well. So you won't be caught by surprise when dining at them, they are:

A & J
C.F. Folks
Crisp & Juicy
Full Kee
Market Lunch
Marrakesh
Pho 75
Ravi Kabob House
Sholl's Colonial Cafeteria
Sumah's
3rd & Eats

HAPPY HOURS

Banana Cafe
Busara
Cafe Deluxe
Carlyle Grand Cafe
Chadwick's
Clyde's of Chevy Chase
Clyde's of Georgetown
Cottonwood Cafe
District Chophouse
Evening Star Cafe
Gabriel
Georgetown Seafood Grill
Jaleo
Legal Sea Foods
Les Halles
Luna Grill & Diner
The Mark
Max's
McCormick & Schmick
Morton's
Music City Roadhouse
Raku
Red Hot & Blue
Rio Grande Cafe
Ristorante Terrazza
Southside 815
Taberna del Alabardero
That's Amore

NON-SMOKING RESTAURANTS

A & J
Asia Nora
Asian Flavor
Bacchus
Bistro Lepic
Bombay Bistro (Rockville)
Bread Line
C.F. Folks

Cafe Olé
Carlyle Grand Cafe
Cesco Trattoria
Ching Ching Cha
Cielito Lindo
City Lights of China
Crisp & Juicy
Ella's Barbecue
Faryab
Hollywood East
Luna Grill & Diner
Malaysian Satay House
Market Lunch
Marrakesh
Matuba
Monroe's
Nizam's
Obelisk
Oodles Noodles
Patisserie Poupon
Persimmon
Pizzeria Paradiso
Pesce
Rabieng
Raku
Red Tomato
Restaurant Nora
Richland
Saigon Crystal
Savory
Shamshiry
Sumah's
Suporn's
Sushi-Ko
Swagat
Taipei Tokyo
Tara Thai
Teaism
Thai Square
Tiffin
Weissblatt's
Xavier & Bruno Patisserie
  Cafe

RESTAURANTS WITH FIREPLACES

A.V. Ristorante
Al Tiramisu
Ashby Inn
Barolo
Bis
Chadwick's
Cities
Eleventh Hour
Jefferson Restaurant
La Chaumiere
La Ferme
L'Auberge Chez Francois
Le Gaulois
McCormick & Schmick
Mike Baker's
Morrison-Clark Inn
Paolo's
Red Sage
1789
Sam & Harry's (Vienna)
Sea Catch
Soper's on M
Stardust
Tabard Inn
Tahoga
That's Amore

RESTAURANTS OFFERING DIM SUM

A & J
Golden Palace
Mr. Yung's
Raku
Tony Cheng's